THE CONSPIRACY AND MURDER
OF MAO'S HEIR

YAO MING-LE

The Conspiracy and Murder of Mao's Heir

COLLINS
8 Grafton Street London W1
1983

William Collins Sons & Co Ltd
London · Glasgow · Sydney · Auckland
Toronto · Johannesburg

First published in the UK 1983
Text and translation Copyright © Alfred A. Knopf Inc.1983
Introduction © Stanley Karnow 1983
ISBN 0 00 217141 4
Photoset in Times Roman
Made and Printed in Great Britain by
Robert Hartnoll Ltd, Bodmin, Cornwall

CONTENTS

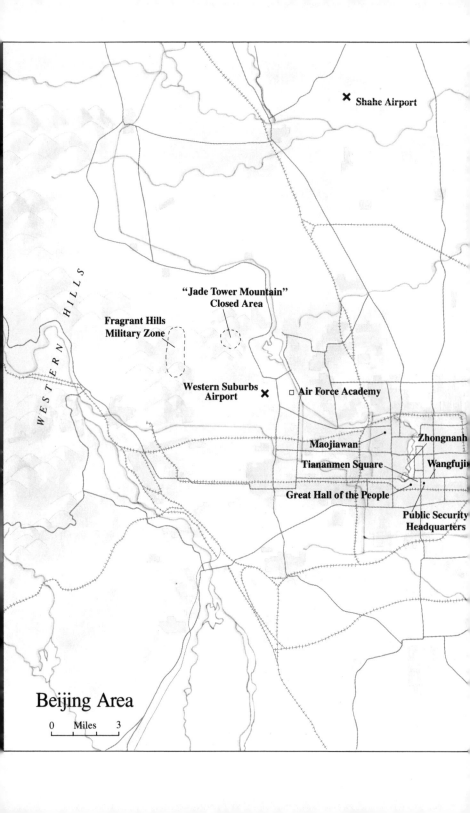

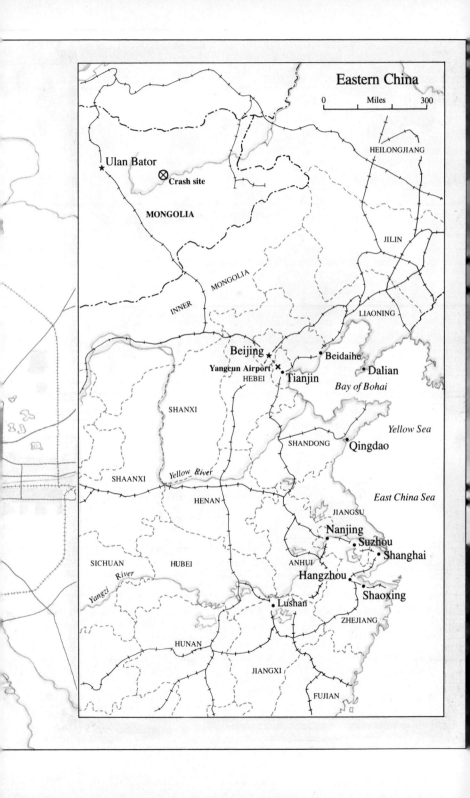

INTRODUCTION

by Stanley Karnow

LIN PIAO BELIEVED TO BE DEAD. That headline appeared above my byline on page one of the Washington *Post* of November 27, 1971. The story that followed was, I believe, the first to disclose that China's highest-ranking official had died after a desperate attempt to assassinate Mao Zedong, the Chinese Communist deity, who had formally appointed him his successor.

The event—and my account of it—came at a critical juncture in world affairs. President Nixon was then looking forward to his spectacular trip to Beijing, and big global stakes hung in the balance. A rapprochement between the United States and China offered both countries the opportunity to check their common adversary, the Soviet Union. Nixon hoped, too, that a deal with the Chinese could accelerate America's withdrawal from Vietnam. The journey, televised exhaustively, would also launch his campaign for reelection.

As far as I can ascertain, nobody in the West at that time fully appreciated the precariousness of the situation. Nor, I would submit, has it been realized since that the dramatic Sino-American breakthrough was by no means a foregone conclusion. As the presumably authoritative documents in this extraordinary book reveal, Lin, if his plot against Mao had succeeded, would have

ix

instead steered China toward a reconciliation with the Soviet Union. Indeed, according to Yao Ming-le, he evidently sought in advance to persuade Leonid Brezhnev, the Soviet leader, to participate in the fantastic conspiracy.

But even though these arcane machinations were unknown outside China's innermost ruling recesses, Nixon was tense as his visit to Beijing approached. He feared that the Chinese might, for whatever mysterious motives of their own, seize on some pretext to abort his journey. He had therefore ordered administration experts not to discuss developments in China with the news media, lest the Chinese penalize him for the leaks—and thus cancel what he planned to call "the week that changed the world." His concern may have been exaggerated, but the Chinese could be unpredictable.

There were plenty of developments to discuss. China during this period was spastically emerging from the Great Proletarian Cultural Revolution, the convulsive upheaval sparked by Mao to purge his Communist Party rivals. The American press was largely barred from China, and those of us who covered the country relied heavily on State Department, Central Intelligence Agency and other government specialists for assistance. Early in the fall of 1971, we were badly in need of help.

According to reports, a British-built Trident jet airliner belonging to China had crashed in Mongolia on the night of September 12, 1971, and all aboard were killed. The incident at first seemed banal. But then further reports indicated that China's entire fleet of military and civilian aircraft had been grounded. Then the Chinese National Day celebration, a great annual event scheduled for October 1, was abruptly and inexplicably canceled. Soon rumors seeping into Hong Kong, the prime post for monitoring China, hinted that Lin Biao had dropped out of sight. Plainly, something important was happening.

Having served as a correspondent in Hong Kong for more than a decade prior to my return to a Washington assignment, I was accustomed to stitching reports and rumors together, then bouncing the conclusions off various official sources who were going through the same exercise. We "China watchers" constituted a kind of club, rather like a group of Talmudic scholars, forever analyzing and interpreting and arguing about the scriptures. It was an imperfect art, comparable to observing the United States from, say, a perch in Bermuda. Still, the results were as a rule remarkably accurate. In fact, Mao himself once paid us an indirect compliment. Late in 1970, commenting on the Western coverage of the Cultural Revolution, he told his American biographer Edgar Snow: "When foreigners reported that China was in great chaos, they were not telling lies. It had been true."

Now, however, information was scarce, and Nixon had put his experts under wraps. But good fortune intervened for me in the person of a Chinese-American friend, who to this day insists upon remaining anonymous. The son of a distinguished Chinese general who had thrown in his lot with the Communists, he had somehow kept in contact over the years with relatives in China, some of whom had attained senior positions. He had just returned from a visit to Beijing, which, he told me, was agog over tales of Lin Biao and intrigue. His uncles and cousins had shown him secret documents that had begun circulating among top party cadres. My friend was visibly nervous about discussing the subject, as if Mao's long hand reached even into the District of Columbia. He insisted that we meet in a secure place. And so, one evening in November, we sat in a car parked on Wisconsin Avenue and talked.

Lin, he said, had been betrayed by his daughter. He had tried to escape to the Soviet Union aboard the Trident, accompanied by his wife, his son and three prominent Chinese military figures, all of them members of his cabal. They, along with two other men and a woman, had died in the crash, their bodies burnt beyond recognition.

It sounded to me at the time like an incredible thriller, a flamboyant Chinese opera cloaked in contemporary Communist costume. But my instinctive skepticism was tempered by two considerations.

First, if I had learned anything over the years about China under Communism, it was that Mao had failed to transform the country's "soul"—the charged word, incidentally, that he himself had used in proclaiming his extravagant goal. His revolutionary zeal had unquestionably altered the political and economic face of China. And yet, despite the frenetic mass drives he set in motion, such as the Great Leap Forward and the Cultural Revolution, the traditional and even feudal nature of Chinese society had scarcely changed. Communist commanders in many regions were really warlords in disguise, and party functionaries often behaved like mandarins. Local ideological conflicts were frequently rooted in ancient clan vendettas, and complex kinship ties underpinned the system of authority in numerous areas. I could not, therefore, dismiss out of hand the notion of fierce internecine struggles roiling the Beijing hierarchy.

Second, I knew better than to accept any story in toto. As I listened to my friend, it occurred to me that this might not be the final word on the fate of Lin Biao. Lin might not have been a casualty of the airplane crash; he was reputed to have been in poor health for years, and perhaps he had simply expired in bed from natural causes. In any case, I concluded, the Chinese leaders would not be reporting his death to their own apparatchiks were he alive, and I had to assume that the story reaching us was the government line. In short, Lin had to be dead. (Little did I imagine the true circumstances of his death, at least according to Yao Ming-le. But to divulge them here would be an injustice to the reader of this book.)

Armed with my friend's story, I arranged a series of equally surreptitious encounters with my official contacts inside the Nixon administration. They were short on hard facts. But they agreed that, whatever else had happened, Lin was gone. I consequently gave my Washington *Post* account a somewhat speculative flavor: "China specialists here now believe" that Lin had died, it began, and the rest of it was hedged with qualifications and conditional verbs.

The Chinese later conducted an investigation of the affair, releasing the findings bit by bit. The entire report was ultimately published in June 1972. It asserted authoritatively that Lin had been killed in the Trident crash, fleeing China after his plot against Mao had been exposed. I felt rather pleased with myself, as any newspaperman would; after all, I had broken the story eight months earlier. But now I realize that my performance may have been flawed. For this fascinating book, while confirming Lin's attempted coup, knocks for a loop the official Chinese line concerning the circumstances surrounding his death. And it will, I would venture to predict, make the present regime in Beijing unhappy.

I cannot vouch for the authenticity of Yao Ming-le's vivid description of Lin's final hours. My guess is that, having punctured the cult of Mao's personality, the current Chinese leaders will not object too strenuously to this unkind portrayal of him. But I would be surprised if they did not protest against the descriptions of life inside their ruling structure. For the account evokes memories of China's imperial courts during their more decadent eras—corrupt, duplicitous, cruel. It is hardly a picture of themselves that the Chinese, with their pretensions to proletarian virtue, want to see projected.

Western illusions about their delicate frailty notwithstanding, Chinese women can be dynamic and ruthless in their quest for power. The wives of both Mao and Chiang Kai-shek are cases in point. So was Lin's wife, Ye Qun. If we are to believe Yao, she was having a love affair with General Huang Yongsheng, the chief of the general staff and one of her husband's co-conspirators, partly to lock him into the plot and partly also to promote the career of her profligate son, Lin Liguo. With Lin Biao named Mao's heir apparent, she dreamed of establishing a dynasty.

Several Chinese have made clear to me the privileges granted to the children of the Communist leadership. They were—and probably still are—accorded special schools, jobs, consumer goods and other luxuries denied to the masses, who are cherished principally in the abstract. Lin's only son, Liguo, was a part of this *jeunesse dorée*. Exactly what this sort of privilege could mean—in Liguo's case, unlimited young women, and even copies of *Playboy* and *Penthouse* smuggled in from Hong Kong—is illustrated with special vividness in this book. So are some of the personal idiosyncrasies of the great Mao himself, including his adherence to the traditional belief that young girls would increase his longevity, his dependence on divination and the *Yi Jing* to help him make decisions, and his insistence on sleeping with his head lying in an easterly direction (because "dong," one of the characters in his name, means "east").

Can we believe all of what Yao Ming-le tells us here? It is obviously impossible to say with any certainty, except to note that his story confirms much of what has been rumored and reported about the Lin Biao Affair in recent years. Focusing as it does on the coup and counter-coup within a specific span in 1971, and coming from a Chinese source, the book does not stress the broader historical perspective behind the events it recounts. Mao and Lin were both veterans of the Long March of the 1930's, the Communists' heroic retreat from their Nationalist enemies. Lin, a brilliant soldier, went on to greater glories during the civil war against the Nationalists following World War II, and in the Korean conflict against the United States. By 1959, Mao needed him for political purposes.

The Great Leap Forward of the previous year had been a disaster. Mao's wild effort to modernize the country overnight by mobilizing the population drove China to the brink of collapse, and in some spots the army mutinied. Marshal Peng Dehuai, the crusty old defense minister, was so appalled that he appealed to Soviet Premier Nikita Khrushchev to help him topple Mao. This treason earned Peng dismissal. But the Communist Party staged a showdown against Mao, stripping him of much of his power, although they left him in office in order to retain the benefits of his prestige. Or, as Mao himself later put it: "They treated me with the respect they would have shown their father at his funeral."

Lin, who supplanted Peng as defense minister, devoted his loyalties to Mao as the intramural tensions in China mounted. One of the more interesting disputes that evolved in the mid-1960's was over Chinese policy toward Vietnam.

The Communist Party machine, suspecting that Mao intended

xiv

to use the armed forces as his instrument to regain authority, favored Chinese intervention in the Vietnam War as a way of depriving Mao of that weapon. Mao, in contrast, opposed involvement. The debate raged through the first half of 1965, culminating in a triumph for Mao. Acting as his spokesman, Lin wrote an article entitled "Long Live the Victory of People's War!," which made it plain that China would stay out of Vietnam. A Washington newspaperman facilely labeled the article "Mao's *Mein Kampf,*" as the Chairman's purported prescription for world domination, and soon U.S. officials were repeating the preposterous phrase. Indirectly, however, Mao and Lin had served the purposes of Lyndon Johnson, who would surely have recoiled from escalating the American commitment in Vietnam had he been confronted by a Chinese threat.

During the Cultural Revolution, Lin became Mao's chief lieutenant. Together, they overthrew the Communist Party apparatus. It was Lin's staff that prepared the celebrated "little red book" of Mao's quotations, and Lin himself who wrote the preface, extolling Mao as "the greatest Marxist-Leninist of our era." His army also organized the Red Guards, the bands of young men and women that rampaged around China, screaming Maoist slogans as they wrecked the country. By the end of 1967, Mao and Lin perceived that China was in no condition to withstand the Soviet Union, then strengthening its forces on their frontier. They moved to restore law and order.

At that stage, as the army imposed discipline, Lin evidently began to fill the power vacuum with his own supporters. China was now becoming a military state. In April 1969, Mao elevated Lin to the status of his official heir. But he quickly realized that he had made a mistake. Mao had operated for decades by juggling his subordinates; now he had bestowed his imprimatur upon a single man. He began to regret his decision, and mutual suspicion grew between him and Lin—Mao suspecting that Lin was pressing to take over from him, Lin suspecting that Mao might be planning to switch to a younger successor. They were like a pair of paranoids, except in one respect: their enmity was real.

We are now told that Lin, like his predecessor, Peng Dehuai, contemplated the cooperation of the Soviet Union in his elaborate conspiracy, and that he even considered unleashing a phony war against the Soviets to camouflage the plot. If so, it is unclear whether or not Brezhnev was aware of this crazy scheme. In any case, Lin did not live to tell the tale—luckily, it would seem, for Richard Nixon. And, I might add, for the world.

The Conspiracy and Murder
of Mao's Heir

PROLOGUE

On September 12, 1971, Lin Biao died. He was one of China's foremost military and political leaders, having first established his legendary reputation on the battlefield fighting the Japanese, and later, during China's Civil War, winning decisive battles against the Nationalists as far north as Manchuria and as far south as Hainan Island.

Following the Communist victory in 1949, Lin Biao had been named one of China's ten marshals. In 1959, replacing Peng Dehuai, he became Minister of Defense. In 1966 he was named Vice-Chairman of the Communist Party. And in 1969 he was officially appointed successor to Chairman Mao Zedong. At the time he died, Lin Biao was by all accounts the second most powerful person in China.

News of his death was at first withheld both from the public and from inner political circles. Only one indication suggested that something unusual had happened: the highest commanders of each of China's ten major military regions received orders from the Central Committee to prepare for an emergency. No explanation was included in the orders, and nothing linked them to Lin Biao.

For weeks afterward the Chinese people continued to worship Lin Biao as Mao's successor and closest comrade-in-arms. The slogans exhorting citizens to adhere to the words of both Mao and Lin continued to loom in giant characters over Tiananmen Square in Beijing (Peking). The October 1971 issue of the official *People's China,* China's largest pictorial magazine, featured on its cover a photograph of Mao Zedong and Lin Biao together. To all appearances, they were as intimate as ever.

But while his public image lived on, the man did not. Lin had been accustomed to make a grand appearance each year with Mao at Tiananmen Square on October 1, National Day; this year the entire ceremony was called off, never to occur again. The only reason given for the cancellation was that a gathering of hundreds of thousands would offer the Soviet Union too easy a target for attack.

Word of Lin Biao's death spread in a slow and controlled manner through the circulation of a series of top-secret Central Committee documents, later compiled under the heading *Criminal Materials of Lin Biao's Anti-Party Clique, Parts 1, 2, 3* and available at first only to top party officials. The first document appeared weeks after the actual death of Lin Biao, and alluded only briefly to it. Later another document was issued calling for the removal of Lin Biao's closest associates—Chief-of-Staff Huang Yongsheng, Air Force Commander-in-Chief Wu Faxian, Navy Political Commissar Li Zuopeng and Chief of Logistics Qiu Huizuo—from all their military and political posts. In November 1971 a document was issued recalling all printed matter by or about Lin Biao, and all photographs of him.

It was not until January 13, 1972, that top party officials received an explanation of Lin Biao's death. A Central Committee report cited an attempt by Lin Biao to assassinate Mao Zedong in a plot called the "571 Project," which had been managed by Lin Biao's son, Lin Liguo. When the plot was exposed, the official explanation stated, Lin Biao had apparently attempted to escape by air to the Soviet Union, and died when the plane he was in crashed in the Mongolian People's Republic.

Finally, on June 26, 1972, nearly ten months after Lin Biao's death, a full and detailed report of the "Lin Biao Affair" was released. Entitled *Criminal Evidence for a Counter-revolutionary Coup by Lin Biao's Anti-Party Clique,* it contained transcriptions

Mao Zedong and Lin Biao on the rostrum overlooking Tiananmen Square in Beijing in 1966, at the start of the Cultural Revolution. (UPI Photo)

of confessions, results of investigations, records of telephone calls, letters, notes, diaries and other evidence of Lin Biao's crimes. This report was shown to all party members with the instruction that they in turn disclose its contents to the Chinese people.

According to this Central Committee document, the events leading up to Lin Biao's death were as follows:

During the Second Plenum of the Ninth Party Congress at the resort of Lushan in August 1970 a noticeable rift developed between Mao Zedong and Lin Biao over the issue of succession to Mao's position of Chairman. Lin, sensing Mao's displeasure with him, began plotting to launch a *coup d'état.* He solicited the help of his son, Lin Liguo, and his son's secret organization, called the "Joint Fleet." Together they worked out a scheme called the "571 Project" involving plans to blow up Mao's train during an inspection tour in the South of China. Mao supposedly learned of the plot and returned suddenly to Beijing. Lin Biao, upon discovering Mao's arrival in Beijing, decided to transfer his accomplices and supporters to Guangzhou (Canton), where he would continue his insurrectionary activities.

From a confession by Lin Biao's daughter, Lin Liheng, the documents stated, Premier Zhou Enlai learned of Lin Biao's plans and issued an order calling for special clearance of all flights to and from Chinese airports. Lin Biao at the time was at the resort of Beidaihe on the Bay of Bohai, some 200 kilometers east of Beijing, and, recognizing defeat, decided to escape to the Soviet Union.

Late at night on September 12, 1971, so the story went, a Red Flag limousine arrived at the naval airport of Shanhaiguan near Beidaihe. There a British Trident jet with Air Force insignia and the number 256 marked on its tail was waiting. Lin Liguo emerged from the car first, shouting, "Hurry! Hurry!" Behind him were his parents, Lin Biao and Ye Qun, who rushed onto the plane. The plane took off without a complete flight crew and disregarded airport personnel who attempted to block its flight. When Premier Zhou informed Chairman Mao of Lin's escape, Mao took no action.

After about an hour the aircraft disappeared from Chinese radar screens. Shortly thereafter, in the early morning of September 13, it reportedly crashed near Öndörhaan east of Ulan Bator in Mongolia, having run out of fuel.

The site of the plane crash was later investigated by members of the Chinese embassy in the Mongolian People's Republic. They discovered the corpses of eight men and one woman. All the bodies were buried at the site of the crash.

This is the story that was filtered down to the people by party members through what was called *chuan da wen jian*, or "document-reading sessions." While some people may previously have heard rumors of a Lin-Mao conflict or even that Lin Biao had died, not until the release of the June 1972 report was the official government line on the events spelled out.

A procedure such as this, employing "secret" documents, is

frequently used as a means of communication between the Central Committee and the "masses." The effectiveness of the method relies on the fact that the masses, for whom knowledge of high-level politics is scant at best, tend to believe anything that sounds like inside information. Their assumption is that whatever warrants treatment in a top-secret Central Committee document must be the truth, and a very important truth. Furthermore, since their information on the matter is invariably limited, they are never in a position to make an independent judgment. Thus, when an incident as extraordinary as the death of Lin Biao occurs, few ordinary Chinese dare doubt what they are told about it.

The situation is vastly different for high-level cadres familiar with the workings of Chinese politics. They are experienced at reading government documents, and often in a position to gain outside knowledge through personal contacts. It was for these top leaders that the explanation provided in the official documents seemed least adequate. It was they who began questioning what they read, both for its seeming failures in logic and for key points left unclarified or unstated.

One major cause for suspicion was the seeming lack of concrete evidence for the crimes Lin Biao was accused of committing. Although the documents contained the confessions of several of Lin's top military advisors, most were devoid of any "hard" information. Nor did the disclosure of the 571 Project reveal facts about any overt action taken. Instead there were only general statements about the prevailing political situation and the conspirators' intention of taking over power.

Surprisingly, much of the evidence dealt with the activities of Lin Biao's son and his followers, the so-called Joint Fleet. The impression created by the documents was that Lin Biao had delegated a great deal of responsibility to his young, relatively inexperienced son. One could not help but notice that this did not accord with what was known of China's "invincible marshal."

Leaders who read the documents also questioned the reasons given for Lin Biao's seemingly quick and unresisting acceptance of defeat. It had supposedly been brought about by Mao's unexpected return to Beijing, yet nothing overtly threatening had occurred to cause Lin's collapse. Furthermore, Lin Biao was supposed to have had elaborate contingency plans for continued resistance in Guangzhou. Yet he never carried them out. Why would he choose to abandon his schemes even before acting on them?

Another puzzling inconsistency in the official explanation involved the statement that the plane in which Lin Biao attempted to escape had taken off from the Shanhaiguan Airport near Beidaihe. According to other original primary sources available to some high cadres, the plane that crashed in Outer Mongolia had departed from Beijing. The documents also neglected to mention that Lin Biao himself had returned to Beijing from Beidaihe before September 12, a fact which some top leaders were aware of.

The reason given for the crash of Lin's plane was that it had run out of fuel. Those who had experience working with aircraft knew that they are allowed to take off only with a full tank. The plane had been parked at the airport for several hours before taking off, and Lin was supposedly planning to use it to fly to Guangzhou, a greater distance from the Shanhaiguan Airport than the crash site in Mongolia. The suspicion was that either the Trident was not prepared to go to Guangzhou (or anywhere else) or it had not crashed due to lack of fuel.

Mao had apparently requested that the corpses be buried at the site of the crash; at least this is what was said to have been done. According to international custom, the remains of those killed in flight accidents are returned to the home country. In this case, where the dead were prominent members of the Chinese military and where the crash took place only a few hundred kilometers from the Chinese border, there seemed to be little justification for burying them hastily in the Mongolian People's Republic.

These are some of the inconsistencies one encounters upon close scrutiny of the official account of the Lin Biao incident. Their significance grows as we recognize—as we must—that the incident occurred against a backdrop of violent political competition. Lin Biao's importance and power at the time of his death make skepticism even more necessary. Why, for example, would Mao, a recognized expert at self-aggrandizement, report the events with such secrecy and vagueness if his deeds were truly heroic and Lin's truly villainous? Why the delay in notifying even high-level cadres? Suspicion of foul play is overwhelming; substantiating that suspicion has been the challenge.

The author of this book was among those shown the official documents concerning Lin Biao's death. The questions they raised seemed unanswerable for a long time until—quite by accident—he chanced to see a document relating to the affair that was different in significant respects from the others. It too was labeled TOP SECRET, and, like the others, it dealt with testimony from a participant in the plot, but the testimony itself was markedly richer and more believable. He was later able to secure access to more of this class of "truthful" documents, and grew to recognize how much they varied from those displayed as part of the official account. Eventually he reached an inescapable conclusion: that Wang Dongxing, Mao's closest aide, and the others who were responsible for the investigation of the Lin Biao Affair had in fact executed a huge cover-up.

The author continued to pursue his theory and with the help of personal connections was able to find much supporting evidence. His principal breakthrough came, however, when he was allowed to see a set of private memoirs written by a man named Zhao Yanji, now dead, who had been intimately involved in many aspects of the investigation of the Lin Biao incident. The memoirs were uniquely comprehensive, clear and reliable. Even in matters of little consequence Zhao Yanji seemed to display exceptional veracity. The memoirs offered a basis for verifying and confirming other materials, and from them much of the information contained in this book is drawn. They are quoted at length, though for the sake of protecting individuals, they could not be used *in toto*.

The memoirs were most valuable in providing the author with a sophisticated understanding of the process whereby the news of Lin Biao's death was made public. The fact is that Mao Zedong had every reason to prevent others from knowing what really happened. The true story reveals uncomfortably much about the power struggles, military maneuvering, secret intelligence operations, violence and life-style of the upper echelons of Chinese leadership.

Because Lin's death was sudden, Mao had little time to develop a plausible explanation for it. He was, however, able to temporize by strictly controlling all information regarding Lin Biao's final days and by severely punishing anyone who violated the news blackout.

Eventually he wove together fact and fiction in an elaborate story concerning Lin's death and began the even more elaborate process of documenting it. He then proceeded to "leak" the appropriate information—more accurately, the misinformation—to convince China and the world that his "explanation" was the truth.

Mao placed Wang Dongxing, as head of the General Office of the Central Committee, in charge of orchestrating the information. Wang set up two basic systems. One dealt with the actual facts of the Lin Biao Affair, including tapes, photographs and unedited interrogatory records. These materials, of the utmost secrecy, were accessible only to the handful of people actually involved in the cover-up work.

The other system contrived a complete picture of the Lin Biao Affair as Mao wished it to be seen. This system likewise generated materials treated as internal documents of top secrecy and were labeled SECRET, CLASSIFIED or TOP SECRET. The difference is, however, that these documents—while in many cases similar to the "true" ones—had been added to, deleted from, supplemented and/or revised. The resulting materials were those used by the Chinese government to disclose the "facts" of the Lin Biao Affair.

To keep these two systems of information distinct, the former was categorized as "Class i Files of the Central Committee" while the latter was simply called "Central Committee Documents." The author would like to note that the doctoring of materials used in official secret documents is not an uncommon practice and was used on occasion by Lin Biao himself. Nevertheless the extent to which doctored sources were used in documents related to the Lin Biao Affair was, in the author's opinion, exceptionally great.

This book incorporates materials taken almost exclusively from "Class I Files" and the memoirs of Zhao Yanji. Thus, while the story in many instances parallels the official account, it is far more detailed and complete, and in several critical respects—the role of Mao, particularly, and the circumstances of the death of Lin Biao and his wife, Ye Qun—radically different from anything that has been reported before.

For the benefit of the reader, supplementary notes to each chapter at the end of the book make plain where and how the sources of information used by the author differ from the official account.

In addition to written materials, the author was able, over the course of several years, to speak with many military and political leaders, some now living, some dead, some who were rising, some who were falling, their spouses, mistresses, secretaries, relatives, friends, colleagues and staff. Most did not know they were being "interviewed." A few needed to unburden their consciences. Still others knew they had nothing to lose by telling the truth.

Why is the story being told only now, a decade after the bizarre disappearance of Lin Biao? Time has allowed the author to check and recheck sources and facts. Time has allowed the incident to take its place in history. And time has confirmed that the deception was intended to be permanent. The perfect and most dramatic opportunity for revealing the true facts presented itself during the historic trials of the "counter-revolutionary cliques" of Jiang Qing and Lin Biao in 1980–81. Yet it did not occur. Despite their symbolic importance as public proof that the forces responsible for the "ten turbulent years" of the Cultural Revolution had finally been expunged, the trials were finally a disappointment, if not a complete mockery, lacking as they were in the presentation of concrete

11

evidence for the actual crimes with which the defendants were charged.

In the case of Lin Biao the chief defendants—Huang Yong-sheng, Wu Faxian, Li Zuopeng and Qiu Huizuo—were the only surviving members of Lin Biao's "clique." All had been imprisoned since Lin Biao's death in 1971. In court, answering charges of conspiracy in the plot to assassinate Mao, all confessed to their "counter-revolutionary" crimes and profusely apologized for them. Their statements, however, begged more questions than they answered. Doubts about exactly what happened to their ring-leader, Lin Biao, were even more pronounced than before.

Both they and the leaders in power today have continued to keep their lips sealed. One perhaps cannot blame them. How would the Chinese people react to the truth? Mao Zedong Thought is still taught, his legend still upheld. Having been so thoroughly deified, Mao can absorb deflationary stabs and still retain his larger-than-life dimensions. Yet the leaders of China now and for a long time to come have a great deal at stake in the founder of the People's Republic. Mao shaped the new China, its party, system and state, the mind and spirit of its people; the leaders today inherited all this from one man, and so they cling desperately to him as a unifying, legitimizing force without which their own identities would be seriously weakened.

Nevertheless the time has come to tell the truth about this episode. One can and must undertake to restore history's original face, for history's sake, for the sake of those who unwittingly helped in distorting it and for the sake of those who wish and deserve to know what sort of masquerade they have been forced to witness.

I

The author of the memoirs excerpted in this chapter was a high-level cadre in the Security Bureau of the Central Committee. His name at the time of his death was Zhao Yanji, but he had many others. For reasons of safety and convenience, he, like all those who do "secret work" in the highest organs of the party, had assumed a professional name. Since the founding of the People's Republic in 1949 he had used as many as seven names. His most recent name had been adopted in 1971.

In that year he was transferred to the Party Central Committee's "Classified Office of the Special Case on Lin Biao" by its head, Wang Dongxing. Members of the Special Case staff were mostly personnel from the Central Committee's affiliate organs, the Ministry of Public Security and the People's Liberation Army's General Political Department. But even they did not know of the existence of Zhao or his work. They were prevented from knowing by his overriding authority and the nature of his duties.

Zhao's new position allowed—in fact, sometimes required—intimate association with and interrogation of those who were personally involved in the Lin Biao Affair. He was, thus, one of the handful of people able to discover the truth behind it. Yet his work, ironically, was covering up the truth.

At the same time that Zhao was acting as an investigator he was also nominal head of an organization called the General Office

Special Investigative Division. This organization also dealt with the Lin Biao Affair. But its function was the invention of events and documents to support them—in short, the manufacture of a cover-up.

Zhao Yanji was already in poor health when he began writing the memoirs and died before finishing them. It can never be known for certain whether or not he intended by means of this document to elucidate the events and correct the distorted information. Clearly, he was reluctant to take his secrets to his grave, for he left the memoirs with a relative. They were later discovered by the Central Committee and sealed in its archives. Our conjecture is that the act of writing the memoirs enabled him to better analyze and reflect upon his investigation as he was performing it. In any case, the memoirs appear to be accurate in all respects, and this is the first time any of the manuscript has been published.

On September 14, 1971, I was bathing at a beach in Dalian in Northeast China called Fu Jiazhuang. It is one of the best beaches in Dalian and belongs to the Shenyang Military Command. Also at the beach were several other Army and Air Force officers in their fifties and sixties. I was suffering from what I had originally thought to be cancer but was finally diagnosed as an intestinal disorder. Thus, whereas medically I had been freed of my death sentence, politically I was a walking corpse, having been exiled, placed under house arrest and finally neglected. I was now being given the opportunity to rest.

At about eleven A.M. a security guard came to say that someone wanted to see me. As I headed back to the recreation room, a man came toward me. He wore a military uniform and appeared to be in his forties. He was of medium build, pale and wore glasses. Speaking with a Sichuan accent, he told me that his name was Chi Yutang and that he was a cadre of the 8341 Unit, the so-called Palace Guards[1] serving the Military Commission of the Central Committee. He was to escort me to Beijing. He provided no reason for the trip.

It had been a long time since I had been asked to move with such haste. I was not to return to the Baqi Sanitorium,[2] so I phoned the person on duty there and left a message. Then I followed Chi Yutang to a car that carried us to the Zhoushuizi Airport. Awaiting us there was an An-24 plane from the 34th Division of the Air Force.[3] Once seated in the cabin, I noticed that there were no other passengers. I thought at first that we would wait for others to come aboard before taking off; but Chi Yutang simply motioned to someone in the cockpit and the plane's engine was started.

The flight from Dalian to Beijing was made in virtual silence. A woman soldier emerged once to ask if I wanted tea. Chi Yutang didn't utter a word. I had no idea whether this trip signified a blessing or an evil omen. All I knew was that it was no ordinary venture.

I recalled that something odd had happened earlier that day. The Deputy Chief-of-Staff of the Shenyang Military Region and I had arranged to play chess. But he had left for Shenyang first thing that morning without a word. His wife came to tell me that he had been called away by Xiao Quanfu, a deputy commander of the Shenyang Military Region. The peculiarity was that his telephone call to his wife had been made from strategic head-quarters in the caves of the mountains. The Deputy Chief and I were good friends, an unusual relationship because he was also my subordinate. His sudden summons struck me as odd.

My own military position was prestigious, but I had not been privy to important military affairs for a long time. I had never held a combat command, but, to quote Mao Zedong on the occasion of conferring my military rank in 1955, I had "made masterful contributions *off* the battlefield."[4] Under the guidance of Zhou Enlai, Li Kenong, Kang Sheng, Wu Defeng, Ye Jianying and others, during the Anti-Japanese Wars, the War of Liberation and the Korean War, I drafted various successful plans for special military aid, intelligence operations and politics of alliance. Had someone rediscovered something of value in my experience and thought to put it to use? This was one of many questions that I asked myself as I descended from the plane in Beijing.

It was about noon and very warm. The sky was empty of

clouds or planes. There were several large aircraft parked at the airport, one of which I later learned was a Trident. A black Red Flag sedan drove down the runway to pick me up. I immediately recognized the license-plate number of the car—it belonged to the fleet of the Jingxi Hotel, which is used chiefly as the headquarters of the General Staff's Administrative Bureau. It had been several years since I had been in one of those cars. As we drove away, I noticed that parked in front of the airport lobby were two "56" tanks and several jeeps, while uniformed, rifle-bearing soldiers patrolled the building.

I was familiar with the Western Suburbs Airport. It was the headquarters site of the 34th Division of the Military Air Transport Service and of the 100th Regiment of the 34th Division. Some of the best-trained troops in the Air Force belonged to this division, and normally their defense of this airport could not be interfered with by any other unit. At first I thought that the soldiers were Central Committee Security troops and were preparing to meet a VIP from a passenger plane. But tanks at the airport? I didn't remember ever having seen that before.

How was I to know that my plane was the first plane to land at the airport since martial law in the air had been proclaimed at about one or two o'clock that morning? How was I to know that all Air Force equipment and activities were being controlled by the Army?

I was given a room on the fifth floor of the Jingxi Hotel. Joining Chi Yutang, the shadow who hadn't once let me out of his sight, was Su Quande, a bodyguard. This thirty-seven-year-old cadre from the Confidentiality Bureau of the Military Commission was slender and short. He was also a chain smoker and was forever bowing to me in a deferential manner.

I waited at the Jingxi Hotel for two days. This caused me to question the urgency of my arrival. I wanted to call the Baqi Sanitorium in Dalian to ask someone to bring my belongings to Beijing. But Chi Yutang reminded me that Central Committee regulations forbade my making telephone calls, writing letters, receiving visitors, going out or talking with others—the so-called "Five Forbiddens." Su Quande had me write a note instead, authorizing someone to pick up my things in Dalian; three days later he brought me all my belongings exactly as I had left them.

So that I would not bump into acquaintances, all my meals were sent to my room. Twice, however, I was caught off guard. Zhou Xihan, Deputy Commander of the Navy, entered my room by mistake one day, recognized me, sat down and proceeded to chat at length. Chi Yutang and Su Quande eased the situation by saying that it was time for us to leave. We made a show of going out, bade farewell to Zhou Xihan and so gave him the slip. The second incident occurred at a barber shop, where I met Xiao Ke, the principal-to-be of the Military Political Academy. We were both getting crew cuts. It was awkward trying to get away from him.

I spent each day in my room and on the terrace, walking around in circles. At six P.M. on September 18 the telephone rang. Chi Yutang answered, then informed me that I had an invitation to meet with "someone." Things certainly had changed: in the past anyone who called, even Mao Zedong, would leave his name. Rather confused, I departed from the Jingxi Hotel in a late-model Red Flag sedan.

The car drove into the underground garage of the Great Hall of the People on Tiananmen Square. We ascended in an elevator, and I was escorted into a small banquet room where a small table was already set. Chi Yutang and Su Quande stood at attention behind me as I turned around and saw someone enter the room. He greeted me with an extended hand and a "How are you?" It was Wang Dongxing. Two or three years had passed since I had last seen him. He had put on some weight, and his face was partially marked with a rash. The two of us dined alone, and our conversation was intriguing. I remember it as clearly as if it had happened only last night.

"I've invited you here tonight to eat," he began, "but not to drink. There is something very important that you can do for us. It was I who requested that you come." I said nothing, merely nodded my head. He glanced at me, then lowered his head and stared at the dishes. He jabbed his chopsticks into the food, shoveled it from side to side, and yawned throughout the meal. His manners hadn't changed a bit.

The meeting was not at all what I had expected. He looked at

17

me with reddened eyes and said, "It's been four or five days since I had a full night's sleep. What do you think of that?"

That busy?

"Busy?! . . . This time the knife has been stabbed all the way through my heart. . . ." He threw his chopsticks down, straightened his back, stared at me unblinkingly and nodded his head.

I was beginning to feel faint with apprehension. Perhaps it was my poor health, but I began to sweat. Something—I wasn't quite sure what—had happened. I waited awhile, then started probing with questions. "What's going on? Is Beijing at war?"

He shook his head, but didn't speak. Then he stood up, paced back and forth across the room twice and, stopping behind me, said, "Lin Biao tried to escape, and his plane crashed."

I cannot describe my shock upon hearing his words. This remains the first and only explanation I was ever formally given regarding Lin Biao's death.

It was precisely to discuss this matter that Wang Dongxing had arranged the dinner. He told me that there were two sections responsible for the investigation of Lin Biao: he headed one, Zhou Enlai the other.

Wang Dongxing's assignment for me involved investigating, examining and reporting on certain materials that would contradict the Central Committee's official statements about Lin Biao. I was to limit the circulation of this material to the smallest possible sphere and, moreover, ascertain and verify its source. I was also responsible for dealing appropriately with those who were implicated as a result of the investigation.

He would give me enormous freedom in my work, including the right to circumvent the Central Committee's Classified Office of the Special Case on Lin Biao (headed by himself) in the investigation, arrest, imprisonment, interrogation and punishment of individuals. He would also make available to me personnel and information from the Public Security Ministry, General Political Security Department (belonging to the military) and the 8341 Guards. I would be reimbursed for all expenditures by the National Treasury itself and could even bypass the Financial

Organ in my requests. The scope of these privileges engendered in me a vague uneasiness.

Almost four months later, on January 4, 1972, Wang Dongxing invited me to his house in Zhongnanhai for dinner. After a brief discussion of my work, he showed me several reports to the Ministry of Public Security and the Central Committee on the reaction of the foreign, Taiwanese and Hong Kong press to the Lin Biao Affair, plus summaries of foreign intelligence service theories about what happened.

"How did they get hold of official Chinese documents so quickly?" I asked. I was understandably concerned about leaks.

Wang Dongxing waved his hand dismissively. The information, he explained, had been leaked to them intentionally for propaganda purposes. The Chairman had said that it was better to let others think they had uncovered the story and worked it out to their own satisfaction. Wang Dongxing reiterated that if information should appear which contradicted the facts as described by the Central Committee documents, I should report it to him, control its circulation and investigate the source and development.

Toward the end of the meal he looked at me very sternly and warned that should the Lin Biao Affair turn out to be far more complicated than I had ever expected, I ought to be mentally prepared. He didn't say what I should prepare for, or how. He only emphasized that I must maintain my full equanimity in any event.

On a later occasion Wang Dongxing's assistant Wang Liangen, deputy director of the Central Committee's General Office and one of the three directors of the Special Case on Lin Biao, came to see me to discuss the technical details of my work. Did I need more help, for instance, or to have personnel transferred? Shortly afterward Wang Liangen contracted a fatal disease and died. I was left with a deep impression of a man whose thin, haggard face betrayed the terrific pressure of working under Wang Dongxing.[5]

I too felt under similar pressure. Not only did the nature of my work restrict my activities, my entire life-style was changed. Wang Dongxing provided housing for my family and an office for me, both in the vicinity of the Imperial Palace and thickly guarded by frequently changed soldiers. But my place of work became more or less my place of residence, as I visited my real home only occasionally.

My work was not without its rewards, though. I worked closely with Wang Dongxing and met periodically with Premier Zhou, who seemed quite convinced of the authenticity of my materials. On a few rare occasions I even met with Chairman Mao himself.

In short, that first meeting with Wang Dongxing changed my life. For a long time I did my work quietly and dutifully. It was only much later, after many puzzles had been unlocked, that I gained some idea about the real objective of my work. Had I found it out sooner, I might not have been allowed to continue.

At the beginning I didn't encounter anything particularly unusual. Sometimes, however, I felt an overwhelming desire to visit the Qincheng prison and meet with those who had lost their freedom as a consequence of the Lin Biao Affair: Huang Yongsheng, Wu Faxian, Li Zuopeng, Qiu Huizuo and Jiang Tengjiao, among others.

I had one unforgettable meeting in the offices of the "Three-Doors" Military Commission.[6] It was with a pale, fragile, plain-looking woman. She seemed exhausted, and in her eyes was a look of doom. Lin Liheng, nicknamed Lin Doudou, was the daughter of Lin Biao. She was later to become instrumental in my investigation.

My investigation of Lin Biao's actual activities during the critical months before his death was severely handicapped by the fact that official records of virtually all his telephone conversations had been destroyed. (Ma Yuying of the Military Commission and Feng Yinjie of the Air Force were the cadres working in the communications stations responsible for burning the records.) Fortunately, over a substantial period of time I was able to retrieve and compile many of the notes kept by the secretaries of Lin Biao and others. These "records of key events" soon filled my vault and ultimately proved more useful than the testimony of individuals.

One thing I was given to understand was that contact between Lin Biao and his peers had been quite normal. It was his son, Lin Liguo, a member of the Air Force and the organizer of a small subversive group in Shanghai called the "Joint Fleet," who was supposedly responsible for the crimes with which Lin Biao had been formally charged. As everyone was told, it was the Joint Fleet that had made plans to assassinate Mao Zedong. When the plans fell through, Lin Biao was said to have attempted to escape in a Trident, #256. The plane crashed in Outer Mongolia, killing everyone inside.

The Chinese Communist Central Committee document *Lin Biao's Anti-Party Clique* contained a great deal of political criticism of Lin Biao but virtually no evidence of his actual activities. Huang Yongsheng and others were similarly declared guilty of criminal acts, but no specifics were supplied. The overwhelming bulk of the information centered on Lin Liguo and the activities of the Joint Fleet, including documentation of the 571 Project and pictures of weapons and equipment.

As I read the accumulated materials, I raised the following questions, among others, that sparked doubts and seemed worth pursuing:

1. Lin Liguo and his Joint Fleet had indeed planned to kill Mao, but their plans had been canceled at the last minute. Why?

2. Mao's sudden return to Beijing from his southern tour coincided with the Lin Biao Affair. What had Mao's intentions been?

3. How did Lin Biao manage his sudden escape attempt if his daughter, Lin Liheng, had previously exposed his activities to Zhou Enlai and the 8341 Guards?

4. How was it that Huang Yongsheng, Wu Faxian, Li Zuopeng, Qiu Huizuo and other close associates were not in any way involved in Lin Biao's escape?

5. Why were orders never given from any post of any rank that the Trident #256 be intercepted?

6. How could Lin Biao have let his wife and son conduct the

key battles in the Lin-Mao struggle while he retreated to his seaside villa at Beidaihe? What made him give up so easily by attempting to escape to the Soviet Union? This last point, because it so contradicted Lin Biao's character and career as I knew them, particularly concerned me.

I first met Lin Biao a year or two after he had achieved his first big victory at Pingxingguan during the Anti-Japanese Wars. The year was 1940, the city was Moscow and I accompanied Soviet friends to see my Chinese compatriot. The young general's name had reverberated sonorously during the Long March and the Anti-Japanese Wars; I had to suppress my excitement and unease.

He was pale and fragile, with the feeble physique of a scholar. He wore a plain gray flannel uniform, and his face beamed an unassuming smile. If not for the thick, jet-black eyebrows and a serene determination in his eyes, it would have been difficult to believe that the young man extending his hand before the Soviet-style fireplace was the famous Chinese Communist general Lin Biao.

After the meeting I was able to establish a relationship with Lin Biao in Moscow. Since he was essentially the liaison between the Chinese and Soviet Communist parties, he was also my superior.

The unusually high esteem in which Stalin held Lin Biao was quite evident. He enjoyed the most privileged living conditions. He was able to meet regularly with first-rate theoreticians while conducting arduous research for his study "The Essence of Victory."

Lin Biao returned to China in 1942 and in 1945 proceeded to march into Manchuria, developing there the Fourth Field Army, our party's strongest. He swept through the country from north to south, winning the Liaoning-Shenyang battles and the Beijing-Tianjin battles. He led the crossing of the Yangzi River and carried away central and southern China, fighting all the way to the Leizhou Peninsula and Hainan Island until all of Chiang Kai-shek's 2,700,000 men were either annihilated, captured or forced to revolt and cross over to us. Lin Biao's victories spanned the larger half of China.

Lin Biao was a great strategist as well as a decisive commander on the field. The strongest element in his character was his confidence in himself alone. He was utterly independent and self-reliant. Lin Biao once wrote a scroll for Liu Yalou, Chief-of-Staff of the Fourth Field Army, that Liu now regards as a creed. The scroll says, "In matters of life and death, others are secondary; you alone are all-important. This is the essence of a winner."

During the Korean War, Lin Biao risked conflict with Mao Zedong by refusing the position of supreme commander. He used illness as a pretext; but later, during several of our frequent meetings, he hinted that he had refused the command because he had neither understood the American Army well nor felt comfortable with fighting conditions in Korea. He had felt no *guarantee* of victory.

While Marshal Peng Dehuai directed the war in Korea, the rumor spread that in fact Lin Biao was the one in command. I knew otherwise because I worked briefly with Lin in China. During one meeting I happened to mention his study "The Essence of Victory." His manner suddenly became cool and stern. He spoke slowly: "If you are confident, then you can expect victory. You must rely as little as possible on the abilities of others, no matter how much experience they have or how superior their strength. This is the key. First, people are not to be trusted. Second, you must not leave yourself empty-handed: you are the nerve center of all war activities. Third, the way to save your own skin is to get your enemy's blood and guts first. To achieve victory, you must leave the enemy behind in the valley of death, and it is best to put him there at the very outset. There is a proverb that says: He who strikes first is ahead."

Mao Zedong called Lin Biao "the unmatched marshal," "the invincible marshal." Stalin praised him as "the foremost Chinese commander, whose intelligence and courage surpass all. He is a red iron wrist." Chiang Kai-shek cursed him as "a demon in war," at the same time acknowledging that he was "someone who held the key to military secrets."

It seemed incongruous, impossible, that Lin Biao, given his character and career, would suddenly withdraw like the head of a turtle in Beidaihe, defer to his wife and son in the life-and-death struggle against Mao and attempt no strategy of his own. Would Lin Biao have placed his career—his very life—in inexperienced hands against the powerful Mao, under whose feet a succession of political enemies had fallen? This Lin Biao simply did not correspond to the Lin Biao of history: he was another person, someone reckless, incompetent and ignorant of both military and political affairs. At first baffled, I was now becoming suspicious.

Unless there was another Lin Biao, I couldn't help speculating. Or . . . perhaps the Lin Biao Affair had not happened quite as the Central Committee had explained it. I suddenly found myself in an awkward position. For my suspicions, justified or not, put me in an impossible position. I had been ordered by Wang Dongxing and Wang Liangen to procure information and coordinate my findings with those provided by the Central Committee documents. If my suspicions were true, reconciliation was out of the question. Yet at the same time the nature of my work gave me an unparalleled opportunity to verify or to dispel these suspicions. It was probable that my efforts would, as in the past, go mainly toward disguising historical truth, deceiving others and protecting hypocrites. This time, however, I wanted to ensure that I myself would not be deceived.

II

It is *de rigueur* in Communist China for children of high-level leaders to join the military. In the military, promotions come fast, privileges are many and family background wields tremendous influence. The Air Force especially is a breeding ground for the elite. It had been this way since the Communist Air Force was first established. Liu Yalou, Lin's Chief-of-Staff in the Fourth Field Army, was chosen as the first commander of the Air Force. He combined old-fashioned discipline with modern tactics, and under his influence the Air Force soon became the *crème de la crème,* the best trained and most devoted of all military forces. Likewise, it was the most richly endowed in everything from personnel to weaponry to "extras."

It therefore came as no surprise when Lin Biao's two children joined the ranks of the Air Force.

The elder of the two was his daughter, Lin Liheng, nicknamed Lin Doudou (meaning "small beans," a favorite food of his). She joined the Air Force Press in 1966. She was a privileged, restless and proud young woman who liked posing as a noble intellectual. As the daughter of the Minister of Defense, she was ceaselessly fawned on and flattered, and within a year had her own following. Among the countless splinter groups formed during the Cultural Revolution, Lin Doudou led one of her own called "The Foolish Old Man Who Moved Mountains," the name of a parable Mao

Zedong was extremely fond of citing. In 1969 she was named associate editor of the Air Force Press, which was probably the peak of her political career.

Younger than his sister by a year, Lin Liguo was the more aggressive of Lin Biao's two children. He was tall—a good head taller than his father—and handsome. While resembling his mother in most respects, Lin Liguo inherited two indisputable traits of his father's: thick eyebrows and ambition. When he joined the Air Force in 1967 at the age of twenty-two, he was said to be "like a newborn calf unafraid of tigers."

Much to the dismay of his colleagues, he turned out to be immature, politically naïve and uninterested in military affairs. Despite efforts by his parents and their friends to indoctrinate him properly, he did not, at first, seem to appreciate his own potential.

For the first few years his connections with the Air Force were highly personal. They began with something called the "search group," organized at the request of his mother, whose gravest concern for her son involved finding him the proper mate. After much urging, she convinced her colleague Wu Faxian to assign several of his men to this duty, while Wu's wife, Chen Suiqi, took charge of them.

Lin Liguo was not sure he was ready for marriage. He had had two unsuccessful affairs. One was with a classmate at the elite Beijing Eighth Middle School, who subsequently died of illness, leaving him grieving. Another romance, with a classmate at Qinghua University, never in fact came to anything because he could not work up the courage to approach her. He was deeply annoyed when she went off with another man, and then blamed his parents for his own pride and passivity.

After he had been in the Air Force for a while, however, Lin Liguo began to grow fond of his privileges and the attention he attracted. It did not take long for him to become swollen with arrogance and egotism, even in respect to girls.

Lin Liguo looked on his mother's matchmaking efforts with unconcern. He did not so much disapprove of the activity as he did of her choices. They were often good-looking but not beautiful;

poised but not sophisticated; nice but not enchanting. They seemed to satisfy Ye Qun's political criteria, but were not the type to get under her son's skin.

Finding the right girl for Lin Liguo was no easy task, and it was getting on everybody's nerves. The best advice on how to proceed came finally from Jiang Tengjiao, the Deputy Political Commissar of the Air Force, who was known as an old hand with women. He suggested to Ye Qun and Chen Suiqi that Lin Liguo himself lead the search, and that he begin in places like Shanghai, Hangzhou and Suzhou. (These places, in his estimation, were by far the "best hunting grounds.") After all, it was Lin Liguo who would finally have to pick his "imperial concubine."

Chen Suiqi's patience was exhausted and she was willing to go along with this suggestion. Lin Liguo felt he had nothing to lose; the prospect of some free-style romancing, in fact, appealed to him.

On his first trip to Shanghai he immediately reorganized the "search group." He sent what he regarded as the orthodox old fogies back to Wu Faxian and replaced them with some of his peers. The new organization was called the "Shanghai Group."

One of the most valuable members of the Shanghai Group was an English translator in the Intelligence Department of the Air Force named Chen Lunhe. He was short and spunky, and on his first private meeting with Lin Liguo concerning some translations, he launched into a vivid and detailed description of a Western pornographic magazine.

The meeting cemented Lin's relationship with Chen Lunhe and pornographic magazines. Soon *Playboy* and *Penthouse* became Lin's regular bedtime reading. He began obtaining them in bulk by sending a courier at short intervals to the town of Shumchun just across the border from Hong Kong.

The diaries of an active member of the Shanghai Group, Xi Zhuxian, records some details of their activities:

> We normally worked individually with our own assistants and made frequent trips to Shanghai, Hangzhou and Nanjing, some-times with stops at Suzhou, Ningbo and Wuxi. We would carry

weapons and special Air Force identification with us at all times. In Shanghai we possessed an additional ID issued by Wang Weiguo and the Military Control Commission that allowed us to travel freely anywhere in Shanghai, call for cars and bypass the usual channels in general. Sometimes our activities attracted the attention of the Shanghai security forces: when this happened, our ID's came in very handy.

We mostly looked for girls in public places: theaters, parks, shopping centers—and sometimes in art and performance circles. After we spotted them, we would find out their names and investigate their backgrounds. If Lin Liguo approved of our choices based on photographs and files, we'd arrange for a meeting. We could easily lure a girl by saying that she had a chance of becoming a secretary in a special high-level military organ. She was usually very willing based on this information alone.

The next step was to observe her nude. This was Lin Liguo's means of judging her. When in Shanghai, he observed women daily. Elsewhere he made special flights and crammed many viewings into one sitting. He said it was the most relaxing form of entertainment, even more enjoyable than watching foreign movies.

The beauty of our system for observing the women nude was that it didn't require the subject's knowledge. We would simply use the pretext of a physical examination. We had occupied, in the name of the Military Control Commission, the residence of a former capitalist. One room was set aside as the examining room, and it was partitioned off with an entire wall of one-way mirrors. Observation took place through these mirrors. Accommodations were continually added for better and safer viewing —sound insulation, amplifiers, adjustable lights, closed-circuit TV, a ball of mirrored lenses which hung from the center of the ceiling.

Similar rooms were set up in Hangzhou and Nanjing, but they were not quite as elaborate as the one in Shanghai. In fact, Lin Liguo rarely visited the other places; he preferred to have the girls taken to Shanghai.

The examination was performed by women doctors who were

carefully selected and frequently rotated. They were not aware of what was behind the mirrors and they never knew where they were, for they were escorted to the examining room in curtained cars at night.

Lounging on a plush divan, imbibing good liquor, Lin Liguo took his time studying each girl, her physique, posture, fitness and beauty. If he liked what he saw, he requested a second and still more intimate examination.

Lin Liguo would often videotape the entire process and then invite his friends to private showings.[1]

From the "patients" who had passed the examination with flying colors, Lin Liguo eventually accumulated about twenty mistresses. The transition from the examining room to the bedroom sometimes met with resistance. As they later found out, being one of the chosen had its degrading aspects. One of Lin's favorite "concubines," a tall and lithe nineteen-year-old named Qi Zhijing, gave testimony that:

> . . . When Lin Liguo got really crazy, he beat me, bit my breasts and legs until I was black and blue. I was left with scars on my genitals. After intercourse he would put on his uniform and, with the airs of a general, reprimand me for being old-fashioned. He said I didn't understand the essence of masculinity. He said I hadn't yet awakened from the ignorance from which he was trying to rescue me.[2]

But more often than not the girls rationalized their submission as an honorable proof of loyalty to Father Lin. They weren't merely chosen as sex objects to occupy Lin Liguo's privately run brothel, as a crude interpretation might have it; they were intelligent and well-bred young women who welcomed this privilege of serving the son of a great leader. Their lives were suddenly "better," less ordinary, more prestigious. They were all given employment in the network of units under Lin's administration and granted nominal military status. They lived in the luxury of the most privileged and the excitement of the most powerful. Except for Lin Liguo's favorite mistresses, called "the Tiger's Angels," none had any direct knowledge of what he did, beyond his activities as a womanizer.

Had it not been for his mother's relentless prodding, Lin Liguo might have done little else but wallow in this decadent and promiscuous life, a life not untypical of others who were the progeny of top military figures. But Ye Qun had grander designs for him, and her colleagues would help him achieve them. She shuttled back and forth between Wu Faxian, Huang Yongsheng and the people beneath them, searching for an "apprenticeship" for her son. She sought a position of responsibility which she hoped would lead to an interest in the world of politics and the military. A somewhat strained mother-son relationship had prevented her from approaching her son directly—until one day when the two had a dramatic confrontation.

Lin Liguo had begun bugging the phones of his family's home. He acted out of rebellion and a love of mischief, enjoying the idea of dabbling in such tricks of his father's trade as espionage. By sheer happenstance he picked up evidence that his mother and Huang Yongsheng were engaged in an affair, and decided to use it as an instrument of extortion.

He played the tape for his mother—a conversation in which she and Huang Yongsheng exchanged words of love and affection. He waited for her to break down in embarrassment or a tear-filled apology. To his surprise, Ye Qun seemed scarcely ruffled by the incriminating evidence, and instead attacked him, accusing him of naïveté and lecturing him about the desirability, if not necessity, of cultivating "that kind" of relationship with the true followers of Lin Biao. She explained how Lin Biao's appointment as Mao's successor months earlier had suddenly made relations with "those" people, Mao's people, increasingly delicate and trying. Under the changed circumstances, she and her older friends experienced a renewed intimacy, political and otherwise.

She then broached a matter she had not planned on revealing to her son: Lin Biao's health. Although kept a state secret, it had been poor for a long time. He displayed symptoms of some unidentified diseases, worrisome enough to cause her to have a new vision of the role of the family. She was determined to conserve and continue the Lin family regime. In much the same way that Chiang Ching-kuo appeared likely to inherit and retain the power of his father, Chiang Kai-shek, Lin Liguo would prepare for and assume the role of crown prince. So Ye Qun hoped.

It was Lin Liguo who felt embarrassed at the end of the conversation. It had jolted him into a recognition of his own mission in life. He had always glided in the wake of his father without thinking ahead to the consequences. His father's ill health meant that he now had to plan and act, quickly.

No longer conniving behind her son's back, Ye Qun continued soliciting help from her well-placed friends. Her biggest achievement came when she convinced the chief of the Air Force Operations Department to make Lin Liguo his deputy chief. She achieved this by suggesting to Chief Lu Min that he might one day become Lin Biao's chief advisor in the General Staff.

Lu Min, as it turned out, was an excellent choice. The first thing he did was to establish a relationship in which Lin Liguo always felt that he had the upper hand. To instill in the young Lin a sense of pride and responsibility in his work, Lu Min had to give up many of his own duties. He also succeeded in getting him excited about war. He proved to him that MiG fighters could be just as sexy as girls.

Lu Min became Lin Liguo's walking encyclopedia. Having achieved fame as a war hero, Lu was extremely well versed in the past battles of the Chinese military (though far less knowledgeable about foreign techniques). His colorful and animated stories contributed to Lin's enthusiasm. Lin particularly liked it when Lu attracted a large audience with his orations. Lin Liguo would then pretend that he was the commanding officer, while the others were his advisors and executive subordinates. He liked to imagine the feeling of power.

When Lu Min's talk turned to current strategic activity and the Air Force control of nuclear weaponry, Lin's impression of power seemed close to reality. On one occasion Lu Min discussed a battle plan drafted and approved by Lin Biao stipulating that if China and America approached serious conflict, China would make the first strike. It would fire air-to-surface guided missiles from transport planes at three targets in Japan and one in Korea where there were large American military contingents.

The crux of the plan was the belief that a weaker China could conquer a stronger America because America lacked nerve. Lin Biao was convinced that any American President would choose to retreat in such a situation. Certainly Western Europe, Eastern Europe, even the Soviet Union were sufficiently interested in preventing the spread of nuclear war to pressure the United States to back down rather than fight.

By now Lin Liguo had terminated his "beauty contest." Rather than worry any longer about the sexual finesse of his women, he began training them in the use of handguns and secret code. He put his Shanghai Group followers through rigorous training, imbuing them with a sense of loyalty and power, flattering them by calling them a new "ruling class."

But while Lin effectively gathered strength in Shanghai, he felt handicapped in Beijing. His position as Deputy Chief of the Operations Department did not afford him the freedom and power he wanted. So he approached Air Force head Wu Faxian with the request that he be allowed to establish his own independent unit in the Air Force; he would call it a "research and investigative group," and it would have the power to hire, bypass immediate superiors and give orders. It would also possess access to intelligence, weaponry, private transportation and other privileges accorded high military officers. Wu Faxian agreed on the spot and thus gave rise to Lin Liguo's "Small Group."

Lin Liguo was proud of the progress he was able to make with the Small Group. Soon he had developed quite a large contingent of supporters who were skilled, courageous and devoted. They were experienced military men, some with lofty titles, others without.

What they brought with them were skills in the use of all sorts

Lin Liguo is supposed to have had this amphibious vehicle for his own use. These pictures, allegedly seized at his secret hideout in Beijing, show Lin trying the vehicle out at the beach at Beidaihe. (From *Criminal Materials of Lin Biao's Anti-Party Clique*)

of light weaponry and vehicles, as well as in kidnapping, murder, disguise, espionage and surveillance. Lin Liguo was going to make sure that their talents did not go to waste. The Group had all the makings of a powerful force; most important of all, it was *his* force, at *his* disposal.

III

For a time the Security Bureau of the Chinese Air Force Head-quarters kept a file labeled Top-Secret Operations Document #7051909 in a fireproof metal vault. The only person who had access to this file was the Air Force Commander-in-Chief, Wu Faxian. Even the head of the Security Bureau, who was in charge of guarding the file, knew nothing about its contents. He assumed it had something important to do with military or intelligence matters.

The file in fact had nothing to do with war or intelligence, or with Air Force command. It contained a detailed report of the clandestine activities of Lin Liguo, the son of the Minister of Defense.

Why was Wu Faxian keeping a file on Lin Liguo? What did he expect to accomplish with it? Was he simply being overcautious —a habit he was sometimes chided for?

The diminutive, obese lieutenant general had a pudgy face as memorable as his remarkably rapid rise to the top of his profession. In the late 1940's, when he first caught Lin Biao's eye, he had been a young, able officer in the Red Army, commanding 50,000 or 60,000 men in the million-strong Fourth Field Army, fighting decisive battles against the Kuomintang.

After the People's Republic of China was established, Wu received the rank of lieutenant general and was assigned to help Lin

Biao's Chief-of-Staff of the Fourth Field Army, Liu Yalou, in organizing the Air Force. He was named political commissar within the new service. On the eve of the Cultural Revolution in 1966, Air Force Chief Liu Yalou became critically ill. Wu Faxian and Zhang Tingfa, the leader of a younger element of Air Force officers, vied for the vacated post. Lin (as Minister of Defense) and Liu together finally decided that Wu was the man for the job.

The Cultural Revolution witnessed Wu's unhindered political ascent. He became one of the most powerful members of the Standing Committee of the Politburo and number-three man in the People's Liberation Army. He was the first deputy chief-of-staff (under Chief-of-Staff Huang Yongsheng) and occupied the second chair in the Administrative Group of the Military Commission. For all this and more, Wu had one person to thank—Lin Biao.

Wu never forgot that his power was only as great as Lin Biao allowed it to be. Defense of his own position meant defense of Lin's. This complementary relationship with Lin, combined with Wu's compulsive, sometimes paranoiac personality, had led the general to keep a close watch on the activities of Lin's son.

When Wu Faxian first learned that Lin Liguo would be joining the Air Force in 1967, he regarded it as a blessing. Ye Qun had assured Wu's wife on several occasions that placing Lin Liguo near Wu would strengthen ties between the two families. Lin Liguo could serve as a conduit of information and ultimately protect Wu. Wu had no choice but to take him under his wing. But there were things Lin Liguo was doing which made Wu nervous. The young man seemed to feel as comfortable as a fish in water, swimming freely back and forth between the highest command organs in Beijing and the elite war troops in major military regions such as Shanghai and Guangzhou. Wu was surprised to see Lin promoted to deputy chief of the Operations Department so quickly. The responsibilities of such a post were large, and Wu wasn't sure the young man was capable of handling them. In the meantime Lin's entourage of aides and staff grew rapidly to include some of the most notable figures on the military roster.

Given his cavalier attitude, Lin Liguo might make a wrong move, offend someone, overstep the bounds; the consequences could be unpredictable. Lin Biao might be adversely affected, and Wu, as Commander-in-Chief of the Air Force, might have to take the blame.

So Wu found himself in the awkward position of simultaneously encouraging Lin's activities and deterring them. He hoped he could tame the boy while still taking advantage of his connections.

One of the ways Wu reduced the risk to himself was to spread it to others. He assigned two trusted subordinates—Zhou Yuchi and Yu Xinye—to watch over the young Lin. What their precise functions were is hard to say: they acted as assistants to Lin, the important military leader; they were advisors to Lin, the inexperienced Army man; for Lin, the son of Lin Biao, they were bodyguards; and for those curious about Lin's activities they were spies.

Zhou Yuchi was a man with a history of solid, reliable work which won him a quick promotion to deputy director of the General Office of the party committee of the Air Force. He was indebted to Wu for helping him out during some heavy bouts of factional fighting, and quite willing to keep Wu informed about Lin's handling of sudden stardom. Zhou managed to juggle his duties well, and in a short time his patience, charm and expertise completely won Lin's trust. Zhou was probably the last person Lin would have suspected of filing detailed reports on his activities to Wu Faxian.

Wu's gnawing doubt centered on his uncertainty about what Lin Biao wanted for his son. How far did Lin Biao want his son to go, and how quickly? Was Lin Biao aware of his son's activities? Wu tried to sound out Lin's opinions through his wife, Ye Qun, his colleague at the Administrative Group of the Military Commission and at Lin Biao's office. They chatted frequently and were on very good terms. But on this matter Wu was frustrated by the way she mixed her own opinions with those of her husband. He was interested in the thoughts of Lin Biao alone.

On the few occasions when Wu Faxian approached Lin Biao directly, he was always met with terse ambiguity and reserve. Then one day the time finally arrived for him to find out.

In the afternoon on that day Wu Faxian arrived at Lin Biao's residence at Maojiawan in his Red Flag car, bringing with him a stack of documents from the Air Force Headquarters. It was a regular meeting scheduled between the Minister of Defense and his Air Force Commander-in-Chief on the use of nuclear weaponry. Wu had prepared a thorough response to Lin Biao's request for information regarding possible nuclear and anti-nuclear warfare in Soviet and Japanese territories. He would propose the use of such aircraft as the MiG-21, Jian-8 (a new fighter, recently satisfactorily tested, with capabilities similar to those of the MiG-23 and F-4) and Du-16 (a Soviet-style fighter bomber that carried Chinese-made air-to-surface guided missiles and bombs).

Lin Biao didn't normally spend long periods of time on official work, but on that day he broke with habit and made the meeting drag on for hours, tirelessly analyzing the military positions of the Soviet Union, America, Japan and the Korean Peninsula.

By dinnertime, when their discussion showed no signs of ending, another Air Force officer entered the room—the deputy chief of the Operations Department, Lin Liguo.

Lin Biao didn't acknowledge his son's presence at first. He continued with what he was saying to Wu Faxian: "I agree completely with the views of the Commander-in-Chief. The People's Liberation Army must prove to the reactionaries of the world that nuclear weaponry is the tiger in our hands. Nor is it a paper tiger, a dead tiger, but a real, live one. Once the nuclear forces of the Air Force take off, the enemy won't have a chance of getting away."

Then, barely catching his breath, he turned to his son and said cajolingly: "Are you a real tiger?"

Wu Faxian answered for him: "Comrade Liguo is a true tiger, all right. Now that we have him in the Air Force, the Air Force is a truly fierce tiger too."

Lin Biao didn't take his eyes off the sheepish Lin Liguo. "Tiger [Lin Liguo's pet name]! See that, tiger? Your Commander-in-Chief thinks you can be a real tiger. What do you think of that? Uncle Wu and I want to see what you can accomplish in three, five, a dozen years. Commanding a division is easy. Commanding a corps is no problem either. But commanding a whole army—now, that's something different, but it's within your reach. When I led the forward units during the Long March, I was only in my twenties. Commanding an entire front army is like climbing a mountain so huge that it may take ten or twenty years, but it can be done."

Lin Biao's words provided the clue for which Wu Faxian had been frantically searching. It was suddenly made clear to him— Lin Biao's voracious ambition to rule the country included full participation on the part of his son. The Air Force would be the young Lin's training ground, his power base. Wu guessed his power would eventually exceed that of anyone else in the Air Force, including Wu himself. Lin could conceivably take over his own post one day. And when Lin Biao made it to the number-one seat of power, his son would be prepared to step into his shoes.

Now that Wu Faxian understood this, he could follow through decisively. When Lin Liguo approached him about starting his own "research and investigative group," Wu did not hesitate to agree. Before long he announced to the Chief-of-Staff of the Air Force, Liang Pu, and other high leaders that Lin Liguo was to be given unbridled privilege, leeway and encouragement to do as he pleased.

Wu Faxian's orders had the weight of the sea; they were beyond question. But Wu himself was disturbed.

Wu Faxian and his wife began to meet with Zhou Yuchi on an increasingly frequent basis.[1] Their agent provided them with detailed reports of Lin Liguo's actions, the group's mobility, its access to information, its private meetings; and, risky though some of its activities seemed, at first no concrete action was taken to curb them.

One day in the spring of 1971, Zhou called an urgent meeting with Wu. Wu sensed the importance of the rendezvous when Zhou refused to have it take place in an office or home. He insisted instead on meeting in the sprawling, wooded hunting grounds in the Fragrant Hills forbidden military zone on the outskirts of Beijing. Guarded by 500 soldiers, the area would provide seclusion and minimize the possibility of bugging.

It was the first and last time Wu ever went hunting, and he

returned empty-handed that day. What he brought back instead was the shocking news that Lin Liguo was preparing to kill and overthrow Mao Zedong. Lin had requested that Zhou not only join in on the coup but that he be responsible for drafting the plans. The project's code name—the "571 Project"—derived from the Chinese term for "armed uprising," *wu zhuang qi yi,* three characters of which *(wu, qi* and *yi)* are pronounced the same as the numbers five, seven and one.

"Lin claims," Zhou added, "that it is his father's idea."[2]

After a moment of silence Wu responded by taking out his handkerchief and wiping the perspiration from his face.

Wu, of course, knew what had inspired Lin Biao's sudden desire to eliminate Mao Zedong. The friction between them at the second plenary session of the Central Committee in Lushan in August 1970[3] had escaped no one. Ostensibly called to plan the upcoming Fourth National People's Congress, the Lushan Plenum neatly served as an opportunity for Mao to redistribute power among the members of China's ruling circle. Lin Biao, as usual, had led his followers in singing Mao's praises. He also brought up the matter of the post of Chairman of the State, which had been vacated by the fall of Liu Shaoqi. Mao had mentioned to Lin that he wished to have the title himself; it had seemed to everyone a *fait accompli.* Yet after Lin stood up to make his protocol speech, after he exalted Mao as the greatest genius in the history of mankind, the very personification of the united forces of the party and government, and therefore the only choice for Chairman of the State, Mao suddenly turned on him.

Surprising everyone at the meeting, Mao accused anyone who called him a genius of being a phony and a betrayer. He then proceeded to dismiss and arrest one of his best theoreticians (and a strong Lin Biao supporter), Chen Boda, along with a high leader in the Beijing military organization, Li Xuefeng. He further ordered the self-criticism of Huang Yongsheng, Wu Faxian, Li Zuopeng, Qiu Huizuo and others. Although Mao didn't point his finger directly at Lin, he systematically omitted mentioning all the other factions equally guilty of engaging in activities reeking of

Mao idolatry. No, Mao would not come out and say so, but it was clear he was intent on clipping Lin's "party feathers."

Mao Zedong's unexpected behavior left Wu Faxian and others who had relied on flattery of Mao to smooth their advancement in agonized bewilderment. Even Lin Biao, who had always prided himself on being able to "see through" Mao, could not, for the moment, grasp what was going on. Mao's closest associates would readily admit that his magic weapon was the creation of a personal cult; now that he seemed to be attacking the very idea of a cult, what mechanism did he expect to use to keep his own position intact and the party unified?

The political quakes in the military and their indication of a dramatic change in the Lin-Mao rapport were disturbing to all of Lin Biao's associates, but they jolted Wu Faxian perhaps more than anyone. Now this announcement by Lin Liguo about a coup.

He had many questions. What was the nature and cause of the conflict between Lin and Mao? Why would Lin Biao have his son resort to such extreme tactics as a coup? And why had he, the number-three man in the Lin Biao clique, never heard a word about a decision of such magnitude?

Before Wu had time to sort out the terrifying implications, he found himself up against the practical problem of covering for Lin's plot without letting others know he knew. That meant he was forced to act rather hastily in cases like that of Ding Siqi.

The low-ranking Air Force officer Ding Siqi had come from Shanghai on March 20, 1971, to meet privately with Commander-in-Chief Wu. He had something of grave importance to tell him regarding large-scale dissident activities. Ding prepared for his meeting the following day by retiring early at the Da Muchang, a hotel reserved for Air Force officials located on a narrow, winding alley at the northern extension of Qian Men Boulevard. That night at around midnight two carloads of enforcement soldiers armed with loaded rifles surrounded the hotel and arrested him.

Ding had come to Beijing bearing news of a conspiracy that he had heard about from one of Lin Liguo's diehard supporters. Li Weixin, the deputy director of the Secretariat of the Fourth Air Force Army Headquarters in Shanghai, had approached Ding hoping to enlist his participation in something called the "Joint Fleet." The list of members, which Li had given to Ding—and which Ding had brought with him to Beijing—were all men from the Fourth Air Force Army.

The reason Li Weixin approached Ding to begin with was that Li was in love with Ding's younger sister. Although Li was married, he hoped that being on good terms with the girl's brother would help promote his affair.

Ding was in turn sure that he could impress Wu with his show of loyalty to Mao Zedong, and possibly even get a promotion out of it.

Ignorant of the true situation, the young officer was marched out of his hotel in handcuffs, questioned brutally (during which he refused to change his testimony) and finally taken to a secret execution grounds and dispatched.

After the execution Wu Faxian recorded the nature of Ding's crimes in a file: "Ding Siqi vehemently opposed Mao Zedong and viciously attacked the Central Committee. For him, even death is too generous. He was an active counter-revolutionary."[4]

For the time being, by eliminating Ding Siqi, Wu had managed to protect Lin. But he realized that he couldn't both cover up the plot and feign ignorance of it forever. If Mao were to discover the conspiracy, nobody would believe that Wu had been unaware of it. On the other hand, if the scheme really did originate with Lin Biao, then how could he oppose it?

While Wu stalled for time, he started the file on Lin Liguo's activities, based on Zhou Yuchi's reports. He wasn't sure what he would do with it, but at least he could produce it should it ever become imperative to do so.[5]

IV

Wu Faxian, as a key member of the Administrative Group of the Military Commission,[1] had always prided himself on maintaining an exceptionally harmonious relationship between the General Staff and the Beijing Military Region command. But now he and Huang, the heads of the General Staff, were being bypassed while Mao was busy shaking up the entire organization of the Beijing Military Region. There was no telling what might happen.

Mao had clearly chosen to strike where it hurt most. The Beijing Military Region was a bastion of military prowess and firmly under Lin Biao's control. Long content with the situation, Mao was now suddenly practicing his "mixing different grains of sand" tactic by himself placing new hand-picked men at high levels.[2]

With headquarters located in a scenic area of the Western Hills outside the city, the Beijing Military Region had always been special. Nominally equal to the military commands elsewhere, it was in reality exceptional in both strength and prestige. Most military regions maintained only two or three field armies; along with the important Shenyang Military Region in Manchuria, the Beijing Military Region had as many as eight or nine. In addition to its field armies, the Beijing Military Region also had troops in Hebei and Shanxi provinces, in Inner Mongolia, in the Tianjin Garrison Command and in the Beijing Garrison Command.

This key military region consistently received the best equipment and the best men. Its 38th Army, a strategic unit, was the first to possess motorized troops. This army, the 39th and the 40th were known as Lin Biao's "three fierce tigers." (The phrase would not be so memorable if it weren't for the fact that the Chinese character for "Biao" [彪] in Lin Biao's name is the character for "tiger" [虎] followed by three strokes [彡].)

Now, with Mao's tinkering, those "fierce tigers" were in danger of becoming very lame indeed, and Wu found the prospect nothing short of disastrous.

He felt like the man who knew too much. The news from Zhou Yuchi of Lin's coup meant that he had an all-or-nothing decision ahead of him. He could expose Lin and side with Mao—that, of course, would mean that down went Lin and everyone else who lined up behind him. The question was, could Wu himself avoid being penalized? Could he truly win the trust of Mao? If he could, the effort might be worth it. He might conceivably land Huang's position as Chief-of-Staff, or perhaps—and he dared let himself think so—Lin's as Minister of Defense.

The prospect was attractive, but it meant making overtures to Mao's vast and diverse pool of confidants. Besides Mao's wife, Jiang Qing, there were Zhang Chunqiao, Kang Sheng, Wang Dongxing and Zhou Enlai. They were all sticky individuals to deal with.

Before the Cultural Revolution, Jiang Qing was on very intimate terms with a man named Ke Qingshi, the Party Secretary of East China. Ke was a powerful figure whose influence was equally felt in Shanghai, Hubei, Jiangsu, Zhejiang and Anhui provinces. But just as Mao Zedong was making plans to launch an attack on Liu Shaoqi and Deng Xiaoping on an ideological front, Ke, the man who would have been ideal for the job, became fatally ill. It was up to Mao and Jiang Qing to find a replacement. They decided on Zhang Chunqiao, who at the time was chairing the Propaganda Department of the Shanghai Party Committee. When Ke died, Zhang had already taken a firm hold on Cultural Revolution work.

Zhang earned his first credits with an article written by his chief commentator, Yao Wenyuan, indirectly attacking Liu Shaoqi.

When Wu Faxian reflected on the fate Liu Shaoqi had suffered —absolute disgrace and death, from a position of the highest authority—and what an enemy like the "cobra" Zhang Chunqiao was capable of, a chill went down his spine.[3]

Kang Sheng, also Jiang Qing's crony, who had been responsible for introducing her to the Communist Party years before, was a different story. He would destroy you in other ways. In the late 1930's and the 1940's he had served in the party's top security organs in Yanan and was in charge of supervising underground intelligence agents hiding in the Nationalist government, military and police. Following the establishment of the People's Republic, his talents went unused for a time. But not for long. He made a comeback as Mao Zedong's "hit man" during the "rectification" of individuals like Peng Dehuai, gradually carving out a domain for himself by employing the methods he had learned in his work against the Kuomintang, and Mao granted him more power accordingly.

Kang Sheng came to be known as a terrifying figure whose scathing reports caused trouble for many people, some of whom seemed to disappear mysteriously. Even those with secure positions avoided him at all costs. Wu Faxian turned pale at the mere thought of the man.

Jiang Qing was a mystery to him. Wu had no way of understanding her volatile political nature. In any case, it seemed likely that if Lin Biao were to fall, there would be no place for Wu in her clique. Zhou Enlai and Wang Dongxing, as Mao's closest aides, were Wu's strongest political opponents. That they would ever wholeheartedly accept him seemed inconceivable.

The problem, of course, was that they all identified him too strongly with Lin Biao. If they had nothing against Wu Faxian the person, they despised the Wu Faxian who was Lin Biao's protégé.

There was no question but that Wu felt more secure playing a role in Lin's empire. Mao's power seemed only mythic, symbolic; Lin's was tangible, real.

Wu was coming to the sad but firm conclusion that without Lin he too was nothing. His power existed only in the military, and only in a military run by Lin. If Lin succeeded in his coup, Wu would have no problem acquiring power. And once Lin was in control, Wu might continue being the number-three man in the new ruling clique. That was nothing to scoff at. It was certainly far better than what waited for him if he turned himself in to Mao.

Wu had more or less made up his mind, but was able and willing to change it if prompted by a reasonable justification. His decision to go with Lin did not become irreversible until Lin Biao called him in one day in the late summer of 1971 to discuss the very matter which haunted Wu.

The meeting took place in the sequestered and heavily guarded Western Hills compound near Xiang Hongqi between the Summer Palace and the Fragrant Hills. Before the Cultural Revolution the compound had been the second home of at least ten marshals and top generals. But recently the cluster of free-standing buildings had served mainly as the meeting ground for Lin and his military chieftains.

The buildings were couched on a slope, each one rising above the next as if symbolizing the ascent to power. The two buildings occupied by Lin Biao were situated at the summit of the hill. Lin Biao and Ye Qun resided in one, while the other was given over to the use of their son and daughter. Both structures were immense and included accommodations for a number of secretaries and guards, offices, conference and reception rooms, dining and dance halls, exercise rooms, massage rooms and screening rooms.

This was the place Lin Biao regarded as his palace, and it was here that he normally held court meetings with his chief advisors under the heavy protection of his personal guards.

Wu Faxian thought it unusual that Lin Biao and Ye Qun had decided to come to the Western Hills when they were so shortly planning a vacation at the seaside resort of Beidaihe. In any case, on arriving that evening at about 6:30, Wu made small talk with Ye Qun in the first-floor reception room before being led upstairs to Lin Biao's reception room.[4]

Lin and Wu first discussed Lin Biao's traveling plans. It was Wu Faxian's responsibility, as Commander-in-Chief of the Air Force, to dispatch the private planes for anyone at the level of Standing Committee member of the Politburo or above. When Lin Biao was traveling, the matter was of top priority.

Wu Faxian said he had prepared three aircraft: a British Trident as a passenger plane for Lin Biao and Ye Qun; a Soviet IL-18 for the security troops; and a Soviet AN-12 transport for cars and other large equipment.

One thing about Lin's pending trip to Beidaihe was unusual: Lin Biao, like Mao Zedong, disliked taking planes, yet even for this short trip from Beijing to Beidaihe, at most an overnight journey by car or train, Lin Biao insisted on flying. Moreover, he requested a "ride around" in the air for three hours before landing at the Shanhaiguan Airport. Wu Faxian didn't voice his surprise, but couldn't help wondering whether this change in standard procedure had something to do with a *coup d'état.*

They dined in Building #11, after which Lin Biao led Wu into his study. Lin Biao didn't sit down, but paced back and forth in the large room as if expecting Wu to begin the conversation. The topic hung in the air without Wu having to put it into words: the Lushan Plenum, where Mao had inferentially attacked Lin. Wu finally spoke. What did it all mean? What were Mao's intentions?

Lin Biao listened attentively, grinning on occasion. When he finally spoke, he did so in a matter-of-fact tone:[5]

"What do *you* think the Chairman is prepared to do with me?"

Wu had never expected him to be so blunt. Caught by surprise, he found himself at a loss for words. Ye Qun, who normally was good at clearing the air during awkward moments, remained silent.

Lin Biao, as if having just awakened from a daydream, walked over to Wu Faxian and stared at him. Finally he said:

"The Chairman is reconsidering his choice of successor."

"Are you sure this news is accurate, Chief Lin?" Wu asked. Though Lin hadn't said to him anything that Wu didn't already know, somehow hearing it from Lin's own mouth caught him off guard.

Lin Biao responded by nodding his head expressionlessly.

From left: Qiu Huizuo, Wu Faxian, Li Zuopeng, Ye Qun, and Lin Liguo. At the Lushan Plenum in August 1970. (From *Criminal Materials of Lin Biao's Anti-Party Clique*)

Ye Qun spoke. "The Chairman has already hinted at this matter with the Chief. He said there was no such thing as immortality. The Chairman has probably gotten it in his head that Chief Lin might reach the end before him, and that even if he didn't, he could serve at most only ten or fifteen years. We think the Chairman intends to designate someone younger, someone in his forties or fifties."

Lin Biao waved his hand and interrupted his wife. "That was

before Lushan. Now the Chairman definitely wants me to go before him. And he wants all of you to accompany me to Babaoshan.[6] He wants us to lie down like stone lions."

"That can't be! The Chairman said so himself?" Wu Faxian asked in surprise.

Lin Biao smiled and shook his head. "By the time the Chairman says so himself, it will be too late. We have to stay ahead of him. As long as time is on our side, the victory is ours."

Wu Faxian said: "Then you've decided to . . . ?"

Lin Biao responded flatly: "Mao Zedong's banner doesn't have to be lowered. But his power does. We must act quickly, though. We must control the situation. We must put an end to this horrendous period in our history, this Cultural Revolution."

Wu Faxian then asked, rhetorically: "You mean using special means?"

Ye Qun spoke excitedly: "Geniuses think alike!"

Lin Biao sat down. He placed both hands on his knees, and his face showed deep meditation. He said softly: "We must act before they do. It's not so much a strategic decision as a response to necessity. We may not be able to play politics as well as the Chairman, but we can certainly compete with him in armed strength."

Ye Qun then said soothingly to Wu: "It is like the eve of the Soviet October Revolution, a turning point. Making revolution is your specialty, isn't it, Commander Wu?"

Wu Faxian couldn't think of much to say. He acted according to habit and military decorum and stood up at attention. He then proceeded to take an oath, but did so haltingly and barely coherently. The only complete sentence which he finally formulated was: "Whatever Marshal Lin Biao says, I will act on to my death."

The words rang and echoed in Wu's ears as if they had been uttered by someone else. He suddenly realized that without really meaning to, without any active premeditation, he had reached an irreversible decision.

Lin Biao proceeded to enlighten Wu about the rationale for a clean break with Mao, evidence that Mao had in fact initiated a break with him. There were the subtle political signs: Madame Jiang Qing and Zhang Chunqiao had reported to Mao that the "three-in-one policy"—the alliance among party, army and masses which was espoused as a Cultural Revolution slogan, and which aimed at a balanced mixture of different segments of society—was rendered impossible owing to a veritable state of military dictatorship under Lin.[7]

Lin's relations with Jiang Qing had become noticeably strained. Whereas she and Lin had once cooperated with each other when charges were leveled by their opponents, now, after the Lushan Plenum, Jiang Qing secretly handled three anti-Lin cases. She delivered trial materials directly to Mao, implicating Lin in Mao's mind, then proceeded to persuade the anti-Lin people to join her faction.

Mao, for his own part, was acting strangely too. He frequently summoned senior regional military personnel without going through the ordinary channels in the Ministry of Defense. And when he met with these individuals, he was heard referring to the Huang-Wu General Staff as "worthless bureaucrats." He often made reference to Lin Biao as "that vice-marshal" instead of the all-embracing appellation "comrade."

Lin Biao himself noticed that his previously frequent dinners and meetings with Mao Zedong had been drastically reduced. Mao claimed that he had cut down on his workload for health reasons, spending more time in solitude with books. But Lin knew otherwise; Mao was as active as ever, meeting frequently with associates to exchange information.

What Lin found most objectionable was Mao's use of humiliation at the Lushan Plenum. Mao had frequently hinted to Lin his desire to step down from the party leadership, becoming instead Chairman of the State and exercising a greater influence on China's international relations. Suddenly at the plenum Mao had acted as if the notion were absurd. It was clear to Lin that it was only a matter of time before Mao pulled his "replace number-two man" trick. Like so many others who had stood beside him, Lin was used up and now must be disposed of. What methods Mao would adopt, judging from his past record, included only the grimmest of possibilities. Even if Lin's dismissal was carried out peaceably, he would never have a chance of staging a comeback —Jiang Qing and Zhou Enlai would long since have started nibbling away at his influence like silkworms on a leaf.

Lin Biao believed that whether or not he could effectively replace Mao Zedong had everything to do with whether or not his military machine could maintain order. Lin predicted that there would be a complete redistribution of power among all factions; if it wasn't the military who came out on top, then it would be Jiang Qing and her Cultural Revolution group.

When Lin Biao had moved into Peng Dehuai's post as Minister of Defense in 1959, Mao hadn't minded letting it get around that he had been cold and imperious in his dismissal of Peng. He, in fact, had boasted that the only way for leaders to deal with their powerful generals was to keep them in line. There should never be an opportunity for a general to rebel.

The warning was still etched clearly in Lin's memory. Lin Biao had maintained supreme military strength, but he had used it to defend Mao, by fostering a Mao cult, shielding Mao from attack by enemies, eliminating those whom Mao regarded as undesirable, fighting many of Mao's battles. The same military prowess had also allowed Lin to rise to a position where he was subordinate to Mao, but to Mao alone. He could not give it up now. He was too close to the top.

"I have been named 'the unconquerable general.' Yet there is nothing that makes me particularly brilliant. In actuality, I have only one talent: I never bungle the chance of winning a battle. A chance must never be lost. Once lost, it never returns. The Chairman and I must have a showdown. The opportunity may never come again."

Lin's confidence inspired in Wu an unwavering conviction of victory. Even in Lin Biao's dim study, the heavy drapes drawn, Wu could see and feel the glow of that conviction. It was one that had developed in him over a period of thirty years—from the Red Army's battles in the Northeast to the final defeat of the Kuomintang. He couldn't walk out on Lin Biao now. Lin trusted him, confided in him, needed him. No, he would stand by Lin as his closest comrade-in-arms until, as he promised, his last, dying day.

Later that evening Wu Faxian learned that Lin Biao had already spoken in the same way to Huang Yongsheng, and that similar private conversations with Li Zuopeng and Qiu Huizuo were to follow. There was little time for vacillation; Lin Biao wanted a basic coup plan developed before he left for Beidaihe.[8]

V

The relationship between Mao Zedong and Lin Biao was a long-standing one, representing as it did a harmonious wedding between party and Army. Though Lin and Mao probably first met when they joined Communist forces in Jinggangshan in 1928, they undoubtedly heard of each other before that. Lin had already made a name for himself commanding the 28th Regiment of the Workers and Peasants Fourth Corps, a unit headed by Mao. When the regiment expanded to form the first column of the new Red Fourth Army, Lin at twenty-three became army commander with Mao's blessing.

Lin Biao continued to gain distinction during the Nationalists' first four unsuccessful encirclement campaigns; following the fifth, in which the Communists were defeated and forced to embark on the historic Long March, Lin Biao commanded the central column. By the end of the Long March, Mao had rewarded Lin by making him deputy commander of the entire Red Army.

In subsequent inner-party conflicts Lin, although sometimes also in disagreement with Mao, ultimately stayed in his camp and gained a reputation as a loyal Mao follower. At the outset of the Sino-Japanese War in 1937, Mao placed him in command of the 115th Division of the new Eighth Route Army. Lin performed brilliantly in a famous attack on a Japanese column at Pingxing-guan, defeating hitherto victorious forces under the command of

Lieutenant General Itagaki Seishirō; it was a critical juncture for the country as a whole and for the careers of Mao Zedong and Lin Biao.

Subsequently Lin spent several years receiving medical treatment in the Soviet Union (for injuries suffered in a 1938 battle, some sources say) and, while there, was designated by Mao to be the Chinese representative to the Comintern. When he returned to Yanan in 1942, his support for Mao was stronger than ever; the Chinese Communist Party could be as successful as the Soviet Union's, he maintained, if Mao continued to lead it.

After the Japanese surrender in September 1945, Mao sent Lin to Manchuria to assume supreme military and political power. Lin managed to hold the Communist positions in the face of severe Nationalist pressure, suffering only relatively minor losses, and eventually, in 1947, brought the entire area under Communist control. From there he moved south to play a major role in the Communist takeover of mainland China. During the next few years Lin fought and won decisive battles in Beijing and Tianjin. His final victory was the capture in April 1950 of Hainan Island, the southernmost part of China. His army by that time had swelled from the 100,000 he commanded in Manchuria to well over a million men. Having won the larger part of China, Lin, at forty-two, was easily the most renowned commander of the newly formed Chinese People's Liberation Army.

Following liberation, however, Lin Biao maintained a low profile. Perhaps because of poor health, he rarely made public appearances, though he was still able to retain several lofty political positions and a powerful backing among military men.

His first real starring role came in 1959 when Mao Zedong launched his public attack on Peng Dehuai, then Minister of Defense. With Peng's removal from office, Lin Biao took his place and managed to dissolve or absorb most of Peng's personal power structure within the armed forces.

But it was the beginning of the Cultural Revolution in 1966 that saw Lin's power base really grow. This period gave him the opportunity to expand his influence by doing once again what he knew so well how to do: wield military strength.

Mao's "Great Proletarian Cultural Revolution" created an unparalleled degree of political unrest. At its height, factions raged through the streets fighting each other with knives, sticks, rocks and whatever they could get their hands on. Schools and factories were closed down; the nation's economy ceased to function. Taking advantage of the confusion, Lin commanded his troops to support all "leftist" factions. He knew perfectly well that virtually all of the factions regarded themselves as leftist; they all held high the banner of Mao Zedong and the Cultural Revolution. Lin's generous contributions of weapons and manpower therefore merely served to transform the initial struggle into an all-out civil war. Soon China's landmass had become a battleground, and Chinese people died by the tens of thousands.

Amid the crossfire and bloodshed Mao found himself getting more than he had bargained for. The Cultural Revolution leaders whom he had personally appointed, most notably his wife, Jiang Qing, and Zhang Chunqiao, were unable to defeat their opponents decisively. Moreover, with Mao's principal opponent, Liu Shaoqi, gone, there was no need to maintain such a pitch of chaos, and for the first time since 1949 Mao felt his control over China seriously endangered. Zhou Enlai told him the economy was on the brink of failure and that he had already exhausted the nation's public funds merely to prevent collapse. At the end of 1967 Mao finally had no choice but to dispatch his trusted "8341" Troops, the "Palace Guards" under Wang Dongxing's personal direction, into several of Beijing's schools and factories to establish order.

Lin took Mao's move as the cue he had been waiting for. In Mao's name, Lin followed suit elsewhere in China, the only difference being that the troops he sent in were his own and, consequently, the military control under which he brought the nation was also his. The various factions that had previously enjoyed Lin's support now felt the lash; their weapons were confiscated and they were forced to merge with the newly established military control commissions. Having paid a heavy toll, the zealous Cultural Revolution factions were now left with neither power nor identity.

Mao was thankful to Lin for bringing at least a semblance of normality to the country again. What he did not realize was that Lin's military control had come to stay. Lin Biao would not voluntarily step aside.

Except for Shanghai, which was firmly held by Zhang Chunqiao, all provinces and municipalities lay under the rule of the military. At the Ninth Party Congress of April 1969, Lin was officially declared Mao's successor, making him in name as well as in fact the second most powerful man in China. He may actually have been the most powerful. His followers made up over fifty percent of both the government and the military representatives at the Congress. Of the 150-plus Party Committee leadership posts, more than 100 were occupied by military commanders; the remainder were largely former military men, most of whom had been at one time or another Lin's subordinates. Even a number of the important ministers in Zhou Enlai's State Council were Lin Biao's men.

In the military sector Lin Biao's power was all but absolute, with his supporters commanding many of the major military regions. The only person who stood a chance of changing any of this was Mao himself, and even his influence on the military was doubtful.

For a long time Mao had let Lin's popularity go unchallenged. But now, rather than buoying Mao up, Lin's expanding circle of supporters had begun pressing in upon the Chairman. The delicate balance of power had been upset and probably could never be restored.

The events of the Lushan Plenum were the result.

Lin tried to consider possible alternatives. He concluded that there were none. Mao had already delivered the call to arms; Lin could either do nothing and be defeated or he could fight and, he hoped, win. To fight the head of the country meant only one thing: a *coup d'état*. Once he reached that decision, there was no turning back.

Not everyone could be so unequivocal. The first person Lin informed of his plans was his wife, Ye Qun; she became nearly

From left: Li Zuopeng, Wu Faxian, Lin Biao, Huang Yongsheng, and Qiu Huizuo, together aboard a plane at Jiujiang Airport in September 1970. (From *Criminal Materials of Lin Biao's Anti-Party Clique*)

hysterical, pleading with him to consider other means. Lin Biao in time became outraged. "Should or should not Lin Biao continue to be a Lin Biao?" he asked. Ye Qun had nothing to say, and after a while showed a more accepting attitude.

The first problem Lin faced was the choice of participants.

Ye Qun helped him prepare a list of about 200 names of potential accomplices. Lin considered the proposed individuals, but ultimately rejected the list. He was afraid such a broad base would cause complications. He then considered a plan involving a few commanders who would be reshuffled. Chen Xilian and Xu Shiyou, commanders of the Shenyang and Nanjing military regions respectively, would be called in to fill the posts of Vice-Ministers of Defense. Lin's confidants would replace them, thus furnishing support for the coup in the Shenyang and Nanjing military regions; these forces would be combined with the Guangzhou Military Region, commanded by Lin Biao's supporter Ding Sheng, to form the nucleus of a coup alliance. But Lin ultimately dropped this idea because he feared that the personnel changes might affect his timetable.[1]

Most of all, he wanted to confine his plans to those individuals he really "understood."

Ultimately, that narrowed his choice down to his "four great warrior attendants": Huang Yongsheng, Wu Faxian, Li Zuopeng and Qiu Huizuo, leaders in the Army, Air Force, Navy and Logistics departments of the General Staff. With their vigilant assistance Lin had managed to assure his strength in the military establishment. There was no one else he trusted as he trusted these four men.

Chief-of-Staff Huang Yongsheng had been with Lin Biao from the start as a commander in the early years of the Red Army; he became commander of a regiment of Lin's troops during the Long March; commander of a brigade in Lin's 115th Division during the Anti-Japanese Resistance Wars; commander of the eighth column in Lin's Fourth Field Army; and deputy commander of the 12th Corps. After the People's Republic was established, he was named commander of the Guangzhou Military Region and Party Secretary of South China.

In the midst of the Cultural Revolution, Huang Yongsheng replaced acting Chief-of-Staff Yang Chengwu to become the permanent Chief-of-Staff. During the Ninth Party Congress he was elected a standing member of the Politburo.

Chief-of-Staff Huang's power was built into the structure of the military itself. Any decision by a military region to move field armies was subject to the approval of his General Staff. The General Staff's orders, on the other hand, had to be obeyed by the military regions.

Li Zuopeng's official status was that of first political commissar of the Navy, but he had in fact assumed the duties of the Navy Commander-in-Chief. The nominal Commander, Xiao Jinguang, was also devoted to Lin Biao, but had been transferred by his mentor into one of the ceremonious but empty positions of Vice-Minister of Defense.

During the Fourth Field Army period, Li Zuopeng helped Lin

Biao accomplish much strategic and tactical planning, earning the respect of the commander. Lin Biao subsequently made him Chief-of-Staff of the 115th Division, Commander of the 43rd Corps of the Fourth Field Army and deputy commander of a column. His ability to execute military schemes was outstanding and he had all the cunning of a good politician.

The Navy under Li's control had Northern, Eastern and Southern fleets totaling 670,000 men, in addition to an elite marine corps and five divisions of naval air forces. Thanks to Li's continuous and thorough purification movements, all the naval leaders were loyal to him and to Lin Biao.

The two together—Huang Yongsheng and Li Zuopeng—made an interesting contrast. Although of similar medium build and physical appearance, they displayed vastly different temperaments and work-styles.

The name Huang Yongsheng has a resounding ring. "Yong" and "Sheng" literally mean "forever" and "victorious." It was his name, in fact, which first drew Mao's attention to the young soldier in the Red Army. His achievements in the military gave substance to the name. The troops in his command were always strong and well disciplined. On the battlefield he took complete charge and inevitably emerged on the winning side. Yet he was courteous with his subordinates, never making a show of his abilities. His greatest talent lay in discovering and promoting excellence. When facing important policy decisions, he acted as though he had no opinions of his own, soliciting instead the ideas of others. After slowly sifting and shuffling through these ideas, he would end up with a sophisticated revision of one of the plans, making it his own. This procedure almost always worked.

Li Zuopeng differed from Huang in that he created his own plans from scratch. When Lin Biao was commanding the Fourth Field Army against Chiang Kai-shek, Li's role was to translate Lin's ideas into specific policy. He was intrepid and haughty, openly deriding those colleagues, including superiors, less able than he. He thought his ideas should be guiding principles for others. Wu Faxian once commented that Li "is extremely shrewd, alert and always the one to come up with the last point." Wu also remarked that "one always has a feeling of confidence when working with Zuopeng; in the end, the reason for this confidence is inevitably justified."[2]

Qiu Huizuo had been a commander in the Red Army, but was transferred to political work in the military. He became the political commissar of the eighth column of the Fourth Field Army under Lin Biao and finally the deputy director of the Political Department of the Fourth Field Army. After the People's Republic was established, Qiu received the rank of lieutenant general and became the chief of the Logistics Department. As such, he saw to the provisions of the entire Army.

Shortly after the outbreak of the Cultural Revolution, Lin Biao encouraged Qiu to eliminate or weaken the power of many generals and lieutenant generals in the Logistics Department. Qiu then proceeded to organize and lead a military clique composed of high-level logistics officers who took orders directly from Lin Biao.

Lin Biao's appreciation for Qiu centered on his loyalty, equanimity and reliability, which made him the perfect person to call upon in dealing with Lin's opponents. He was healthy, vigorous, severe and extremely demanding of his subordinates, inspiring in them fear and respect. His units had more women employees than any other (most of them occupying posts in the military hospital), a fact which earned him his nickname, "Playboy of the Century."

Huang, Wu, Li and Qiu—these were Lin Biao's four "iron brothers." Their "diehard" alliance stemmed from the early days of the Cultural Revolution when the four were verbally and physically attacked by Red Guards. It was Lin Biao who helped them survive and prevail. On May 13, 1967, they formed a secret pact with Lin and Ye Qun to solidify their devotion to one another, and each year subsequently gathered together on that day to commemorate the alliance.

Convinced as he was of their devotion, however, Lin had to

prepare for the possibility that one or more of them would refuse to go along with his decision to execute a coup. As was his usual practice in matters of such importance, Lin arranged to call them in one at a time to test their reactions. The procedure was very systematic: first Huang would be summoned; then Wu, who would be told of Huang's agreement to the plans; then Li; then Qiu. Each would be notified of the decisions made by those who had come before him. If any of them balked, that would be considered a sign of disloyalty and would lead to immediate kidnapping and assassination, with the death announced as due to illness. As a precaution, Lin had two experts on hand capable of inducing immediate apoplexy or an acute heart condition.[3]

When Huang Yongsheng had his meeting, he was frightened and moved to tears. He and Lin Biao embraced and consoled each other.

Wu Faxian seemed a bit flustered, but remained stoic.

Li Zuopeng commented that it had occurred to him Lin Biao should take such actions, but that he had been reluctant to suggest it himself first. He said he felt relieved.

Qiu Huizuo remained calm and firm. Lin Biao was particularly pleased.

The first time Lin met with the four of them together, he emphasized that if Mao were to learn of the plot, none of them would be able to escape. He used the examples of Liu Shaoqi, Peng Dehuai and Wang Ming—all destroyed on Mao's orders—to remind them of the old man's vengefulness. The older he gets, Lin added, the more vicious he is. Then he made the men vow that they would die before revealing their secret. Lastly, he commanded each of them to decide, on the spot, his own method of suicide.[4]

VI

The plan for the "imperial *coup d'état*" was conceived and designed by Lin Biao alone. Even after his associates were told of his intention to kill Mao Zedong, no one could predict what method he would adopt to achieve that goal. When he finally made his plan known to Ye Qun, Huang, Wu, Li and Qiu, they agreed upon its brilliance.

Lin had mulled over many different ideas before finally deciding on one. The central problem was this: a subtle, small-scale operation would never create the kind of widespread public support necessary to make the coup succeed, while grander operations would be difficult to slip past Mao's vigilant eye. Lin Biao hoped not only to bring about Mao's death but also to guarantee his own subsequent control over the entire nation.[1]

Lin was sure he could mobilize the troops necessary to end Mao's life. Assuming supreme power, however, meant that he had to think of a way to place the nation under a temporary military dictatorship. In one more leap of imagination, Lin at length decided that the ideal national crisis for his purpose would be a Sino-Soviet confrontation. The gravity of the conflict would have to be such as to convince Mao Zedong and Zhou Enlai that China and the Soviet Union were actually on the verge of open war— that, in fact, a mere skirmish would be sufficient to start such a war. Only then could Lin Biao fully exercise his military power without raising suspicions.

Lin Biao liked to think of his battle plans in terms of "models," and, like any battle he had ever fóught, this one required both a "strategic model" and a "tactical model."[2]

Lin Biao had come up with two strategic models. The first called for China to initiate surprise attacks on the Soviet Union. This plan was inspired by actual Sino-Soviet armed conflict which had taken place following the Zhen Bao (Damansky) Island border dispute in 1969. The small-scale military activities of Soviet troops in the frontier provinces of Heilongjiang and Xinjiang had been fairly predictable. But at that time, intending to elevate his personal prestige and position at the upcoming Ninth Party Congress, Lin Biao deliberately overreacted to the pressure, and the aggressive response of Chinese troops caught the Soviets by surprise.

Xiao Quanfu, Lin Biao's deputy commander of operations in the Fourth Field Army of the Shenyang Military Region, had originally ordered his troops to shell a group of low-ranking Soviet officers concentrated in a training area. When the Soviets struck back with equal violence in Xinjiang, Lin Biao and his troops took the opportunity to flex their muscles.

As a result of these events, Mao Zedong had called Lin Biao in to express his concern over the prospects of a Sino-Soviet war. But he concluded the meeting by encouraging Lin Biao to, in effect, prepare for war. Lin Biao had known what to do. On September 30, 1969, the eve of the twentieth anniversary of the People's Republic of China, accompanied by several bodyguards, he drove to the command tower of the Beijing Military Airport, where the 34th Division of the Air Force was stationed. In person, he directed the on-duty guards to prepare for a state of emergency. Wu Faxian, as commander of the Air Force, immediately transmitted the Number 1 Alert to all the Air Force posts throughout the nation.

Three days later Lin Biao, as Minister of Defense and Vice-Chairman of the Military Commission, dispatched a similar order via the General Staff to the entire military establishment. China thus efficiently fell under a general state of emergency.

Lin's order, as well as the decisive personal manner in which he delivered it, had surprised everyone—including the Chairman. To

Lin, however, the whole episode had been like a dress rehearsal. He was left with full confidence in his ability to exercise authority in the event of a real emergency—or, if need be, an artificial one. That particular Sino-Soviet dispute had been real enough, but there was no reason the same situation couldn't be created deliberately. Initiating a conflict would merely require sending a few troops to attack Soviet border forces. If necessary, Lin could stage attacks on Chinese forces with their own artillery, preferably in some remote area, thereby supplying evidence of Soviet belligerence and a *casus belli*.

Lin Biao had a second strategic model. He considered it preferable to the first, but it required even more meticulous and delicate planning. It called for engaging in secret contacts with the Soviets beforehand, offering them special rewards for cooperation in "making war" according to Lin Biao's plan.

Lin Biao called in his Chief-of-Staff, Huang Yongsheng, to discuss this idea.[3] They met one day in an unusual room annexed to Lin Biao's villa in the Western Hills. The floor of the room was covered with a forty- by eighty-foot rug in deep red and gold. This rug, which cost $200,000, was a gift to Lin Biao from the Ministry of Defense and Military Commission, presented on the tenth anniversary of his being named marshal.

The most striking feature of the room was not the rug but a large sand table, the size of about six Ping-Pong tables, equipped with several computerized demonstration boards. With a push of a button, comprehensive tactical simulations of battles involving China, the Soviet Union, Japan, the United States or any number of domestic or international regions could be displayed. Also included was information on numbers and types of aircraft available, points of departure and destination, and air routes and times.

On that day the Minister of Defense and his Chief-of-Staff concentrated on the model's depiction of China's North (Huabei) and Northeast (Manchuria) and related border regions. The key military areas represented were the Beijing and Shenyang military regions in China, and the Soviet military presence in Khabarovsk, the Lake Baikal region and Mongolia. The troops activated for the display included Chinese field armies, tank divisions, airmen, airborne troops and naval vessels.

Lin Biao's "discussion" with his Chief-of-Staff was actually an excuse to use him as a sounding board. He spoke without pause or interruption, always positively, like a prophet.

"When Brezhnev gives the word," Lin began, "the Soviets will aim their rockets and cannons at the Chinese fortifications and border sentries in the northern military regions. The Soviet tanks will cross China's borders while the infantry waits to follow on the opened roads in armored vehicles. The attack will be made on a totally unprepared China.

"The Soviet Air Force in the meantime will send MiG's and tactical bombers toward Chinese military installations; Soviet submarines will appear in the waters of Lüshun and Dalian and launch missiles onto the shores and into the harbors.

"What Mao Zedong has feared all along will finally have occurred—the Soviets will be playing bully, but he, the almighty ruler of China, will not permit surrender. He possesses an invincible commander in Lin Biao, a commander renowned throughout the world, and he will temporarily ignore his dispute with him to let him wage war. He will listen to Lin's advice attentively. Lin will report that the Northeast is seriously endangered by an imminent Soviet attack on the Beijing military. Lin Biao will recommend that Mao protect himself by hiding in the Jade Tower Mountain* installation.

"While Lin Biao and his military advisors are in the nearby command center directing the fighting, Mao Zedong will observe the development of the war from his palatial refuge. Mao and Zhou, much as they did during the Civil War of the '40's, will discuss strategies from their 'command tent' and look forward to victory. Little will they know that for them victory will never come, that all that awaits them is an inglorious death."

*What is here called the "Jade Tower Mountain" actually bears another name which the author has changed for security reasons. The area, to the west of Beijing, contains secret installations that were—and still are—intended for use by China's leaders in the event of a national emergency.

Lin lowered his voice. "The exit to the underground Jade Tower Mountain installation will be sealed by my men, and before Mao has time to realize what is happening, gas bombs will have suffocated him. His body will soon be nothing but ashes.

"This is the Jade Tower Mountain Scheme."

Huang Yongsheng sat and listened with close attention. He was impressed by Lin Biao's utter confidence. It seemed as if the events he described were actually about to occur. Yet after many years as Chief-of-Staff, Huang could think only of the perils and problems. He posed many questions which Lin proceeded to answer evenly and without obvious signs of worry.

Huang asked about casualties. Lin answered that Soviet losses might be anywhere from two regiments to a division. Chinese losses would be greater. But if all went well, no more than three weeks should be necessary to accomplish the coup. Lin Biao rapped the sand table with a long pointer: "Is this not merely a joint military exercise? Can it be helped that it ends in casualties?"

Huang then expressed skepticism about compliance with orders that would result in attacks on China's own men. Lin Biao said it didn't have to go through the ordinary military channels. He claimed that the Shenyang troops could prepare for defensive action with supplementary preparations for retaliation. He would confuse them by issuing a number of different orders, all of which would contribute to the ultimate end. Lin added: "We'll get someone to handle this matter who can be really cold-blooded when it comes to the Russians. Somebody who has a way of making their hair stand on end."[4]

Huang wondered if it would not be possible to wage war without first contacting the Soviet Union. Negotiations with the Soviets could be set up after the coup. Lin replied that he had considered this approach and, although he hadn't ruled it out entirely, was worried about the unpredictable outcome. The Soviets might respond coolly and indifferently or, worse still, put the Chinese on the defensive by a too-vigorous response.

In later interrogations Huang Yongsheng described the rest of their conversation that day:

"Lin Biao was wearing a lavender robe faded gray, terry-cloth cap and slippers. He walked over to the sand-table model and began manipulating the elements in demonstration of the activities he had just described. He became totally absorbed by his maneuvers. At some point he realized that there was no need to limit the military exercise to a simple armed conflict with the Soviets. He could exploit the situation to pull off something far more impressive, more permanent, more far-reaching. He became ecstatic imagining the possibilities.

"After the fighting had stopped, China and the Soviet Union would enter into a friendly armistice agreement. Moscow would prepare a grand ceremony to welcome the highest ruler of China, Marshal Lin Biao, while Beijing would be opening up its own Tiananmen Square to none other than Comrade Brezhnev. He said the world would be waiting breathlessly for the next step.

"He estimated that the 1,200,000 Chinese troops now stationed in the four large military regions near the Soviet border could be relocated in the Soviet maritimes to establish new socialist countries there. Vietnam would expand its holdings across Southeast Asia—Cambodia, for example. The Soviet Union for its part could transfer its million troops from the Sino-Soviet border to Europe to upset that balance of world power. The entire Eurasian landmass, now merely a conglomerate of splintered nations, would become a vast and terrifying fortress of Communism. The new imperial nation would swallow its neighboring countries and advance Communism across the entire globe. It would use nuclear power, infiltration, subversion and military invasion to expand the Sino-Soviet coalition. Yes, the imminent coup would indeed alter the forces of world power.

"Lin Biao declared that the tragedy of modern China lay in its reign by a wildly ambitious Mao Zedong who desired most of all to head the international Communist movement and who therefore alienated all other Communist countries; China as a result had fallen off the track of Communism altogether. The strength of the proletarian, revolutionary Chinese Army had been turned around to threaten other socialist countries. The Chinese military had become an unofficial stronghold of NATO, serving as the lackey for capitalist countries. In his view, the PLA had been turned into an abominable mockery and was in drastic need of a new direction.

"Lin Biao was solemnly convinced that the coup would represent the first—perhaps the only—time in history that China reversed its image of weakness, isolation and internal strife. Not only would this ancient Eastern country build a new life for itself, it would do so through its own terrifying' military strength.

"The last statement I remember Lin Biao making that day was: 'Our new relation with the Soviets, the transition from war to armistice, hostility to alliance, secret contacts to open public relations, requires that great efforts be made to change the attitudes and beliefs of our people.' "

VII

Wu Zonghan, the man chosen to make the Russian contact (the name is a pseudonym), was a thin, frail man who seemed often lost in his thoughts. His quiet and introverted manner seemed more profound than that typical even of China's intellectual class.

Wu had studied mechanical engineering at Qinghua University during the 1950's. Upon graduation, he was assigned by the government to work with Soviet military experts helping to develop China's war machine. His work frequently took him abroad, especially to the Soviet Union, East Germany and Czechoslovakia.

It was while in Moscow that the capable and unassuming young Chinese fell in love with a Soviet woman of German descent. She had blond hair and blue eyes and she was known as La-la. Splendid while it lasted, theirs was a love story without a happy ending. Just as quickly as the honeymoon between Mao and Khrushchev ended, so did that between Wu Zonghan and La-la.

Without any assurance that he might be reunited with his lover, Wu returned to China in 1959 after having agreed to become a Soviet spy. His decision stemmed partially from coercion by Soviet authorities and partially from the vague notion that working for the Soviets might somehow, someday, bring him closer to the woman he loved.

Wu had not anticipated the tremendous pressure of espionage work. Nor did he suspect that relations with China's onetime close ally would become so steeped in acrimony. Affection for his lover across the border was still strong, but he settled for a normal low-keyed life, got married, had children and savored the warmth and tranquillity that family life brought.

One day Wu received some news from La-la. She could arrange for him to be relieved of his dangerous work and join her in the Soviet Union. She had received the promise of her father, a high-ranking member of Soviet intelligence, that he would try to make things easy for them. It would be up to Wu to make the move.

At the time, Wu was preparing for a business trip to a Western nation that had no formal diplomatic ties with the People's Republic of China. As the leader of a technical research delegation, he could slip away from the group and into the Soviet embassy. The procedure would be fairly simple, and there didn't seem to be much holding him back.

Wu had few relatives in China. There was a half-sister by his father who was almost twenty years older than he, and of course his wife and children. He had married out of convenience, and on the assumption that he would abandon his family if the need arose; he had never expected to grow to love his wife and children. Yet he had done so.

He was thus torn between attachment to his family and country on the one hand, and the lure of leaving the world of espionage and joining his lover on the other. He had long since tired of the dangerous work; moreover, there seemed no longer to be any purpose in it. But it was difficult and dangerous to give up. If he stayed behind in China, he would be very vulnerable to exposure.

He remained undecided until the last minute. Then, finally, he rejected the offer. When he returned to China from his business trip, the first thing he did was to write a long letter of confession about his clandestine activities on behalf of the Soviets.

The letter made its way to the highest intelligence organs in the General Political Department and General Staff of the military.

Soon a meeting was arranged, in the name of the standing body of the National Defense Council, between the Soviet Military Intelligence Section of the General Staff and the man who had voluntarily turned himself in as a spy. By the end of the interrogation the Chinese intelligence people felt they knew enough about the man to reach a decision: they would turn him and make him their own spy against the Soviets.

So, rather than ceasing to feed information into the Soviet intelligence machine, Wu Zonghan continued to do so, with one difference: the information was prepared by the Chinese authorities.

Wu continued to lead a double life—as an undercover spy and as a government technocrat. He was an excellent worker, such a model of diligence and precision that in the ordinary course of things he would have received a high position in the defense industry. Much to his superior's dismay, however, his secret work made him "unpromotable"; he had to remain completely inconspicuous.

Before long, however, Wu entered a "hibernation" period. Believing that he was not unwilling but unable to escape to the Soviet Union, La-la once again stepped in and let Wu know he could be relieved of his espionage duties. The earlier offer of asylum in the Soviet Union still held good.

Wu worried at first about how this news would sit with his Chinese intelligence superiors. But he found them understanding and helpful in his desire to resume a normal life: they not only allowed him to withdraw from espionage work altogether, they showed him a secret document regarding his case which cleared him of any crimes.

Wu Zonghan felt as if he had wakened from a long and somber dream. He finally began enjoying life, and memories of La-la dimmed with the passage of time. Everything was placid for several years until 1971. That was a bad year for Wu.

Wu had been relatively unaffected by the violence of the Cultural Revolution, thanks to the protection offered by the military intelligence organ. Thus, he was surprised when two men arrived uninvited at his office one day, saying that they had come to call him into action again. He was asked to re-establish contacts with Soviet intelligence. The matter was of paramount importance, but the purpose of his assignment remained undisclosed.

Wu realized he had been naïve in thinking that the secrets of his past had been forgotten. He was still a weapon of the intelligence system, even if for a time the weapon had been shelved.[1]

When Wu Zonghan had first become a spy for Chinese Military Intelligence in the earlier 1960's, the Ministry of Public Security had been notified and told to assist Wu in his work. By 1971, however, both the military intelligence organ and the Ministry of Public Security had undergone drastic structural changes as a result of the Cultural Revolution. Leaders who had been familiar with Wu Zonghan, by sight or by name, had been imprisoned, reassigned to other work units or locations, or forced to resign.

The Ministry of Public Security and the General Staff were successively headed by a single person: Luo Ruiqing. During the Cultural Revolution, Luo had become one of Lin Biao's prisoners. His former positions were now occupied by two different men, both standing-committee members of the Politburo: Huang Yongsheng was Chief-of-Staff, Xie Fuzhi Minister of Public Security.

Xie had managed to keep up his relations with all factions—Mao, Lin, Jiang Qing and Zhou Enlai. As he had been used by Mao to foment conflict during the Cultural Revolution, Xie was accustomed to spending a great deal of energy on politics at the upper echelons. His work at the ministry was largely left to another man named Li Zhen. Li, one of only two Chinese generals who held the title without a military career dating back to the Red Army period, had proven himself doing political work in the Shenyang Military Region. During the Cultural Revolution, Lin Biao managed to get Li appointed head of the military control commission of the Ministry of Public Security after all real, suspected or potential followers of Liu Shaoqi and Luo Ruiqing had been eliminated. Lin Biao had effectively beaten Jiang Qing in the race to fill the vacated posts.

The leadership changes made for much confusion when Wu Zonghan began his new undercover project. The problem was that the military was not willing to divulge to the Ministry of Public Security what the project entailed. Lin Biao might have asked Li

Zhen to ignore Wu Zonghan and his dealings with the Soviets. But although Li was considered one of Lin Biao's confidants, apparently even he could not be entirely trusted.

As a result, even though Lin Biao attempted to disguise his actions while soliciting the protection and cooperation of Public Security, the ministry did its job too well, and learned of the Soviet contacts. It became suspicious that Wu was in fact working for the Soviets and that the military high command was ignorant of his real identity. It began an investigation. Security men followed Wu one day to the guest house of the State Council, where they observed him dining with another gentleman and slipping him a small black leather case. This second man, middle-aged and casually dressed, walked out and climbed into a car with Beijing plates that was waiting for him at an elite hotel at Xizhimen. Ministry agents followed the car to the western part of Beijing; it drove down onto Bei Hai Front Street, then onto Dong Guan Fang Road and turned a sharp corner into the forbidden military region. It passed through the heavily guarded courtyard of the Ministry of Defense without any difficulty. The men from Public Security last saw the car approaching the General Staff compound, at which point they had to give up.

The detailed report of the counter-espionage section of the Ministry of Public Security landed on the desk of Li Zhen on August 24, 1971. It stated that Wu's orders to establish secret negotiations with the Soviet Union had apparently originated with high officials in the Security Department of the General Staff—namely, the deputy director of the Security Department, the deputy chief of the office of the General Staff and the Chief-of-Staff himself, Huang Yongsheng.

The report concluded that any and all of Wu's clandestine activities should be cleared by related departments of the Ministry of Public Security beforehand. Without the ministry's prior approval, Wu's contacts would be "unlawful," acts of treason and, as such, punishable by death.

Even for a professional like Li Zhen, this kind of report was unprecedented. The timing was uncanny. During the past few months Li Zhen had been working on security measures for secret negotiations between China and America. Dr. Henry Kissinger and Premier Zhou Enlai had already met secretly as a prelude to the American presidential visit that would end the decades-long separation between the two nations. Secret contacts with the Soviet Union might jeopardize or altogether subvert the attempts at a Sino-American détente. Surely Mao would be shocked and angered at the news.

While Li Zhen's own investigation confirmed that Mao had no knowledge of the Soviet contacts, he could not prove conclusively that Lin Biao did. It was merely a logical assumption on Li's part that if Huang, the chief of the General Staff, was involved, Lin must be too. He conjectured that while Mao was trying to present a smiling face to the Americans, Lin was purposely extending a hand to the Russians.

Li considered two alternatives: to present the true facts of the situation to his superior, Xie Fuzhi, or to confront Huang. Neither option seemed very attractive. Xie, he knew, had no scruples; he wouldn't think twice about turning in some of his own subordinates, accusing them of being followers of Liu Shaoqi or advocates of imperialism. He would throw anyone to the lions if he could get something out of it. Li didn't want trouble for Huang or Lin to be turned into an advantage for Xie. Lin Biao had helped him rise in the Shenyang Military Region and succeed in Beijing. Li was indebted to Lin; he was supposed to be a follower of Lin's, if not a diehard supporter.

Approaching Huang directly wasn't much better. If whatever plans Huang had went awry, then it was just a matter of time before their boat—with Li in it—capsized.

Li came up with what he thought was the best solution. He would put a halt to the counter-espionage investigation, then pretend ignorance of it. He would ask no questions about the purpose of Wu's activities. He didn't want to get involved.

The first step was to remove his counter-espionage team from the case. On September 4, 1971, he called in the five-member team one by one and had each arrested and imprisoned for "criminal activities." It was simple for him. Over the years Li had made more than a thousand arrests within the ministry at the behest of Xie Fuzhi, his superior. In the process he had also developed his own blacklist—subordinates who could be randomly accused of such crimes as "illicit foreign relations." Their cases were, in effect, perpetually pending. At times like this Li could simply and conveniently refer to their "crimes" and arrest them.

After the investigators were put away, Li planned simply to slip the explosive document he had received into the files, hoping no one would ever lay eyes on it again. One could say Li was protecting Huang and possibly Lin Biao. But it would be more accurate to say that Li was protecting himself, by way of sacrificing five lives. In a less critical period he might have acted differently. His greatest concern now was to avoid confrontation.

But by another twist of fate one of the five men arrested, in an attempt to exonerate himself and prove his loyalty, decided to set down the facts of the investigation in which he had participated. This written account fell into the hands of Li's assistant, Yu Sang. Yu was one of the few remaining of the original thirteen Public Security vice-ministers. He had been shielded from attack by Premier Zhou Enlai, who praised him for his diligence. Yu was appalled by Li Zhen's attempt to wash his hands of the affair, and took it upon himself to relay his knowledge to two others: Minister Xie Fuzhi and Premier Zhou Enlai.[2]

On September 7, 1971, Zhou sent his longtime secretary Yang Dezhong to the Great Hall of the People to meet with Yu Sang.

Yu had always admired Yang from afar. He found his loyalty to Zhou and trustworthiness remarkable. Their meeting was very brief. "The Premier has the matter under control," Yang said. "Apart from Xie and him, don't let anyone else know. The Premier is very grateful to you." Yu felt reassured and pleased with himself. He was glad to have had the opportunity to reciprocate the favors Zhou had done for him. And he was sure Zhou would handle the case wisely.[3]

VIII

Zhou Enlai, the first Premier of Communist China's State Council, a post he held until his death in 1976, had one of the most remarkable political careers of any premier the world over.

He was a suave, cosmopolitan man as well as a shrewd politician. His administrative abilities and dignity won him the support of many high-level Chinese leaders. His charisma and down-to-earth nature made him tremendously popular among the people. His good looks and charm gave him a reputation as a ladies' man.

Zhou had reached a lofty political position in the Communist Party long before Mao's star rose during the Long March period. He organized a series of workers' riots in Shanghai in the 1920's; he led the August 1 uprising in Nanchang in 1927, subsequently commemorated each year by National Army Day; he participated in the Long March; he represented the Chinese Communist Party in its protracted negotiations with the Kuomintang. Later he was Mao's chief strategic ally in the war against the Nationalists; and finally, after 1949, he became the head of official government affairs as China's Premier.

What the outside world has little knowledge of is Zhou's vast underground work. In the early years of the Communist Party he was often involved in confidential work in the large southern cities such as Shanghai. His activities included recruitment of underground party members, the organization of secret rallies, espionage, kidnapping and murder. During the Second World War, when the Communist Party and the Kuomintang entered a second period of coalition against the Japanese, Zhou Enlai was designated the highest representative of the Communist Party in the Nationalist government in both the nation's capital of Nanjing (Nanking) and the war capital of Chongqing (Chungking). While being carefully observed by the intelligence organs of the Nationalist government, he managed to establish his own intelligence net. He proved to be quite good at espionage, and even the counterintelligence operations of the Kuomintang were unable to interrupt Zhou's activities.

After being named Premier, Zhou stood firmly by Mao's side through all the dizzying spins of political fortune. The sudden purge of high-level party leaders Gao Gang and Rao Shushi in 1955; the call, through the mass media and other "voices" of the party, to intellectuals to express their views in the "Hundred Flowers Campaign"; the subsequent suppression of the thousands of teachers, scholars, scientists, students and administrators when Mao decided he didn't like what he heard; the "rectification" of Mao's devoted Minister of Defense, Peng Dehuai; the split between China and the Soviet Union; finally, the attack on Head of State Liu Shaoqi and leader of party affairs Deng Xiaoping which culminated in the huge Cultural Revolution—in all these important episodes Mao had asked for and received Zhou's cooperation.

But it was the Cultural Revolution which put the most strain on Zhou's abilities. Hoping to increase his own influence thereby, he applied tactics of pressure and persuasion against Mao's enemies; behind the scenes he managed to keep the non-productive national economy from going completely under; when in public view, he always carried his Little Red Book, loudly shouted "Long live Chairman Mao" and joined in the "dances of loyalty."

Zhou's ability to work closely with Mao for so many years without becoming the target of his periodic rectification attacks stemmed from his profound, almost intuitive understanding of the Chairman. Zhou understood the importance of avoiding the number-two seat, and was content to play number-three or even number-four man. He knew how to take Mao's hints, how to read his mind, how to make him happy.

Mao, for his part, appreciated Zhou's willingness to do a great deal of the concrete dirty work. Mao needed somebody who could clean up after him. Zhou was reliable, not a threat. He didn't ally himself with any particular faction, so Mao could talk to him about anything. Still, it was remarkable that they were able to remain friends until Zhou's death.

Zhou's relationship with Lin Biao was not nearly so clear-cut. For a long time Zhou had been the senior of the two, being older in both age and experience. When Zhou was a top instructor at the Whampoa Military Academy, Lin Biao was merely a student. When Zhou was leading the August 1, 1927, Nanchang uprising, Lin Biao was a platoon leader.

Yet Zhou, like most people, grew to admire the young Lin Biao for his military achievements. In Chongqing (Chungking) during the war, a reporter once asked Zhou his opinion of Lin Biao, who was already known for his exploits at Pingxingguan against the Japanese. It was typical of Zhou Enlai's tact that he replied: "Division Commander Lin Biao is a winner of important battles. Though younger than all of us, in military affairs he is more able than we are."[1]

Although his true feelings were not revealed until the relationship between Mao and Lin began to sour, Zhou never wholly trusted Lin. He did not care for the way Lin Biao had expanded his influence in the Fourth Field Army. He believed it to be the worst form of "military-stronghold sectarianism"—that is, the attempt to gain political power through military infiltration and subversion. Zhou was familiar with unbridled greed on the part of the military, and wary of it.

It was not until the Cultural Revolution that Zhou found he was able to use the military to his own advantage. He knew that few others besides Lin were in a position to stabilize the political turbulence. So when Lin replaced Liu Shaoqi to become the number-two man in China, and then Mao's designated successor, Zhou supported him in factional disputes out of political necessity. He did this even when Lin came into conflict with such military leaders as Minister of Foreign Affairs Marshal Chen Yi and Physical Education Committee Head Marshal He Long, men with whom Zhou had formed tacit alliances.

On the surface, it appeared that Mao's behavior in attacking Lin at the Lushan Plenum had been completely unprovoked. Zhou knew better. In November of 1969 and June of 1970, Mao received detailed medical reports on Lin Biao's health. The reports were jointly prepared by doctors from Army Hospital #301 under the Logistics Department, and from the Military Medical Academy. They stated that Lin's health was exceptionally good, and that although he had suffered many injuries in the past, he was as strong as a person twenty-five years his junior. One report concluded that Lin Biao could live to be anywhere from 98 to 117 years of age!

Mao doubted the truth of the medical reports, and suspected Qiu Huizuo, head of the Logistics Department, of exaggerating or distorting the actual findings. Mao was also quite annoyed by the attempt at deception. He didn't know exactly how badly Lin's health had declined, but now that he was sure there was something worth concealing, he wanted to find out what it was.

In July 1970, Mao called Zhou in for a private discussion. He requested that Zhou select a group of reliable doctors from the vast medical network at the Health Department of the State Council to perform a thorough check-up on Lin Biao. Unwilling to let Lin know of his intentions, Mao suggested that Zhou issue a circular announcing that all high-level Chinese leaders were required to undergo thorough physical examinations as a result of an increase in cancer cases. Given this pretext, Lin Biao would have to comply.

The report this team of doctors finally submitted differed vastly from that which Army Hospital #301 had prepared. According to the State Council team, Lin Biao displayed symptoms of a number of diseases. He had arteriosclerosis; his kidneys and pancreas were inflamed to the point of affecting his urinary tract; his endocrine system was blocked and malfunctioning; his mental capacity was deteriorating and he could safely work only three hours a day (according to standard government health regulations for high-level leaders); and, finally, he was suffering from an unusual bone-marrow disease which was spreading up and down from his waist and could result in partial paralysis.

The reports, which confirmed other information about Lin's bad health and extended medical treatment, both stunned Mao and relieved him. He had guessed correctly, and these reports now offered him an ideal excuse for reconsidering his choice of successor.

Mao had originally thought that by choosing the proper successor he could guarantee his influence in China for generations to come. He was just beginning to realize that he would actually be forced to relinquish control over the future leaders of China to his successor. The very thought devastated him.

Zhou Enlai was the first person Mao consulted about the matter, for Zhou himself was clearly not in the competition. Nor was he in Lin's camp. In fact, Zhou was pleased to find that Mao was no longer committing himself to Lin. If Lin were to become the next leader of China, Zhou couldn't imagine serving as Lin's Premier or political advisor. On the whole, it seemed preferable to Zhou for someone younger and less experienced to occupy the top position and wear the laurels while Zhou himself wielded the real power behind the scenes.

But now that Mao's trust in Lin was obviously dwindling, Zhou might be able to influence his choice of a successor. He encouraged Jiang Qing and Zhang Chunqiao to recommend Wang Hongwen, the Cultural Revolution mass leader who had risen to notoriety inciting armed riots in Shanghai.

Nevertheless Zhou would have continued to maintain relations with Lin Biao had it not been for the report from Yu Sang at the Ministry of Public Security. When he heard about the General Staff's attempts to establish secret negotiations with the Soviet Union, Zhou had been in the midst of the delicate preparations for

President Nixon's historic visit to China.[2] By successfully achieving this, Zhou hoped to accomplish at least two things: give a jolt to the Soviet Union, and increase his own influence in China's foreign affairs.

Now these grand plans were in severe danger of being wrecked by the military's covert mission. When Zhou met with Xie Fuzhi in August of 1971 to discuss the methods of handling the matter, they decided to replace the Public Security agents eliminated by Li Zhen and to continue their own investigation. Rather than involve personnel from the Ministry of Public Security, however, Zhou called upon the 646 Group from the Fifth Investigative Research Office in the Security Bureau of the State Council. A number of men in this unit had backgrounds similar to Zhou's and had done confidential work with him in the past. They were professionals of the sort that few other departments could boast. They also worked almost entirely undercover, so that very few people knew of their existence. Their superior was a man who doubled in the role of Zhou's principal bodyguard: Yang Dezhong.

Zhou ordered his Fifth Investigative Research Group not only to pursue the Wu Zonghan case but to expand its sphere of observation to the "Three Doors" Military Commission as well as the General Staff. He also encouraged it to use the most sophisticated devices and methods of investigation. Eventually the entire sequence of events related to the Chinese military's attempts to "make friends" with the Soviet Union was revealed to Zhou.

Had whoever in the Soviet Union first received the message of the planned Chinese military *coup d'état* taken it seriously, the news would immediately have been passed on to General Secretary Leonid Brezhnev. And if Brezhnev gave it any credence at all, he probably would have consulted with Yuri Andropov, the leader of the KGB, a neighbor in his apartment building, where they often held meetings under conditions of deep secrecy. Had they agreed upon a response and proceeded to channel a message back to the Chinese military leaders, the first step toward a reconciliation between the two hostile neighboring countries might thus have been taken.

But the Soviets did not choose to act, forfeiting a unique opportunity. They perhaps regarded the whole thing as a hoax and simply ignored the overtures. Perhaps technical errors kept the proposal from reaching them. Possibly the ever-suspicious KGB wanted more time to gather evidence of the authenticity of the apparent intentions of the Chinese military. Personnel changes or bureaucratic errors may have prevented the channels of information from flowing to the right places. Or it may be that the Soviets simply could not decide how to respond until it was too late.

Whatever the reason, Huang Yongsheng was anxious about the lack of progress being made in the secret contacts with the Soviet Union. Although he didn't necessarily interpret the non-response negatively, he was afraid of the increased chance of leaks as the Chinese waited for word.

After repeated discussions with Huang, Lin too finally agreed that perhaps their actions had been a mistake. Even if the Soviets were finally to make a move, it would probably be a long time before the conspirators could establish the necessary dialogue with those Soviet leaders who had actual decision-making power. Neither Lin Biao nor Huang Yongsheng liked the risk involved in waiting; they decided to discontinue attempts to make contact.

Zhou Enlai was a late sleeper, for his prime working hours were from midnight to five in the morning; normally his bodyguard-aide Yang Dezhong never woke him from his slumber. But Yang had just received an urgent message from the team of investigators. They had learned that Wu Zonghan had been taken to the Shahe Airport near Beijing, along with two other military officers from the intelligence organ of the General Staff who had been instructing Wu in his work all along, and escorted into a helicopter. The aircraft, which belonged to the 34th Division, had taken off and shortly thereafter crashed in the mountains 290 kilometers west of Beijing. None of the passengers survived.

Zhou and Yang drew one inference from the helicopter crash: for some reason, it had been necessary to dispose of Wu Zonghan. Why now, after he had been dormant for some time? What might follow? What were the implications? Should Mao be alerted?[3]

Zhou decided that he had better inform the Chairman. He asked Yang to go to Mao in Hangzhou with a secret document wrapped in a brown paper envelope which bore the seals of the State Council. The document included secret photographs, copies of intercepted written materials, and transcriptions of wiretapped conversations bearing witness to Wu Zonghan's attempts at contact with the Soviet Union. The most alarming piece of evidence was a transcription of a phone conversation between the vice-chairman of the intelligence organ of the General Staff and the officer in the Soviet Military Intelligence section of the same organ, Chen Dayu. In it the vice-chairman said: "Huang Yongsheng told me that Vice-Chairman Lin is getting very impatient. He said to try it one more time, and if it still doesn't work, then come up with something else."[4]

Zhou included with the document a letter warning Mao to keep two essential points in mind: first, the General Staff and others involved in the secret contacts with the Soviet Union would probably discover that the State Council investigators had been on the case; and, second, the plotters would probably step up their activities to more threatening levels.

Yang was also to give Mao orally a message Zhou did not dare put down on paper: that Mao should immediately conclude his inspection tour and return to Beijing. Moreover, before arriving in Beijing, Mao should make a firm decision about his counter-move.

Mao received the information on September 8 in Hangzhou. Until that time he had planned on spending a few days in Guangzhou. Zhou's news caused him to change his mind.

IX

Lin Yamei was an eighteen-year-old Shanghai woman whose angelic features and lithe physique had always made men's heads turn. In another time film directors would have tried to place her in leading roles in their movies, but it was the period of "model operas," and workers, peasants and soldiers dominated the stage and screen.

After graduation from high school Lin Yamei managed to avoid getting sent to the countryside to work and stayed instead with her parents in Shanghai. She lived a simple, idle life, exploring her father's vast book and music collection, studying ballet. Sometimes she visited her brother in Qingdao, where she enjoyed the beach and sun.

It was at Badaguan, a beach in Qingdao, in the summer of 1970, that she and Lin Liguo first crossed paths. (Their surnames are the same, but they were not related.) Along the beach, one of the most pleasant places in the city, many villas had been built by Germans and Japanese before World War II. Most of the villas stood empty except for the servants required to maintain them. One exception was Lin Biao's villa, whose staff had been increased to serve Lin Liguo and several Air Force friends he had invited to vacation there.

Lin Liguo and his friends Chen Lunhe and Liu Peifeng had just returned from a cruise in a motorboat. As they strolled across the

Badaguan beach, they were struck by the beauty of a girl walking toward them with two of her friends.

"Must be from Shanghai," commented Chen Lunhe, tipped off by her distinctly accented speech.

Lin Liguo purposely did not turn around to catch another glimpse of her. But he did say, "Wherever she's from, make sure you get her to Shanghai."

When Lin Yamei returned home to Shanghai, she received by mail a notice of recruitment into military service.* She passed the preliminary examinations and was summoned again for further exams. Arriving at the Military Commission building on the Bund at the designated time, she was met by two officers. They served her tea and pastries while carefully scrutinizing her. That evening she was driven to an undisclosed destination. All she noticed as she got out of the car were the fully uniformed guards stationed in the courtyard.

She was led into the examining room and introduced to two women doctors. The doctors questioned her, checked her vision, hearing and lung capacity; undressed her, weighed her and took her measurements. Finally she was asked to perform various calisthenics in the nude.

After the exam Lin Yamei learned that she had passed and would be given a privileged status in the military service. She was warned, however, that her new position required extreme confidentiality in all matters.

She was provided with a military uniform—a green jacket and cap and blue slacks—and advised that she was a bona-fide member of the Air Force. Her immediate superior was Zu Fuguang, a cadre in the Nanjing command, who made her feel very much at home. She learned that Zu's superior was the director of the Military Affairs Bureau of the Fourth Air Force Army in Shanghai, Jiang Guozhang.

She was accommodated at a small military guest house, where she immediately began her training. She learned military discipline

*Military service is a much-prized career for Chinese youth.—Translator.

and responsibility, as well as how to play billiards, drive a car and use a gun. Sometimes her superiors allowed her to make use of the facilities of the French-built International Club, preserved since China's colonial days as a retreat for the higher government and military classes. There her tennis improved considerably.

After three months of training and a three-day furlough at home, she was sent to Beijing, to another military guest house located at 5 Fandi Road. There she continued to receive instruction, this time in how to be a secretary to high-level military commanders. She thought it odd that her secretarial duties should include techniques of massage, cooking and—most embarrassing of all—sex. Her "required reading" included sex manuals and pornographic magazines published in Hong Kong and abroad. She was also instructed to watch pornographic video tapes. Having grown up during the Cultural Revolution, she had been much influenced by the puritanical attitudes that prevailed. Thus, all this seemed very strange to her.

It wasn't until November 1, 1970, that she met Lin Liguo face-to-face. The young officer was tall, confident and spoke beautiful Mandarin. He seemed considerate and proper, and under his thick eyebrows his eyes were penetrating. Her first impression was good.

One night Lin Liguo invited her to dinner. They dined alone and discussed Shanghai evenings and Qingdao beaches. It was as if they had known each other a long time. After dinner they headed back, arm in arm, toward 5 Fandi Road in the cold November wind. When they arrived at the entrance to the courtyard, Lin Yamei said she had to go back to her quarters, and that she was under strict military regulations. As she was to be evaluated soon, she was concerned about what her superiors would think.

"You have already passed the test. I'm the one who had you come to Beijing and I am the one who will assign you your work," Lin Liguo told her.

From that evening on, Lin Yamei was a regular resident at the officers' hotel in Lin Liguo's section of the courtyard. On some occasions she stayed with him at the Air Force Academy, or the

Second Professional Training School, where Lin Liguo had special quarters. She became a regular part of his life.

It is difficult to say how this relationship would have progressed had Lin Yamei not been used by Wang Dongxing to spy on Lin Liguo.

While the Chinese government decries the beauty contests of the West as a symbol of decadence in capitalist countries, it carries on its own. In China there was and continues to be a tradition of collecting beautiful girls for its most powerful leaders. Mao Zedong was no exception—he continued the practice of concubinage with zeal. The difference was that he used girls for two reasons— for pleasure and for the procurement of information. Those who most loyally served Mao with women were Wang Dongxing, Wu Faxian, Senior Deputy Commander of the Air Force Cao Lihuai, Kang Sheng and some of the provincial leaders such as Hua Guofeng in Hunan.

Several months before, just after Lin Yamei had been inducted for training, Wang Dongxing had approached Mao to recommend her services. Wang had known her family a long time, he said. The girl's maternal grandfather had been an early member of the Chinese Communist Party—a man trained at the Whampoa Military Academy who died during the Long March.[1] Because of his chronic illness, he had never been given much responsibility, but he had made valuable contributions in his own way. He befriended many poor children from the countryside and recruited them into the Red Army to work and study. Those whom he initiated into the Army all harbored fond memories of him, and many went on to become important party members. Among them was Wang Dongxing.

Mystified by the sudden and unexplained offer of a military career, Lin Yamei had originally asked her mother to find out why. Her mother got in touch with Wang Dongxing. Wang learned that Lin Yamei had been chosen as a likely candidate for marriage to Lin Biao's son, Lin Liguo. He realized that she would be in an excellent position to spy on the entire Lin family, and went to Mao with the proposal that she be so employed.

Mao was very much interested. He didn't have any reason at that point to suspect Lin of wrongdoing, but he was curious to learn how Lin Biao had reacted to his attack at the Lushan Plenum. He had long ago made attempts to spy on Lin, even before he named him his successor. But Lin's extreme caution prevented Mao from learning anything of real value. So Mao was glad to take advantage of the eighteen-year-old, even though he did not think it likely that she would produce much information.

During Lin Yamei's three-day furlough before departing for Beijing, she met with two of Wang Dongxing's subordinates. She was nervous talking to the plainclothes special agents, but her devotion to Chairman Mao made it inconceivable that she would refuse what they asked. In addition to instructing her in the basic methods of espionage work, they also spoke of the need for a certain psychological strength. She would have to exercise control over her emotions.

Once in Beijing, she began exchanging messages in secret code with Wang Dongxing as her intimacy with the Lin family grew.

Lin Liguo might have chosen to let one of his favorite women know a little about his secret activities, but he did not. In the end almost all that Lin Yamei learned came from others, including members of Lin Liguo's group who were susceptible to her flirting. Her most valuable contact, however, was actually someone she had not pursued, not even noticed at first.

He was the secretary in the office of the party committee of the Air Force Headquarters. Cheng Hongzhen, an authentic country bumpkin, had never had much contact with beautiful women. Eventually, overcome by emotion, he seized her hand and boasted, "I am going to be a minister in the State Council someday."[2]

Lin Yamei did not disdain him as she might have under different circumstances. Encouraged by her reaction, he proceeded to blurt out a number of secrets about Lin Liguo's private life and the political activities of his clique. Lin Yamei allowed the hopelessly infatuated Cheng to ramble on. He continued to court her and in the process revealed more secrets. In due time she reciprocated with vows of love. They agreed that they would marry after the coup was accomplished. She found the whole situation ridiculously funny, but played along convincingly.[3]

Lin Yamei's secret work came to an end on September 11, 1971. That day she relayed some information she received from Cheng Hongzhen to her immediate superior. Within ten minutes an urgent telegram had arrived in the hands of Wang Dongxing in Shanghai, where he was with Mao's party. The cable to Wang—which employed a secret code never used before, one specially devised before Mao left Beijing for his tour—contained a phrase that struck Wang as odd and completely unfamiliar: "Jade Tower Mountain Scheme."

X

Lin Liguo was not necessarily an alarmist—it was obvious that Mao was out to get Lin Biao—but he was particularly sensitive to the humiliation his father had suffered.

Lin Liguo had always hated Mao. Lin felt that Mao wanted the fame of a Marx and the power of an emperor, but lacked the wisdom to get either. He felt that Mao was kept afloat by blind idolators and obedient soldiers.

Unfortunately, Lin Liguo told his colleagues, my father can't see the man objectively. He has bowed down one time too many, and as a result I have been forced to take the matter into my own hands. It's a pity, Lin concluded, that my father and his friends are too old and stuffy to do what has to be done.

Lin Liguo's first action after the Lushan Plenum had been to combine the forces of his "Small Group" in Beijing with the "Shanghai Group" of his followers. They became the "Joint Fleet," a name inspired by one of his favorite Japanese World War II films. As an avid viewer of such films, he had developed both an appreciation for the Japanese art of war and a passionate hatred for the Japanese people. In one particular film the Japanese warriors were divided into a "small joint fleet" and a "large joint fleet." Lin Liguo decided to adopt the name "Small Joint Fleet" for himself, reserving the name "Large Joint Fleet" for his father. (The term was never used, so "Small Joint Fleet" is herein referred to simply as "Joint Fleet.")

The Joint Fleet was strictly an Air Force entity. Lin Liguo established its headquarters in Beijing and subdivided it into three major units: one headed by Lin himself and Zhou Yuchi, who were designated the highest "commanders" of all activities; another led by the Air Force Deputy Chief-of-Staff Wang Fei, who was primarily in charge of liaison work with other military units; and a third under the direction of Air Force Deputy Political Commissar Jiang Tengjiao, who was in charge of planning.[1]

Meeting places for secret activity were established according to need. The principal ones were: the Y-shaped office building in the Air Force compound; a row of one-story barracks belonging to the 34th Division at the Western Suburbs Airport; the residence of the former head of the Air Force Academy; a large building in the Second Professional Training School of the Air Force; the Air Force guest·house at 5 Fandi Road; and Lin Biao's house at Maojiawan in the western district of Beijing.

In addition to the units in Beijing, there were two special detachments in Shanghai and Guangzhou. The detachment in Shanghai was under the direction of Lin Liguo's original Shanghai Group and its very active secret service. The training unit of about 200, all members of the Fourth Army in the Air Force, was rigorously manned and trained. The secret service and special detachment in the Air Force of the Guangzhou Military Command were styled after those in Shanghai.

The final Joint Fleet roster included about 375 names. Many were well-placed military men with ranks of major or lieutenant general, which represented real power and authority in the General Office or Military Affairs Office (as opposed to men of similar rank in combat units, who receive orders from superiors). Others were skilled and loyal soldiers.[2]

Lin Liguo wasted no time in defining for his men the main project at hand for the Joint Fleet. As an extra precaution, he told a small lie. Afraid his own name did not bear enough weight, he attached his father's name to the scheme. "This *coup d'état* against Chairman Mao is a direct order from my father," he claimed. Once that had been said, no questions were asked.

He explained to his men that his father was confident about

Some of the secret hideouts allegedly used by the "Lin Biao–Lin Liguo Anti-Party Clique" in Beijing, Guangzhou and Shanghai.

succeeding Mao eventually, but that waiting the five or ten years for Mao to die was not appealing. Anything could happen in the interim. It was clear to everyone, he said, that Mao had a tendency toward irrational outbursts, causing the fall of those closest to him. And now that Zhang Chunqiao was so powerful, Lin Biao could conceivably get squeezed aside.

Everyone agreed heartily. They were willing to take part in the coup.

On March 20, 1971, Lin Liguo summoned Zhou Yuchi, Yu Xinye and Li Weixin to his office in Shanghai to discuss the Joint

Equipment seized from the conspirators. (Pictures above and opposite from *Criminal Materials of Lin Biao's Anti-Party Clique*)

Fleet project. He told the men that his father had encouraged him to proceed full speed ahead. From March 22 through the 24th, they met repeatedly to fix their plans. The results of that meeting have been immortalized, in the handwriting of Zhou Yuchi, in the famous "571 Project Outline."

The outline was subdivided into nine categories:

1. Potential
2. Necessity and Inevitability
3. Fundamental Situation
4. Timing
5. Available Strength
6. Mobilization of the Masses
7. Implementation
8. Policy and Strategy
9. Security and Discipline

The outline, which refers to Mao as "B-52," justifies its plan of a military *coup d'état* as a natural manifestation of revolutionary activities against the "corrupt, muddled and incompetent" ruling group that was already developing. It calls the prevailing socialism in China "social fascism," and adds that Mao has turned China's state machine into a kind of meat-grinder for mutual slaughter and strife. It accuses Mao of "donning Marxist-Leninist clothes but implementing the laws of Qin Shihuang," the despotic first emperor of the Qin Dynasty (221–209 B.C.). Students, workers and peasants alike had been exploited; now there was restless discontent. The entire country, moreover, was sunk in permanent economic stagnation. Unfortunately, "B-52" still had the blind support of the masses. Changing that would be difficult.

Nevertheless the Air Force, with its geographic mobility and superior strength, was in a better position to undertake the coup than any other group.

The outline spelled out the rebels' main resources: the Fourth and Fifth Air Force armies controlled by Wang Weiguo, political commissar of the Fourth Air Force Army in Shanghai; Chen Liyun, political commissar of the Fifth Air Force Army in Zhejiang province; and Jiang Tengjiao, political commissar of the Air Force in the Nanjing Military Region. There would be several auxiliary groups elsewhere.

The three stages of coup activity were to be:

1. Preparation—e.g., the training of troops, the assembling of weapons, the investigation and analysis of intelligence reports

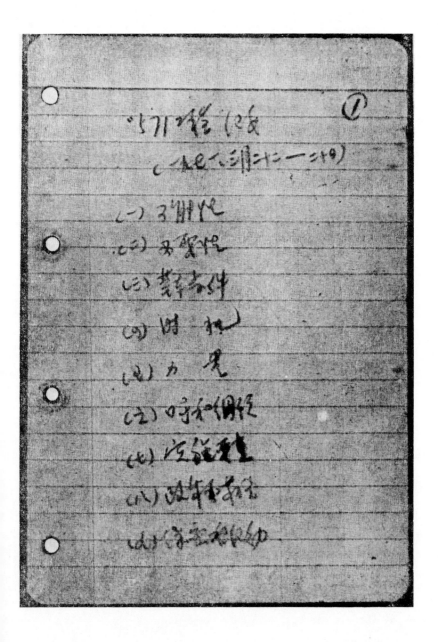

The first page of a notebook setting forth the details of the "571 Project." The handwriting is that of Zhou Yuchi. (From *Criminal Materials of Lin Biao's Anti-Party Clique*)

2. Implementation—e.g., when and how to strike

3. Follow-up—e.g., expanding and consolidating the military control of the populace, directing airborne units and air transport and managing public opinion

All this was planned in the name of liberating the Chinese people. Although the coup would be undertaken while waving "B-52's" flag, everyone would realize after Mao's death that he had been nothing more than a paranoid and a sadist.

Lastly, under the heading "Security and Discipline," came the statement: "Be prepared to die for the cause if we don't succeed."[3]

One problem mentioned only briefly in the outline but of obsessive concern to Lin Liguo during the next few weeks was how precisely to get at Mao. The Chairman lived in almost total seclusion, associating rarely with others. He maintained a few secret establishments outside Beijing, scurrying to one or another from time to time like a rabbit. They would have to encircle him somehow, and kill him by means of "poison gas, biological weaponry, bombs, car accidents, assassination, kidnapping or urban guerrilla warfare."

Lin Liguo's investigation of Wang Dongxing's security measures found them to be absolutely iron-clad. Mao Zedong was planning a trip to the South, probably in the summer. It was already late spring, so Lin Liguo set immediately to work, flying frantically between Beijing, Shanghai, Hangzhou and Nanjing to research the methods of travel normally used by Mao. In the course of this he learned of a man who had been responsible for Mao's rail-travel arrangements five years before. This man, brought from the "cadre school" (it was more like a labor reform camp) where he was being held, was lavishly entertained and questioned for two days and a night. Then, on the way back to the cadre school, Joint Fleet personnel murdered him.

The highlights of the conversation between Mao's former travel secretary and Lin Liguo were recorded by Lin's assistant:

He said: "Mao's travel schedule was passed down to us in the form of detailed top-secret documents. When we were planning one of his trips, we were not allowed to go home at the end of the day's work. When the Railway Department sent for me from Beijing, I couldn't even tell my wife the location, much less the purpose, of my business trip. Everything that went on in the control room was under protective surveillance. All was for the sake of security.

"The irony was that often our plans were completely futile. Regardless of schedules, whenever and wherever Mao wanted to go, the train moved. We would have to request other trains to let his pass, or make last-minute changes in the existing schedules. He might close off an entire route for himself, and either travel only a very short distance on it or not travel on it at all.

"Obviously, this was the safest of methods. Except for the engineer, no one in the entire rail system could know beforehand the comings and goings of his train. Even if you could recognize the car and spot it at a station, you would have no way of predicting what his next move would be.

"Sometimes while Mao was on the last leg of his trip the orders to re-schedule trains still kept coming in. We would not have realized that Mao had already returned to Beijing until after the fact."

Lin Liguo would prepare for both possibilities: that Mao would travel according to schedule, and that he would not.

On July 25, 1971, Lin Liguo called a meeting for chief members of the Joint Fleet at the Air Force Academy in the western suburbs of Beijing, the same institution that would, ironically, serve as the site for the trials of Lin Biao's "counter-revolutionary clique" ten years later.* The academy's normal business was to train its stu-

*The opening and closing sessions of the trials of the Lin Baio clique and the Gang of Four took place at the Public Security Ministry compound in the center of Beijing, but the court dealing specifically with the Lin Biao clique sat at the Air Force Academy.

dents—high-level cadres and important commanders in the Air Force—in battle tactics, nuclear warfare, chemical warfare, Army–Air Force cooperation, Army–Navy–Air Force cooperation, airborne and helicopter operations and combat-troop command. The academy was also responsible for drafting and revising plans for actual Air Force operations.

On this evening, about six P.M., a variety of automobiles headed for the northeast corner of the academy courtyard. Here gardens of bamboo, pine, cypress and flowers surrounded four charcoal-colored two-story buildings. These were the residences of the former academy principal and the academy political commissar. The courtyard was guarded by both uniformed and undercover personnel.

Key members of Lin Liguo's group arriving there included Liu Peifeng, the middle-aged deputy director of the General Office of the Air Force, with experience as both combat soldier and commander. Then there was Zhou Yuchi, who was doing meticulous work as Lin Liguo's aide-de-camp. Jiang Tengjiao and Wang Fei arrived together. They had been using their good contacts in the Army and Navy to facilitate the preparations of the Joint Fleet. There were the six who actually shared offices with Lin and Zhou at the academy: Liu Shiying, deputy director of the party committee of the Air Force General Office; Yu Xinye, head of the first department of the party committee of the General Office; Zhu Tiesheng, head of the second department of the party committee of the Air Force; Li Weixin, deputy director of the secretariat of the Fourth Army of the Air Force; Cheng Hongzhen, secretary in the office of the party committee of Air Force Headquarters; and Wang Yongkui, director of the Administrative Bureau of the Air Force.[4]

Once they had assembled, Liu Peifeng was asked to respond to Lin Liguo's intelligence from his father about Mao's travel plans. Was Mao indeed planning a trip to the South? According to Liu, yes. He was able to add that the trip was scheduled for mid-August, that Mao would be accompanied by Wang Dongxing and that it was an "inspection tour" of Shanghai, Hangzhou, Nanjing,

Changsha and Wuhan with possible stops in Nanchang and Guangzhou. He would probably travel by train, with special Air Force planes to transport guests receiving him and seeing him off.

Jiang Tengjiao, who was formerly political commissar of the Nanjing Military Region, spoke next. He knew the areas covered by the tour intimately. His conclusion, simple and predictable, nevertheless jolted everyone present. "The ideal place to attack B-52 is Shanghai or Hangzhou and the ideal time to do so is . . . right now, on this trip," he stated.[5]

An all-night meeting ensued and produced the following possible schemes:

> 1. While Mao was aboard his special train on the Nanjing-Shanghai-Hangzhou route, the train would be blown up on the tracks and a shock brigade would move in to assassinate Mao.
>
> 2. The assassination would take place while Mao was away from the train.
>
> 3. In the event that Mao boarded a plane at any point in his trip, the Air Force Operations Corps would order surface-to-air guided missiles to shoot the plane down.

Eventually the second plan was dropped when Wang Weiguo received more information about Mao's traveling habits from Wang Dongxing. (Wang Weiguo, as a top local military official, had been assigned by Wang Dongxing to take charge of Mao's security in peripheral areas.) Apparently when Mao received guests it was always in a car of the train equipped with a complete security system. No one was allowed to bring arms onto the train. Any violation of these regulations immediately activated the alarm system and alerted security personnel. Because Mao relied so heavily on these security measures, he rarely left the train. The palatial accommodations built for him in Shanghai were almost never used.

The third plan, to attack Mao's plane, would allow for the smoothest execution. In the event that Mao decided to travel by air, the Joint Fleet, as an Air Force–based organization, would have no trouble bringing under its control everything from the type of plane in the 34th Division used by Mao to the choice of pilots, the route of the plane and the type of fighter planes used in the convoy.

The plans stipulated that the flow of information on Mao's air travel would pass through the Air Force emergency communication system. As its chief, Lu Min would sign all orders delivered to the Operations Department, while Wang Fei, as deputy chief-of-staff and proxy for Chief-of-Staff Liang Pu, would be responsible for information relayed to the Air Force command post of the Fourth and Fifth armies. Both men were Joint Fleet members.

The attack on the plane would be accomplished either in Shanghai by the missile regiment of the Fourth Army commanded by Wang Weiguo, or in Hangzhou, where the job would be left to the missile regiment of the Fifth Army commanded by Chen Liyun. Because the two missile bases in Shanghai and Hangzhou were responsible for protecting Shanghai and Nanjing, cities designated as top-priority defense areas, their officers were unconditionally bound to follow orders received from the Air Force command.[6] There was little possibility of something going wrong on that front.

The missile to be employed in the attack was also good, a Chinese version of a middle- and long-range Soviet-made weapon called the SM. It was first imported in 1960 and updated, under the name "Red Flag," for the third time in 1969. The missile was used during the Vietnam War and records of its performance show that without electronic interference from American transport planes and fighters the missile hit on target 75 percent of the time. With the Joint Fleet's plan to shoot three Red Flag #2 or #5 missiles at a time, the chances of a hit were raised to 98 or 100 percent. Air Force records also cite instances in which several American-made reconnaissance planes (some of which were used by the Kuomintang Air Force) and pilotless reconnaissance planes had been shot down by this same missile in less than one minute from the time of command to shoot.

Lin Liguo hoped that the same excellent performance could be achieved in the attack on China's leader. He wanted the event to take place so quickly that no one would have time to discover who was behind it. He wanted to blame Jiang Qing.

For further security, the missile bases scattered throughout the Northeast military regions were placed under continual military drills and ordered to stand by.

There was no question but that the plan to attack Mao's plane was both the simplest and the one most likely to succeed. As soon as Wang Weiguo and Chen Liyun received word that the plane bearing the insignia of the red sun had taken off, they would pick up the command telephones and deliver Mao's death sentence.

There was only one thing that could thwart their plans: Mao's decision *not* to fly. And everyone knew, judging from Mao's past traveling record, there was every likelihood that he would so decide.

If plans two and three were eliminated, that left plan one: an attack on Mao's train.

XI

When Mao Zedong finally departed from Beijing for Wuhan on August 15, the commanders and political commissars of the Fourth and Fifth armies changed their normally relaxed postures and kept a hot line open to their command posts. Wang Weiguo and Chen Liyun spent anxious days and nights, but all they received was information about the aircraft used to carry Mao's guests—military and political bigwigs of the southern military regions and provinces. Everyone but Mao himself.

That meant that plan number one would probably have to be used. The result was a great deal of pressure on the man at the center of the activities on the Nanjing-Shanghai-Hangzhou railway—Yu Xinye.

Yu Xinye was the forty-three-year-old director of the first department of the party committee of the Air Force Headquarters.[1] He had a pale face but penetrating eyes. He was of a sturdy, medium build and always wore the orthodox military crew cut. Yu carried with him two things at all times: a 1959-model pistol and a razor-sharp paratrooper's knife.

Yu Xinye didn't appear to be brilliant, but he in fact possessed a sharp and rational mind. His analysis of Japanese, Israeli and German military techniques was unequaled. He liked to draft plans and—to the delight of Lin Liguo, who was desperately in need of such people—liked to take responsibility for the execution of his plans.

Yu recommended that the Joint Fleet take full advantage of the exceptional equipment available to the troops defending Shanghai. As China's largest city, responsible for about one quarter of the nation's industrial production, Shanghai was defended not only by its own Fourth Air Force Army, but by some of the best troops from the Nanjing and Beijing military regions as well. Among these troops was an exceptionally strong missile division armed with a special surface-to-air missile modified fo shoot ground or sea targets in cooperation with the Army and Navy. The modified missile was one of China's most reliable.

Shanghai's missile troops had the organizational system of a regiment. They shared two missile bases and three missile units of sixty-five launchers. During battles they used an automatic control system of command. Against surface radar-traced targets they had a 70-percent hit rate; when the target was pre-measured, the hit rate was 82 percent; when the target was followed with a supplementary, automatically controlled device (with which the Joint Fleet was equipped), the hit rate was close to 100 percent.

Information about the movement of Mao's train would be the responsibility of the Shanghai Group and other special detachments, such as the Fourth Army Training Corps, to be stationed along the tracks. The accuracy of the attack would be contingent upon the accuracy of the targeting information supplied.

Based on his father's experience, Lin Liguo was able to make certain assumptions about Mao's manner of traveling. Given the fact that both men were of extremely high rank, there were bound to be similarities. The assumptions Lin made proved to be quite true.

Mao's train, a formation of six cars, was drawn by the finest-quality diesel engine. The middle two cars were those used by Mao himself—the facilities were luxurious, beyond the normal level of comfort, and soundproof, bulletproof and lead-shielded for radiation protection. Both cars were equipped with security and emergency devices. One car contained Mao's bedroom, study and a living room which doubled as a dining room; the other car contained a reception room and a recreation room that could also be turned into a dance hall, projection room or small theater. Also included in the train was a high-powered communications center which enabled Mao to contact any of the military regions; should anything unexpected occur, the car could be strongly defended to stand off an attack.

At the front end of the train two cars held hundreds of Mao's best security personnel and their sophisticated equipment. At the rear were one car for his staff and attendants and another for his fifty or so bodyguards.

The leaders of the Joint Fleet had devised several different ways of attacking Mao's train. None of them was entirely foolproof. Mao's bodyguards were well organized and they had sophisticated sighting devices; the aim of their light and heavy machine guns was extremely accurate. Any attacking force would certainly be faced with a violent counterattack, rendering anything other than a sudden blow unlikely to succeed; if Mao Zedong had time to mobilize other troops, the attack could fail completely. In light of these circumstances the leaders of the Joint Fleet believed that only the heaviest weapons should be employed to achieve their goal.

The unreleased confession of one of the participants in the plot contains details of the activities:

> For security reasons, our identities were carefully disguised. We arrived near the bridge,* where the Fourth Army has military installations, as an intern group receiving training in the protection of these installations. We also prepared secret documents and special identification cards to support this disguise.
>
> We established observation posts at each end of the bridge. They were separated by a distance of about one kilometer. Both posts were occupied by the Shanghai Group in the name of the Shanghai Military Control Commission and were equipped with cable and radio communications. Our unit could receive reports from the other small groups stationed along the Shanghai-Hang-

---

*This bridge is not named in the documents, but simply referred to as "No. 1 Target." It is apparently a bridge on the rail route between Hangzhou and Shanghai.

zhou-Nanjing railway. The communication system had been tested by each of the observation posts and proved to be fast and reliable.

Our equipment included a nighttime tracking device and speedometer. At either end of the bridge we had placed under the tracks, at fifteen-meter intervals, pressure-stimulated magnetic coding devices to activate the speedometer. In addition, we were equipped with submachine guns, flame-throwers and 60 mm. anti-tank rockets.

Our orders were as follows: As soon as Mao's train entered upon the bridge, we should contact the other observation post and the command post of the Shanghai Group.

On September 4, at 5:15 P.M., a train heading for Hangzhou from Shanghai started across the bridge. There were diesel locomotives at each end and six beautiful cars in between. The windows were distinctive. I immediately notified Jiang Guozhang of the Shanghai Group, giving him a detailed report, and then alerted the observation post at the other end of the bridge.

Two days later, in the early morning of September 6, Jiang Guozhang and Yu Xinye from the Beijing Air Force Headquarters came by jeep to our observation post. I was called in for a private discussion with them about the train that had crossed the bridge on September 4. I then accompanied them for an on-the-spot investigation of the bridge. Yu Xinye said nothing for a long time. When we left the bridge, he drove us in the jeep to the bend in the river. From there you could get a long-distance view of the bridge. Yu then said, "The train that passed through here on the afternoon of the 4th was the Chairman's. It's possible he'll take the same route back to Shanghai. We'll have to do it this time."

Jiang Guozhang then explained that on the earlier occasion Wang Weiguo had been unable to establish that Chairman Mao was aboard the train. Thus, no action had been taken, for obvious reasons.

Yu Xinye said: "The train is now parked at the Jianqiao Airport in Hangzhou. Of that the Fifth Army is certain. The critical moment will come shortly, and we shall be well prepared."

Then in a whisper he explained the specific plan of attack to us. (Until then Jiang Guozhang had not known that we were to use missiles.)

As we returned to the observation post, Yu ran over the details of our tactics. He said that our duties were most crucial.

The observation post nearest Hangzhou was to give us continual reports on the location of the train. When it entered our range of observation, we were to switch on our electronic computer equipment in order to pass on the data, via a transmitter-receiver, to the Air Force missile-base command post. The command post would in turn analyze the information received and make the necessary evaluations to determine the exact time of firing. Because extensive preparations had been made to attack the bridge, so long as the observation information was correct the train on the bridge and the bridge itself could be destroyed without difficulty.

Yu Xinye said that the observation posts on the bridge would be under the control of Jiang Guozhang and Yu himself. The missile base was the responsibility of Lin Liguo and Wang Fei; Zhou Yuchi and Jiang Tengjiao would stay in Beijing, waiting for orders and orchestrating the connections; Xi Zhuxian and Zu Fuguang (a member of the Shanghai Group) were to lead a shock brigade organized within the training corps to a secret place near the bridge, where they would hide and wait for orders; Li Weixin and Han Hongkui would assist Chen Liyun in Hangzhou.

The plan and order of the attack were as follows: When Chairman Mao's train left Hangzhou, troops on the entire route would begin final preparations. As the train approached within ten kilometers of the bridge and within our sphere of observation, we would pass on the details and the missile troops would prepare to attack. There would be five groups of fifteen missiles each; the objective was the simultaneous destruction of both the train and the bridge.

Except for my men at the observation post, all the others would retreat immediately after the explosion of the train. My men and the shock brigade would be responsible for sifting through the ruins to find the bodies of Mao Zedong and Wang Dongxing, destroying them completely with flame-throwers. We had to also make sure that there would be no survivors alive in the train.

After our task was completed, we too would withdraw from the attack area by helicopter and go to Hangzhou. We would then board military transport planes to take us back to Shanghai and Beijing.

Yu Xinye, Jiang Guozhang and I kept our lines open. Lin Liguo was at the command post of the Air Force missile base 6.5 kilometers from the bridge base, which was connected to our communication system.

Late at night on September 7 we received a secret coded message from the command post of the Shanghai Group saying that Lin Liguo had been summoned to his father's villa at Beidaihe. He would be back within a day or two and all systems were go.

Wang Fei got in touch with us from the command post of the Air Force missile base to say that in Lin Liguo's absence he would assume command of the actual firing. His message was conveyed in the code language we had earlier devised.

Yu Xinye was in a very peculiar mood. His face was terrifyingly pale. Day or night, he never seemed to rest. He was afraid something would suddenly go wrong with the equipment. He installed a few range-estimation indicators at either end of the bridge just in case the electronic computers failed. He tested the system by directly reporting the distance and speeds of the train based on his personal observations.

When he saw some soldiers from the Nanjing Military Region patrolling the railroad tracks, he remained very calm. He had met them before and their previous social contacts would keep them from making trouble for him.

On September 8 in the early morning Hangzhou sent over a report. The day before, Mao Zedong had mentioned that he would like the train to be moved from the Xian Qiao Airport farther south, to Shaoxing. On the morning of the 8th the train was moved.

Yu Xinye expected that Mao might come back to Shanghai

imminently and told us to prepare to take action. He sat motion-less, observing any movements on the tracks, waiting for news. He worried that the other observation post might be getting comfortable or negligent.

All was quiet on September 8 and the morning of the 9th. At three P.M. on September 9 there came a coded message from Chen Liyun to the Shanghai Group. He and other top leaders in Zhejiang had just been in Hangzhou to see off the Chairman. His train was heading toward Shanghai.

Then news of the train came bit by bit. The Chairman was coming closer and closer to us. The speed of his train had reached ninety-five kilometers an hour.

Yu Xinye looked terrible. His hand clutched a microphone as he cleared the lines for radio and cable communications. He talked incessantly with Wang Fei at the command post of the missile base and with Lin Liguo, who had just returned to the missile base from Beidaihe. Their conversation was confined to simple utterances and reports on the number of kilometers still left for the approaching train to reach the bridge.

Two security trains of four cars apiece ran in advance of Mao's train. They reached the bridge. Two minutes later Chairman Mao's train appeared in our view (on the screen as well as directly). It was traveling at a high speed. It was a tense moment for all of us as we stared at the train without blinking.

Yu Xinye whispered, "He's here." The train was now within one kilometer. The computers had recorded the data accurately. The communication between us, Lin Liguo and Wang Fei was smooth and unobstructed.

The six cars pulled by two locomotives would soon be on the bridge. There was at most nineteen or twenty seconds to go when Wang Fei suddenly blurted out from the command post: "Bridge! The attack is off!"

We were all shocked. Yu Xinye shouted in a rage: "Shoot! You're crazy. Hurry up and shoot!"

With Yu screaming like a maniac, the train continued crossing the bridge.

There was no sound from the command post.

I could see the train cross the bridge safely; it then passed quickly out of our range of vision. Yu Xinye cried out again: "It's all over, Goddammit."

Now Lin Liguo's voice came through on the earphones: "I order. Bridge, shut off!" He then used the secret code to explain that the plans had been changed.

Yu Xinye yanked the wire of the microphone. He cursed and wailed, pounding his fist against the walls. Then, exasperated, he went by jeep with Jiang Guozhang to the missile base to see Lin Liguo.

At eight P.M. Yu Xinye phoned (I'm not sure from where exactly) and told us: "Take the whole crew out of the target area and go to the Shanghai Number One New China Village base to wait for orders there."

The following day, just after we had reached Shanghai, Yu Xinye and Jiang Guozhang arrived. Yu Xinye said that Jiang Guozhang would lead us to a hiding place along the Shanghai-Beijing railway line at a point 185 kilometers north of Shanghai. We would establish an observation post there and carry out the same instructions we had been given at the first target area. Apparently we were to attack Chairman Mao in his train on his way back to Beijing from Shanghai.

While Yu Xinye was giving us the new orders, I asked him why the other attack had been canceled.

Yu simply answered: "We decided to get Mao on the last leg of his trip back to Beijing."

Then he proceeded to drill us on the specifics of the new attack. "We are going to strike at a point 185 kilometers away from Shanghai. We will use surface-to-surface guided missiles with remote-control devices. At points fifty and a hundred kilometers away from our target we will install computerized tracking instruments to monitor and project the train's movement. Within thirty kilometers both north and south of the target a remote-controlled automatic launching device will be installed. As soon as the train enters this range, the missiles should be able to hit right on target."

For additional coverage Yu brought in two experts to install supplementary tracking equipment within a range of thirty kilometers from the target in case the computerized equipment failed. This would provide a system whereby the existing railroad communication system and the missile-launching command system could be interconnected.

I didn't understand the technical aspects. We were there simply to guard the delicate devices and, after the attack, to coordinate with the activities of the shock brigade. The shock brigade was hiding out in an arsenal warehouse 1.5 kilometers from the 185-kilometer mark.

It was my understanding that the equipment was to be tested and adjusted remotely from the command post at the missile base.

According to Yu Xinye, the missiles prepared were five times more powerful than actually needed to destroy the train. They would be launched consecutively, not simultaneously as we had planned at the bridge. The first salvo would consist of fifteen missiles aimed at the target. Then a second salvo would cut off the tracks at points eighty kilometers north and south of the target to prevent any troops from moving in.

Yu Xinye was hiding somewhere near the target along the Beijing-Shanghai tracks when he received a message from the observation post ahead that Mao Zedong's train was heading for the 185-kilometer mark. It was September 11, about noon.

Yu Xinye hadn't heard from Wang Weiguo (whose job, as before, was to confirm Mao's presence on the train) in Shanghai yet, and kept placing phone calls and radio messages in an effort to contact him.

The train was indeed approaching the 185-kilometer mark. Still no word from Wang Weiguo. Yu was understandably desperate.

Yu Xinye then tried to get hold of Lin Liguo, who had again returned to Beidaihe. When he finally got through, Li Wenpu (Ye Qun's secretary) said that Lin was on the phone with Wang Fei at the missile command post.

Yu Xinye cursed heaven and hell. He urged us to try every means possible to get in touch with the Shanghai Group. We finally did, and they told us they weren't certain whether Chairman Mao was on the train. Wang Weiguo was nowhere to be found.

In twenty minutes or so the train would pass the 185-kilometer point. Wang Fei then called to say he had just spoken to Lin Liguo, who ordered that they halt all activities. He said the Shanghai people should go back to Shanghai and the Beijing people should return to Beijing to await further orders.

Yu Xinye said he wanted to keep the lines open to Wang Fei, and wanted also to speak directly to Lin Liguo. Just as he was placing another call to Beidaihe, the call from Wang Weiguo arrived. He said that Chairman Mao was definitely on the train.

Yu Xinye ordered us to make preparations. Jiang Guozhang, Wang Fei, Xi Zhuxian and I were supposed to stay in touch.

Yu Xinye urged us to use all three lines of the Air Force, Navy and Nanjing Military Region to call Beidaihe. When the operator asked me for my military designation, name and position, I replied, "I am Vice-Chairman Lin's secretary, Yu Yunshen, number 09109."

Yu also ordered us to keep using the transmitter-receiver to call the Air Force station at the helicopter airport in the western hills of Beidaihe. When we finally got hold of the Air Force station, they said they were not familiar with our code and could not transmit our message. After we pleaded with them, they finally agreed to take the message, but much time had been wasted.

We hadn't yet reached Lin Liguo when we heard the sound of the train. Yu Xinye got hold of Wang Fei and told him that we should just go ahead and attack and worry about the rest later. Wang Fei wasn't willing to give the order. Yu Xinye was enraged and didn't stop screaming into the phone.

At this point Jiang Guozhang and I told Yu we could see the target.

It was the same train that had crossed the target bridge the other day. This time the speed of the train was much slower, probably about fifty-five to sixty kilometers an hour.

Yu Xinye stared at the train as he continued to shout into the phone to Wang Fei: "Do you see it? Do you see it over there?" Wang Fei said the apparatus indicated that the train still had 1600 meters to go before reaching the 185-kilometer mark.

"Prepare to attack! It's suicide if we don't hit. Do you understand? Answer me!" Wang Fei answered: "Prepare for drills." This was Lin Liguo's code for canceling the attack. "You're crazy!" shouted Yu Xinye. "It's a crime! It's suicide! I'm going to fight this one out with you, Wang Fei."

Yu Xinye banged his gun on the table. Jiang Guozhang, the others and I were silent as we observed the train. Wang Fei was also silent on his end.

Just as the train was crossing the 185-kilometer mark, Yu Xinye threw the phone onto the floor and hissed through his teeth: "Come on. Prepare for attack."

We had long ago prepared. But while we waited, there were no further orders. There was no missile bombardment. Except for the roar of the train, there were no other sounds.

Chairman Mao's train had once again passed safely through our target area. And then it gradually left it behind.

Xi Zhuxian called to ask us what was going on. He said Wang Fei had already called to tell us all to return to Shanghai. Jiang Guozhang asked Yu Xinye to pick up the phone and talk. Yu refused. He just stared at the 185-kilometer mark, his face ashen, his body trembling.

About ten or fifteen minutes later, we finally received a call from Beidaihe. I answered. It was Ye Qun's secretary, Li Wenpu. Li said Lin Biao and Ye Qun had already left for the Shanhaiguan Airport, and that Lin Liguo was accompanying them back to Beijing. Lin Liguo said that if there were any calls from Yu Xinye in Shanghai, the message was "Don't worry."

When I relayed the message to Yu Xinye, he had no reaction. After a while he again pounded on the desk with his gun and said: "I really should have held my gun to Wang Fei's head. If I had only done that, we would have been victors by now."[2]

XII

To understand why the operation was canceled at the last moment, it is necessary to go back in time and follow the doings of Lin Liguo.

In the early planning stages of the 571 Project, when the idea of using Air Force missiles to kill Mao Zedong first arose in a discussion with Yu Xinye, Lin had been excited by it, but had little notion of its practicability. Although occupying the second highest post in the Operations Department, he was not yet completely familiar with the technical information that Lu Min, the department chief, had tried to teach him. He tended to apply himself only to subjects that interested him, and what interested him most at that time was flying. The particulars of the missile attack that Yu proposed eluded him.

Yet once he began reading in detail the top-secret reports prepared by the Air Force missile troops for Wu Faxian and other top military officers, he became convinced that the use of missiles was the most promising tactic for the 571 Project.

The documents provided countless details on the arrangement and positioning of the missile troops, their numbers and capability, advisory data to commanders regarding tactical use of missiles, the biographies of commanders at every level and specific commands for times of emergency. The net effect on Lin Liguo was an unshakable faith in the viability of the plan.

For practice, Lin Liguo decided to conduct a drill in which troops would shoot explosive warheads. Normally, such a drill required the approval of the commander-in-chief and had to take place on a special range. Both regulations were violated, but the success of the drill confirmed Lin's expectation of success.[1]

When Lin Liguo and Wang Fei finally left Beijing to set up their command post at the missile base near Shanghai, they armed themselves with a suitable top-secret document to show to the missile troops. The document stated that the number-one and number-two commanders of the missile troops should take orders from the vice-chief-of-staff Wang Fei and the deputy director of the Air Force Operations Department Lin Liguo in a drill for sudden attack.

The number-one commander was the head and the number-two commander was the vice-head of the regiment. Although they were under the command of the Air Force, they had never worked with high-level officers from Air Force Headquarters, and they were prepared to accept the authority of Lin and Wang. If given the word, they would without asking questions simply press the button to launch the missiles. Lin Liguo was after all the son of the military leader whom all of them worshipped. This fact alone ensured a certain degree of obedience. Although it was extremely risky for Lin Liguo to be commanding such activities himself, his presence added assurance that things would proceed as planned.

The command office of the missile troops had been set up in a small cement building with one floor above ground and one floor below. The command posts in the office were in front of the automatic-control desk with a huge monitoring screen to one side.

When Lin Liguo finally arrived at the command post, his first order was for the troops to remove the aerial warheads from the missiles, replacing them with the more powerful warheads designed for surface detonation and produced expressly for these missiles by China's Fifth and Seventh Machine-Building ministries. Although the troops were surprised that the railroad tracks had been chosen as the target in their drills, they were not suspicious.

At noon on September 7, 1971, Lin Liguo sat in the command office in the heat that had settled over the area. There was no air-conditioning. He wore a short-sleeved silk shirt tucked into the waist of his blue Air Force slacks. In his leather holster was a small Chinese-made "8–1" pistol. He continually wiped away the sweat, drinking cold water and cursing the heat.

Beside him was the duty officer, Hou Tingfang. He was fifty-five years old, a first-rate commander with long experience as a company and battalion leader, and an expert marksman. He wore glasses, liked his tea strong and wouldn't deign to remove his hat even in the heat. Because of ulcers, he looked jaundiced and haggard, but always maintained a high degree of vigor.

Lin Liguo and Hou developed an excellent rapport. As soon as Lin received word that Mao's train was heading for Shanghai, he was to send out the order to prepare. Hou would then immediately position the troops and equipment ready to fire. Once Mao's train approached the No. 1 Target bridge between Hangzhou and Shanghai, the speed of the train was calculated by a tracing instrument at the observation post. Once the command center received the data, it had ten to fifteen seconds to make the final decision about launching.

Wang Fei and another missile commander slept in the lounge, ready to take over the next shift. If the word that Mao's train was leaving for Shanghai arrived after they came on duty, Lin Liguo would be awakened to execute the attack.

At 1:15 P.M. that same day Lin Liguo's telephone rang. As soon as he heard the voice on the line, he knew that it was not the news he had been waiting for. The call was from Beijing, and the caller was Zhou Yuchi.

Zhou told Lin that his mother, Ye Qun, wanted him to come to Beidaihe immediately. Lin Biao wanted to speak with him. Zhou Yuchi added that he had already arranged for a plane. First a helicopter would take Lin Liguo to Shanghai; there a plane would be waiting for him at the Hengqiao Airport.

Lin Liguo worried that perhaps the problem was his father's health, but Zhou assured him it was not. Lin Liguo nevertheless sensed it was something very serious. He concluded that simply telephoning Beidaihe wouldn't suffice. He told Zhou Yuchi not to bother with the helicopter; landing in the middle of the missile base would attract too much attention.

Lin Liguo then called in Wang Fei, granting him absolute and complete command over the Joint Fleet operations while he was gone.

Lin Liguo and two bodyguards immediately climbed into a jeep and sped toward Shanghai. They arrived at a desolate parking area of the Hengqiao Airport to find a Soviet-made AN-24 transport plane waiting. The 34th Division plane had been heading for Shanghai for a refueling when it received orders to reroute to Shanhaiguan Airport near Beidaihe.

When Lin Liguo's plane arrived at Shanhaiguan, it was already 9:50 P.M. Lin Biao had sent a car to meet him. It was driven by one of Lin Biao's personal drivers.

Set amid fine sands and lush scenery, and cooled by a breeze, the western hills of Beidaihe were the resort area occupied by China's highest leaders. Lin Biao lived in a two-storied gray building called the #69 Building. The layout of the building was H-shaped and the surrounding trees, lawns and hills were all part of a forbidden zone patrolled by Lin Biao's personal guards.

When Lin Liguo arrived at Beidaihe, his father was already in bed. He let himself into Building #65 to spend the night and tried twice to call Wang Fei at the missile base near Shanghai.

The next morning, September 8, Lin Liguo met his father for breakfast in the #69 Building. In the afternoon they took a ride in their Red Flag limousine to the Dongshan oceanfront to watch the waves. Not until late that afternoon, after returning to the villa, did they begin to talk in earnest.

Lin Biao's secretary, Yu Yunshen, a participant in the "Jade Tower Mountain Scheme," was present for the discussion. He was there to protect Lin Biao, who could not bring himself to trust even his own son totally. (Unlike Mao, however, Lin Biao didn't go so far as to disarm all his visitors. In this case he regarded his son's weapons as a proper form of decoration.)

The conversations that day were recorded by Yu:

> . . . While at the beach Lin Biao asked Lin Liguo what he thought of when he saw the ocean's waves. Lin Liguo hesitated. Lin Biao then warned him that this was a test.
>
> Lin Liguo, after a moment's thought, could still think of nothing to say and laughed sheepishly.
>
> Lin Biao said that he had answered very well.
>
> The puzzled Lin Liguo asked what he meant. After all, he hadn't said anything.
>
> Lin Biao said that to have no answer was the correct answer. He said a mistake was anything that wasn't absolutely correct. One shouldn't make believe one understood if one did not.
>
> They continued to watch the ocean's waves ebb and flow from the car, and Lin Biao still hadn't inquired about Lin Liguo's private activities.
>
> At five, after Lin Biao had rested for an hour, he had me call Lin Liguo into his bedroom, where Ye Qun was also waiting.

Lin Biao's bedroom was not luxurious. It was quite large, but cold and bare. With all the custom-made athletic equipment, it looked rather like a gymnasium. There was, for instance, a set of steel monkey bars welded together and covered with yellow-and-green gauze, looking as though it belonged in a children's playground. Lin Biao liked to climb up and down the bars for exercise. The carefully heated room, insulated by triple-pane windows, a thick wall and extra soundproofing equipment, was as still as a tomb. Lin Biao felt that too much sunlight was bad for you, and the curtains were drawn all day long. The only light in the room came from the controlled rays of ultraviolet lamps.

> Lin Biao didn't change his habits when his son was visiting. Draped in a brown blanket, he slouched in his chair of wood woven with palm and cattail leaves. I turned on the interference

unit. (Ye Qun was afraid the room was bugged, and they used three different kinds of equipment to counteract listening devices.)

Connected to the bedroom was a smaller room where Lin Biao had his frequent medical examinations. Before Lin Liguo arrived, Ye Qun had me hide in this smaller room and pay close attention to whatever happened in the next room. I was to stay ready to help the marshal at any time.

When the young Lin first arrived, he and his father discussed the difference in weather between Shanghai, Beijing and Beidaihe. Then Lin Liguo said, "The comrades who work with me send their regards. They wish you longevity."

Lin Biao laughed as he responded: "Longevity! Longevity?! Isn't there only one person in this country who can boast of that? How could they wish that to the number-two man? What can they possibly mean?"

Lin Liguo replied, "But you are the successor to the Chairman. . . ."

Lin Biao countered, "Successor? What do you think of this successor business?"

Lin Liguo, for the second time that day, had no answer.

Now Lin Biao wasted no time getting to the point. "Tiger, you once asked me whether Chairman Mao's word was good. That was after they publicized what happened at the 'Big Nine' [the Ninth Party Congress]. At the time, I just said, 'Think about it yourself.' It's obvious that you have been doing some thinking about it, doing some good, hard thinking. You've also been very brave. You can't have any delusions about this man. So many events have proved that the sly fox can never keep his hands away from evil and deception. He couldn't survive a day without trickery. We have to give him a taste of his own medicine. We must smash his schemes."

Lin Liguo replied that he agreed one hundred percent with his father.

"But," Lin Biao said, "our methods are different. I would never have thought of resorting to such rash measures as blowing up a train with missiles."

118

Lin Liguo could not believe his ears.

"How did you know?" he stammered.

Lin Biao smiled without answering immediately. He let Ye Qun help him up and walk him over to the sofa behind the coffee table where he normally did his paperwork. He put on his glasses and searched through his drawers as he said: "I know more than just that."

He flipped through some documents and then handed them to Lin Liguo. "Look these over for yourself."

Lin Liguo's hand trembled as he took the documents.

The first document, as I knew, included three photographs. The first was a casual picture of a military man, the second was a dossier photo of the same person and the third a picture of this man's corpse after he had been shot to death. The head of the man in the third picture bore visible bullet holes, but one could still discern from his features that he was the Air Force officer from the Nanjing Military Region who had reported to Wu Faxian his knowledge of the armed *coup d'état* planned by the Joint Fleet. He was Ding Siqi.

The pictures were accompanied by a detailed text.

The second document was a report approved and commented on by Wu Faxian. The authors of the report were Zhao Shangtian, chief of the political office of the missile regiment in Shanghai, and Bi Ji, chief-of-staff of the missile regiment. Their report praised Lin Liguo's behavior at the missile base, calling it exemplary for all commanders. Their motive in filing the report was apparently to curry favor with Lin Liguo by praising him behind his back, hoping he would eventually find out. What they succeeded in doing instead was to reveal the existence of the secret drill.[2]

Wu Faxian had decided to use the report to pass the burden of Lin Liguo's activities back to his father. Ever since he had committed himself to Lin Biao's coup and abandoned the opportunity of selling out to Mao Zedong, there seemed to be no purpose in remaining silent about his knowledge of Lin Liguo's clandestine doings. But he knew he would have to proceed in a gingerly fashion. The Lin father-son relationship was a delicate one indeed, and he did not want to be caught in the middle of it.

Wu claimed that he had run across the report by happenstance; he did not hold a grudge against Lin Liguo for his activities, he said, but instead felt worried for him. He hinted to the authors of the report that they should keep silent in the future, and he then submitted a copy of it to Ye Qun.

Ye Qun was shocked by its contents and asked Wu to investigate further. Wu was able to say that he had assigned Zhou Yuchi to follow up on the case. Through Zhou's outstanding work, which sometimes involved going outside his normal duties, they were able to protect Lin Liguo from the worst consequences of his activities.[3]

Later Wu showed Ye Qun many of the materials he had gathered and recommended that she and Lin Biao confront their son. He asked that they not reveal the source of their information, and they agreed.

Yu Yunshen's report continues:

> Ye Qun's voice was very tense as she spoke to Lin Liguo: "Baby tiger, don't you see how dangerous this is? Why didn't you mention it to your father before going off and risking your life like this? This is no joke. If you don't act wisely, we'll all lose our heads."
>
> Lin Liguo answered, "Well, what can we do? We can't just sit around and wait for them to come by with the ax."
>
> Lin Biao cut in. "Hurry up and tell those people in Shanghai to end it all right now. You young people always think things through too quickly. The old man isn't that senile yet. You think he'd give his life away to a punk like you? Of course we have to do something. But not that way. It's not that easy. I've been making my own preparations for some time now."
>
> Lin Biao had earlier considered using a method very similar to that of his son. But in Lin Biao's book, one doesn't fight a battle unless assured of winning. The success of a sneak attack like that was contingent on the technical reliability of the missiles. Lin Biao tended to believe more in people than in modern weaponry.

Lin Liguo insisted: "You don't know the whole story. All he has to do is pass through the area and we've got every certainty that we can get rid of him."

"What if your intelligence isn't accurate? How can you be so sure the Chairman is on that train? If you attacked the wrong train, wouldn't it be like beating the grass to alert the snake? We wouldn't have anywhere to retreat."

Lin Biao tried to reason with him, then sighed and concluded the discussion. "There's no use discussing it any longer. No one, least of all you, is going to ruin my plans. The 'Jade Tower Mountain Scheme' is the only way. Even if you were able to get rid of him, it's not the right time. You have to think about taking over power too. It's troublesome if a coup looks too much like one. There might be war, a huge civil war. Then what? Don't you think I would be the one to take the blame?"[4]

By the time Lin Liguo left Beidaihe for Shanghai, he had learned all about his father's so-called "Jade Tower Mountain Scheme." He knew that his father was behind it and that he was supported by virtually all of the highest military leaders. He also knew that his father fully expected him to participate, now that he was privy to the secret. The temptation was great. His father's pressure on him was even greater.

Yet when he first returned to his command post on September 9, he could not bring himself to cancel the whole operation. He had learned that Mao was definitely on the train. Everything was in order. It wasn't until the last minute that he passed up the opportunity to attack. Knowing how furious his comrades were, and being deeply reluctant to forfeit a project he had sweated over and which had come so close to success, he proceeded to set up a secondary operation along the Shanghai-Beijing railway. Then, returning to Beidaihe a second time on the evening of September 10, he tried to convince his father once again of the wisdom of his plans. But once again Lin Biao wouldn't hear of it, and Lin Liguo had to give up for good.

XIII

It was only after Mao's train had passed safely through the gauntlet erected by the Joint Fleet on the first-target bridge that Yu Xinye learned the real reason for not attacking it. He was furious to find out it had nothing to do with technical problems, as he had assumed, but with "the people upstairs"—that is, Lin Biao.

Lin Liguo did not reveal to his associates that he had falsely used his father's name to sanctify the Joint Fleet missile operation. Nor did he let anyone know that his father was developing plans of his own and had vehemently opposed, upon discovering them, those of the Joint Fleet. Taking Lin Liguo's words at face value, Yu never bothered to ask the question: "Why did Lin Biao suddenly change his mind?"

Yu consequently pleaded with Lin Liguo not to cancel the whole missile operation, but to transfer it instead to a point along the Shanghai-Beijing railway. It might then serve as a contingency plan, in case Lin Biao could be brought around at the last minute. Yu argued that fundamental aspects of the original scheme—the intelligence-communication system and the actual attack on Mao's train, for instance—could remain completely intact.

Yu was not a person who had much interest, or expertise, in politics or strategy. What he craved was adventure and excitement. His faith in the missile attack was total; he saw it as a spectacular event as well as one which promised a successful launching of the *coup d'état*. Yu argued ceaselessly in favor of it and, at one point, threw himself at Lin Liguo's feet with a passionate pronouncement that he would sooner commit suicide than go along with Lin Biao's rejection of the missile operation.

Under Yu's urging, Lin Liguo finally agreed to the contingency plan. For his own part, he wished to have a greater understanding of his father's scheme before committing himself to it. He believed that he could temporize, waiting for specific orders from Lin Biao before making a final decision.

On the night of September 10 Lin Liguo took a private Air Force plane from Shanghai to the Western Suburbs Airport in Beijing. At dawn he and Zhou Yuchi boarded a French-made Skylark helicopter which took them to the temporary heliport in the western hills of Beidaihe. While in the helicopter they reminisced about earlier days, when the Joint Fleet was in its gestation period and the two of them learned to fly helicopters together under one of the best pilots in the 34th Division, Chen Shiyin.

On September 11 Lin Biao called his son in for a meeting. Lin Biao was wearing his uniform, not typical for him, and seemed to be in excellent spirits. The meeting was held in Lin Biao's office at the #69 Building. It was a large office but not nearly so elaborate as that of many other high-level leaders. There were no maps, sand tables or other displays in the room.

Present at the meeting were, in addition to Lin Biao's bodyguard and secretary Yu Yunshen, Joint Fleet members Zhou Yuchi and Liu Peifeng. Lin Biao had deliberated at length before finally deciding to incorporate the forces of Lin Liguo's Joint Fleet into his plans. Now, when he called Lin Liguo in, it was not as a son but as the commander-in-chief of his assault team.

Lin Biao commenced the meeting by outlining his own "Jade Tower Mountain Scheme," spelling out the major points of the tactical model and the role of the Joint Fleet. He said that by late September Mao would have returned from his trip, presumably with no further plans for travel until after the National Day celebration on October 1. It would be during this interim period— September 25 was set as the tentative date—that a Sino-Soviet armed conflict would break out. In the course of about five days the conflict would escalate to five to ten times its original size (in terms of length of front lines and number of forces engaged). By then the situation would have become so critical that the anniversary celebration of the People's Republic of China, normally held at Tiananmen Square and attended by some 650,000 people, would be called off. The cancellation would prepare the people of China psychologically for an epochal event.

Within two weeks from its outbreak the war would have expanded to include, at the least, Manchuria and much of North China. Lin Biao and Mao Zedong would have to sit down together to map the counteroffensive strategy.

On the pretext that the Soviets might penetrate North China with airborne attacks, Lin Biao would recommend that three divisions of his loyal Field Army be stationed at the Western Hills to defend Beijing. Mao and his top advisors would be advised for safety's sake to enter the underground Central Committee command center in the "Jade Tower Mountain." Lin Biao was counting on the likelihood that if a Sino-Soviet conflict broke out, neither Mao nor Zhou would have much knowledge of the actual situation. Lin would have no trouble convincing them that there was a severe and imminent threat and that Mao had no choice but to seek refuge in the underground installation.

While Mao was in the "Jade Tower Mountain," Lin Biao would retreat to the adjacent "Number 0" installation* to assume the highest command.

The two installations had been constructed following the breakdown in Sino-Soviet relations in 1959, when Mao and his advisors felt that war, perhaps nuclear war, was inevitable. Over the next few years millions of people had been mobilized to construct emergency underground shelters in four major cities. Beijing had two —the "Jade Tower Mountain" installation and the "Number 0" installation in the Western Hills.

"Jade Tower Mountain," in the suburbs of Beijing, is the site of

*Not its true name.

numerous ancient temples where emperors of the Ming and Qing dynasties used to pay tribute. After the Communists came into power, many of the imperial temples were turned into supplementary residences for high-level leaders. In the early 1960's the underground shelter was added. At a depth of three to ten meters below ground level, the elaborate structure was primarily intended as a large administrative complex where the organs of the Central Committee could conduct party, military and State Council affairs. The structure was equipped with first-rate ventilation and disinfectant devices and comfortable living accommodations. Vast storage areas for foodstuffs and daily necessities held enough to supply inhabitants for at least three years. Large underground tunnels were later extended from the shelter in several directions. The longest of these tunnels ran ten kilometers and took more than eight years to complete. It emerged at the foot of the Western Hills and connected the "Jade Tower Mountain" installation to the "Number 0" underground military-command center.

Similar to the "Jade Tower Mountain" shelter in its construction and facilities, the "Number 0" shelter was designed for the use of the highest military command. It was equipped with sophisticated cable and wireless communication systems that could transmit orders to military headquarters throughout the country in an emergency situation.

Lin Biao explained that both a supreme headquarters and an operations command office would be established in the "Number 0" installation. The supreme headquarters would assume overall control and make critical decisions. Lin Biao would act as Commander-in-Chief while his wife and four lieutenants assisted him. He would make such important decisions as the timing of the coup, the making of concessions to the Soviets and the shuffling of individuals in leadership posts.

In the operations command office Lin Liguo would be the highest commander, with Huang Yongsheng, Wu Faxian, Jiang Tengjiao and Zhou Yuchi as his deputy commanders. The operations commanders would be responsible for providing detailed orders to the troops involved in the attack on "Jade Tower Mountain."

Lin Biao then proceeded to describe the troops to be deployed for the coup. They would be divided into an emergency strategic force and an emergency tactical force. The strategic force would be composed of three Field Army divisions, two from the 38th Field Army and one from the 40th.

The 38th Army was normally stationed along the railroad line between the cities of Baoding and Shijiazhuang in Hebei province, and was largely made up of men transferred by Lin from Manchuria at the beginning of the Cultural Revolution in a major long-term shift. The troops were motorized and organized on a "4–4 reinforcement set-up" basis; that is, there were four divisions, each composed of four regiments; each regiment in turn had four battalions; and each battalion, four companies. It was a far stronger line-up than the usual "3–3 set-up" employed in most field armies. The army had a total of about 66,000 troops, including 12,000 in logistical support, and was equipped with 460 tanks of which 118 were of first-rate quality. In addition, it had automatic cannons, surface-to-surface guided missiles and other heavy equipment.

Like the 38th Army, the 40th Army was made up of motorized troops, loyal Lin supporters. They were called Lin's "ace card" in the Shenyang Military Region. They would be sent to the Jingzhou-Shanhaiguan area and placed under the command of Huang Yongsheng.

Lin Biao said that the Field Army divisions would be dispatched to the Western Hills. Their job was to surround and disarm the 8341 Guards stationed at the "Jade Tower Mountain." And once the area was completely under their control, they would close off all the points of access with the exception of the passageway to the "Number 0" headquarters, with the appearance of rescuing Mao Zedong.

At this point the tactical force—the assault team made up of Joint Fleet members—would enter the "Jade Tower Mountain" shelter through the single open tunnel. They would proceed to kill Mao and other leaders trapped inside.

Lin Liguo suggested that after the shelter had been surrounded and Mao's 8341 troops neutralized, it was perhaps preferable to weaken those inside the sealed installation by injecting liquid fuel and poison gas before sending in the assault team to finish the job. Lin Liguo predicted: "This way we can avoid some messy fighting. The annihilation will be cleaner—and more certain."

Lin Biao liked the proposal and accepted it. He added that the vast and solid underground structure was virtually immune to outside attack, giving their men a great advantage.

As soon as the attack had been made, tactical troops would occupy Beijing's public-utility plants and cut off all communications, except for those needed by the command posts. Mao's 8341 troops and the Beijing Garrison Command would be unable to call in help from outside the city.

Lin Biao explained that just as soon as the coup had begun, the Central Chinese Broadcasting Stations would make an official announcement on behalf of the Military Commission. It would state that Mao Zedong and Lin Biao were together the target of attack by a subversive group, and that defense of the nation against the vicious counter-revolutionaries was being effected through a military coup. Only after the situation had stabilized would there be a gradual disclosure of Mao's wrongdoings and Lin's role in eliminating him. Those who had suffered under Mao's tyranny would be given a chance to recover their reputations.

The commanders and political commissars from all the major military regions would be summoned for a meeting. Lin would take advantage of the opportunity to replace many leaders with his own favorites.

Lin Biao and Lin Liguo discussed responsible members of the Joint Fleet who could be counted on to support the "Jade Tower Mountain Scheme." They included:

Wang Pu, Guangzhou Military Region Air Force Commander
Gu Tongzhou, Guangzhou Military Region Air Force Chief-of-Staff
Liang Jun, Political Commissar of the Second Technical Institute of the Air Force

Lu Min, Chief of the Operations Department of the Air Force

Wang Shaoyuan, Lanzhou Military Region Air Force Commander

Hu Ping, Air Force Deputy Chief-of-Staff and 34th Division Head

Liu Jinping, Chinese People's Civil Aviation Bureau Chief

Wu Dayun, Air Force Headquarters Security Officer

Wang Bingzhang, Air Force Deputy Commander and Head of China's Seventh Machine-Building Ministry

Zeng Guohua, Air Force Deputy Commander

Shi Niantang, Air Force General Aviation Dispatcher's Office Head

Pan Jingyin, Air Force 34th Division Deputy Political Commissar and Pilot

Zhang Yonggeng, Shenyang Military Region Air Force Political Commissar

Li Jitai, Beijing Military Region Air Force Commander

Wang Weiguo, Air Force Fourth Army Political Commissar

Chen Liyun, Air Force Fifth Army Political Commissar

Bai Chongshan, Air Force Fifth Army Head

Liang Pu, Air Force Chief-of-Staff

Lin Biao also indicated that in order to gain absolute political control over the entire nation, an official pronouncement, purportedly signed by Mao, would be issued placing the nation under military control and designating Lin Biao as China's supreme leader. The public statement would help prevent any armed insurrection and dissatisfaction among the masses. Huang Yongsheng and Wu Faxian had already prepared all the necessary documents.

Under Lin's leadership, all military and police personnel would receive orders directly from the supreme headquarters. In addition, the military control commission would set up an *ad hoc* court to punish those who defied the prevailing laws and regulations.

Lin Liguo asked Lin Biao what plans had been made to deal with unexpected or unfavorable circumstances. Lin Biao replied that four basic alternative programs had been developed.

The first was the "Red Program," which provided for the possibility that Mao would refuse to enter the "Jade Tower Mountain" installation. (The actual details of this plan—for example, how Mao would be killed—are not known to the author.)

The second was the "Black Program," which did not require that a Sino-Soviet armed conflict occur for the coup to begin. This program stipulated that Lin would launch a mutiny, have Mao killed, then blame and suppress "anti-Mao" forces for the rising.

The third plan, the "0101A Program," called for Mao to be assassinated prior to the eruption of a Sino-Soviet conflict.

And, finally, the fourth alternative, the "0101B Program," called for the assassination without a subsequent Sino-Soviet conflict.

In addition to these alternative plans there were other measures which could be adopted under conditions of dire emergency. Two involved civil war: the first called for a military offensive against Mao while he was away from Beijing; the second had Lin Biao leaving Beijing and engaging in an open military and political struggle against Mao. If Lin were forced to retreat and admit defeat to Mao, he would escape either to the Soviet Union or to the West via Hong Kong.

But, according to the later confessions of Huang Yongsheng and Wu Faxian, everyone, from Lin Biao himself to the more peripheral characters in the grand plot, had overwhelming faith in the primary plan. No one expected to have to resort to any of the alternative measures.

XIV

On September 11, 1971, a Red Flag limousine pulled into the compound of Taijichang, near Qian Men Boulevard in Beijing. Inside the heavily guarded gates was a small residential-like building that Premier Zhou Enlai often used. It housed one of his key secret meeting places.

Two of the people who got out of the car were a couple engaged to be married. The girl's name was Lin Liheng, nicknamed Lin Doudou, daughter of Lin Biao; her fiancé was Yang Dingkun, an officer in a military hospital and Lin Biao's onetime medical consultant.

According to several sources, Lin Liheng was born in 1941 in the Soviet Union. (There has been some speculation that her real mother is not Lin's wife, Ye Qun.) Her upbringing was, naturally, privileged, but also steeped in traditional Chinese values. Her parents' expectation for her was that she would become a good wife and mother in a respectable family.

In the meantime they lavished attention on her younger brother, Lin Liguo. As the only son, he was regarded as the more important of the children and watched closely. Lin Liheng, on the contrary, was often allowed to wander outside of official circles. Her freedom contributed to her sense of alienation from her family. She grew to resent her brother and to disdain her mother. Some affection did seem to exist between her and Lin Biao.

Lin Liheng realized that one way for her to break away from the family was to do just what was expected of her: get married. But even that was not easy. The men whom she seemed to attract easily almost always struck her as superficial; they did not appeal deeply to her and often had difficulty adapting themselves to the elite ways of the Lin family. Men who completely captivated her tended to have very strong, stubborn personalities that didn't bend with her demands, despite her prestigious status. Yu Boke, Wang Yuanyuan, Hu Xiaodong and Di Xin were a few of the young men whose names had at one time been linked with Lin Liheng's.

It seemed that her younger brother, whose romantic entanglements were far more numerous, had a far easier time with them than she did. With Lin Liheng, unsuccessful relationships often ended in tragedy, sometimes death. Yu Boke was killed during the Cultural Revolution after he refused to leave his other girlfriend for her. Other boyfriends were washed ashore, killed in car accidents, fell suddenly and fatally ill, or died for other reasons that somehow were never adequately explained.

Among her frustrating attempts to catch the right man, sometimes with open coercion, there was only one which met with success. Yang Dingkun was twenty-nine years old, a graduate of China's best medical academy and the youngest doctor in the team which advised Lin Biao on his health.

Yang Dingkun had been one of the first men to make advances to Lin Liheng. That is why her family was so surprised when she announced, after seeing several other men, that she and Yang were engaged to be married.

As a potential member of Lin Biao's family, Yang necessarily became the subject of extensive inquiry. After the wedding announcement his file was immediately sent by the Cadre Department of the General Political Office to the Organization Department of the Central Committee. Thereupon Kang Sheng, the main administrator of organizational work in the Central Committee, ordered a special political investigation.

Within a short time Yang was summoned to the guest house of the Central Committee's Organization Department at Donghuamen, off Wangfujing, the main shopping district in Beijing. This forbidden compound, shut off behind red lacquer doors, is reserved for high-level leaders to live, work and receive guests in. It was here that Kang Sheng often carried on his activities.

Yang found himself meeting with one of Kang Sheng's protégés, a military leader named Guo Yufeng. Guo had risen to fame during the Cultural Revolution when, given a lucky opportunity to work with Kang Sheng, he impressed Kang with his ability to "handle people." Kang Sheng subsequently had him transferred to his own office. Guo at first assisted Kang Sheng's wife, Cao Yi-ou, who specialized in creating artificial evidence for the crimes of high-level Chinese leaders. Guo proved himself quite capable and ruthless in his work, as well as unfailingly faithful to Kang Sheng. He quickly became an important figure in the Organization Department, and eventually indispensable to Kang Sheng in nearly all his schemes.

During the meeting, set as a trap by Zhou Enlai, who orchestrated the investigation, Guo showed Yang a document dealing with his political investigation. It revealed the personal background that until now Yang had successfully concealed.[1]

Yang Dingkun's real father, Chen Shou, had been a low-level officer in the Nationalist Army at the time of the Communist takeover of the mainland. He had also been a wealthy landlord who at different times served both as head of the police bureau in the prefecture and as head of the prefecture itself. Since childhood Yang had lived by choice with a stepfather, Yang Jida, for reasons unknown. Yang Jida was a military officer at the division level in the local troops of a provincial military region. Yang Jida had once told his stepson about his real father's checkered past, but had made him swear to keep it a secret. Yang Jida knew that it could be extremely dangerous were his stepson's true background to be revealed, while Yang Jida's own revolutionary military background was most advantageous for anyone growing up in modern China.

By the end of Guo Yufeng's interrogation Yang Dingkun had readily admitted the heinous crimes of his real father, as well as the crimes committed by himself and his family in deceiving the party about his true background.

Guo Yufeng made it clear that the results of the political investigation made Yang not only ineligible to become the son-in-law of Lin Biao, but also subject to a severe punishment, perhaps even death, because of his close association with the Lin family. Guo said he had the authority to lock him up, but was considering measures short of that. He was willing to help Yang Dingkun— if Yang would agree to certain terms.

After three hours of mental torture Yang Dingkun surrendered to Guo, practically sobbing with gratitude. By that act he placed himself in the hands of a most astute manipulator.

After the meeting Yang Dingkun was taken to a special banquet room in the Beijing Hotel to meet with Zhou Enlai and Kang Sheng. Zhou was charming and the dinner elegant, but Yang continually felt the strain of the leash that had been tied around his neck.

Under Kang Sheng's direction and with Zhou Enlai's approval, the Central Committee Organization Department had in the past exploited many individuals like Yang Dingkun. Kang called his rapport with such subjects a "transparent relationship." Once Kang Sheng had established a "transparent relationship" with someone, it could be years or even decades before he actually made use of it. In some cases the person might be required to work for him immediately.

Yang Dingkun received no special assignment at that time. Weeks, perhaps months passed before Kang summoned him again, to give him precise instructions. Yang's job was to ingratiate himself with the entire Lin family, gain a thorough understanding of Lin Liheng's relationship with the others and induce her to take an interest in their activities.

Kang claimed that they were conducting a "routine checkup" on several high-level leaders, under Mao's direct orders. Yang realized it was unthinkable to defy Kang's orders; if he did so, the political sentence declared against him by the Central Committee Organization Department would immediately be put into effect. As long as Kang Sheng and Guo Yufeng were involved, any attempt to remain loyal to Lin Biao would almost certainly lead to his own destruction.

He began with real diligence, evaluating Lin Liheng's attitudes and character objectively. It was sometimes difficult to spy on her without rousing her suspicions. It helped that she was willing, for the most part, to go along with his plans.

For instance, Lin Liheng's mother, Ye Qun, wanted her to travel to Shanghai, Guangzhou and Shumchun (in Hong Kong) to buy her trousseau. Ye Qun had arranged a special plane and appointed several escorts from the staff of the Logistics Department living in Hong Kong and cadres from the Central Committee Military Commission. But Lin Liheng pleaded serious bouts of anemia and stayed instead at Beidaihe or Beijing, close to Lin Liguo. Her decision was entirely due to the influence of Yang Dingkun.

On September 11, 1971, Kang Sheng summoned Yang Dingkun to Diaoyutai (the government guest-house complex in Beijing), where he occupied an entire building. Kang wanted to introduce Yang to another individual who would be instructing him in his work: Zhou Enlai's guard and secretary Yang Dezhong.

At Yang Dezhong's request, Yang Dingkun telephoned his fiancée at Army Hospital #301, where she was getting a checkup, and arranged to pick her up. Then the three of them—Yang Dingkun, Lin Liheng and Yang Dezhong—drove to Taijichang for a meeting with Zhou Enlai.

Zhou was no less dignified and suave than usual, exhibiting the manners of a perfect Chinese gentleman and the authority of a top political leader as he broke the news to Lin Liheng that Mao Zedong was planning to have it out with her father. He revealed to her that the Central Committee's Political Bureau had been engaging in dialogue with the United States in an effort to unite forces in opposition to the Soviet Union; Lin Biao, even knowing that, had had the audacity to attempt secret contacts with the Soviet Union. For this reason Mao had decided to undertake an investigation of him.

Zhou Enlai said he hoped Lin Liheng would voluntarily divulge what she knew of Lin's feelings toward Mao. He also warned her that from this moment on she was not to see anyone from her immediate family. She would be specially "protected" and sent to Tianjin, where she should call home to say she was shopping for wedding necessities.

Zhou Enlai then allowed Lin Liheng and Yang Dingkun to spend about two hours together alone. At the end of the two hours Lin Liheng was upset but willing to talk. Zhou Enlai had achieved the anticipated results.

While Lin Liheng did not utter one negative word against her father, she had a great deal to say about her brother and mother. For one thing, Ye Qun had indeed devised a plot to kill the Chairman. Although she wasn't clear on the details, she knew definitely that it involved a military *coup d'état*. Lin Liheng also spoke about Lin Liguo's tapping of Ye Qun's phone. After being exposed, she recalled, Lin Liguo had complained to his sister. He said that it was too bad she had not been born a boy, because then she would have had the opportunity to witness his instant political and military stardom personally, and perhaps even participate in the activities of the Joint Fleet. After more prodding by his sister on that occasion Lin Liguo admitted that he harbored ambitions of ruling China and, in fact, was in the process of realizing these ambitions. Lin Liguo made her promise that she would keep her lips tightly sealed.

Most recently, she reported, Lin Liguo had called the house looking for Ye Qun, who was out, and talked for a while with his sister. They first discussed her wedding plans. Then Lin Liheng asked him about where he was and what he was doing. Lin Liguo avoided answering her questions directly, but did admit that the day he had been preparing for was getting very close.

Zhou Enlai continued questioning Lin Liheng and Yang Dingkun about the Lin family. He was interested in such specific points as Lin Biao's mood, appetite, sleep patterns and the number of phone calls he made and received at any given time.

Zhou was also particularly interested in Lin's recent dealings with Huang Yongsheng, Wu Faxian and others.

As Mao's train approached Tianjin from Shanghai, after passing safely through the second of Lin Liguo's aborted ambushes, the Chairman received what would be the last message from Zhou Enlai before his arrival in Beijing. In it Zhou told Mao that Lin Biao's secrets (which Zhou had already guessed in part) had been revealed by his daughter. He also relayed to Mao the unexpected news that Lin Biao had suddenly decided to return to Beijing from Beidaihe and that he was calling a secret meeting of his military supporters at his home upon his arrival.

The last part of the telegram contained the answer to a question Mao had posed earlier to Zhou regarding the safety of his arrival in Beijing. Zhou responded: "I've already announced that the Chairman is arriving in Beijing day after tomorrow. It should be perfectly safe for you to arrive tomorrow."

XV

On the evening of September 10, when Lin Biao was still at Beidaihe with his son, he placed a call to Premier Zhou. Lin asked him about Mao's latest travel plans and when he might be returning to Beijing.

Zhou replied that he didn't know precisely when Mao was expected, but that Wang Dongxing had promised to notify Lin before Mao started back from the South.

Lin asked Zhou to make arrangements for him to greet Mao upon his arrival in Beijing.

Zhou discouraged Lin from making a special trip to Beijing from Beidaihe for Mao's arrival. He said it was more important that he rest up for the National Day celebration.

At about eleven P.M. Lin called Zhou again to tell him he was planning to return immediately to Beijing so that he could greet the Chairman appropriately.

At about midnight Air Force Commander-in-Chief Wu Faxian reported to Zhou that Lin's special plane was scheduled to arrive in Beijing at about three P.M. on September 11.

Lin had intentionally spoken to Zhou before his departure in order to fix the impression that his trip to Beijing was intended solely as a show of loyalty to Mao. In reality, he was returning to Beijing to make final preparations for the coup. After about a month of planning, the "Jade Tower Mountain Scheme" seemed more or less in order. Mao's imminent return would provide a good time to open hostilities with the Soviet Union.

At 8:10 A.M. on September 11, when Lin Biao and Lin Liguo were still discussing their plans for the coup, a Trident bearing the number 256 took off from the Western Suburbs Airport in Beijing and headed for the Shanhaiguan Airport near Beidaihe in order to pick up the Lin family. The commander of #256 was the most skilled pilot from the 34th Division of the Air Force, Pan Jingyin. Pan, a man in his fifties who was developing a paunch, was the favorite pilot of China's highest leaders.

Just as Lin Biao, Lin Liguo and Ye Qun were preparing to leave for the airport, Lin Liguo received news from the Joint Fleet that Mao was about to leave Shanghai for Beijing. Lin Biao was surprised by Mao's sudden departure. Perturbed, he remarked: "I almost didn't get there before him."[1]

Just a few minutes later Wang Fei called, urging Lin Liguo to give the order to attack Mao's train. Lin replied that he had made up his mind to abandon the missile attacks. He ordered the Joint Fleet members to return to their posts in Beijing or Shanghai. He gave Wang Fei instructions for dismantling the Joint Fleet operation.

Wu Faxian and Li Zuopeng were the first to arrive at the Western Suburbs Airport in Beijing to greet Lin Biao. Huang Yongsheng and Qiu Huizuo arrived later. The airport was very quiet. Security guards were patrolling in cars and by foot along the lawn. A few minutes after two P.M. the Trident #256 landed and rolled to a stop.

Wu, Li, Huang and Qiu were on the tarmac to greet the marshal as he disembarked from the plane. Nobody said much as Lin descended the stairs. They merely marched silently behind him to the line of cars.

Before long they arrived at Lin Biao's home. It was a fortress-like structure that had once belonged to Gao Gang and had since been renovated. It now boasted a tall gray wall wired with electronic protective devices. The men crowded into Lin's small meeting room. Lin Biao and Huang sat at either end of a long wooden conference table, while Ye Qun, Li, Wu, Qiu, Lin Liguo, Yu Yunshen and Li Wenpu (Ye Qun's secretary) took seats along the sides. They were joined later by Jiang Tengjiao, Zhou Yuchi and Liu Peifeng.

Huang Yongsheng spoke first, on the question of when to touch off the Sino-Soviet dispute. With Lin's approval, Huang had made special arrangements through the Intelligence Department of the General Staff to supply false information to be included in what was later called the "1577 Document"; this was designed to provide the spark for an outbreak of fighting in the border region. Lin approved Huang's proposal to proceed. They decided to increase the number of strategic troops involved to include six border regiments and four divisions of the field army. On the pretext of "recovering" territory lost to the Soviets, the forces would surround five Soviet border-defense areas, then open fire with cannon, rockets and explosives. In addition, near the Soviet harbor of Vladivostok, submarines would launch a sneak attack, forcing the Soviets to respond militarily. In the end, two more field armies and tank divisions would be used against the Soviet counteroffensive.

The Chief-of-Staff expected that within two to three weeks the Soviet Air Force and Navy would have been dispatched to aid the Army. The situation would have reached the necessary and desirable degree of intensity. The information sent to the Chairman would proclaim that Soviet military forces were densely deployed in the border regions of northern China and Manchuria and that they were preparing to invade northern China.

Wu Faxian spoke next. He had prepared packets of essential materials for seven of the highest leaders (Lin Biao among them). These included maps of the defense garrison systems; pictorial manuals of the geography of major military regions; a list of all military designations, code names and cross-references; a roster of cadres at the level of field army and above; a list of cadres in the elite troops; a manual of secret codes; the account names, addresses, numbers and secret codes of all accounts opened by the

People's Republic of China in foreign banks; and a manual of nuclear weapons used by staff officers.

Wu Faxian also submitted to Lin Biao a reference list, used by the Organization Department of the Central Committee Administrative Office and the Beijing Garrison of the Central Committee, of leaders who lived in the Beijing area, including their phone numbers, addresses and number and type of military troops guarding their homes.

Subsequently Huang Yongsheng and Li Zuopeng described the surface and underground characteristics of the "Jade Tower Mountain," and explained—especially for Lin Liguo's benefit—the tactical and disciplinary measures to be adopted during the preparatory stage between September 13 and the coup date, September 25.

The meeting was interrupted by a phone call from Zhou Enlai. Zhou expressed his wish to call on Lin that evening if it was at all convenient. Zhou then relayed the unexpected news that Mao was on his way to Beijing and would arrive some time the next day. It was not necessary, he said, for Lin to greet Mao at the station, but Mao would certainly wish to meet him after his arrival.

The meeting shifted from planning to speculation about what the phone call from Zhou signified. Lin was quite annoyed by Zhou's attempts to keep Mao's arrival time a secret.

The next day, September 12, upon learning that Mao had indeed arrived in Beijing, Lin decided to pay him a visit as a show of respect. He went to Mao's residence at Zhongnanhai with Ye Qun, two bodyguards and a gift of some shellfish from Beidaihe. The effort was wasted, for Lin did not succeed in meeting with the Chairman on that visit. He was received instead by Wang Dongxing, who told him that the Chairman had gone to sleep and probably would not get up for another four or five hours. Wang went on to speak of Mao's physical condition during his trip. About twenty minutes later, when Lin stood up to leave, Wang extended on behalf of the Chairman a dinner invitation for that evening. The banquet would be held at "Jade Tower Mountain," where the Chairman was intending to stay until after the National Day celebrations on October 1. Wang suggested that Lin arrive about eight P.M. Wang said he had planned on calling on him later with the invitation, at Mao's specific request. He added that Lin should expect a phone call from Mao's wife, Jiang Qing, with the same message. She and Zhou Enlai had also been invited to the dinner.

After Lin returned to Maojiawan, Huang Yongsheng was the first person to call him. Then Wu called. Lin irritably reported what had happened at Mao's home, explaining that he had not been received personally by the Chairman. The news called for immediate discussion, and before long Huang, Wu, Li and Qiu arrived at Maojiawan, where Ye Qun, Lin Liguo, Yu Yunshen and Li Wenpu waited for them.

Wu Faxian made the following notes of the events that day:

> I was the last [of the four] to arrive. The atmosphere at Lin's home was frightful. Huang Yongsheng and Li Zuopeng were utterly silent. Qiu Huizuo was downcast. Ye Qun looked at me with an expression of despair and cried, "You must think of something to do. It's possible he [Mao] has got some plot."
>
> I thought it odd that Lin Biao wasn't present. Lin Liguo was there for a while and seemed very calm. He looked at all of us somewhat impatiently, left, then returned with Zhou Yuchi and Liu Peifeng. This was the seventh time I had met with them under these grave and secret circumstances.
>
> They greeted me with a perfunctory "Commander Wu" and then stood off to one side of the room.
>
> Ye Qun was called several times into another room by her secretary, Li Wenpu, to receive phone calls. One of them, she reported, was from her daughter. "Doudou is really impossible. Without so much as a word, she and Yang Dingkun took off for Tianjin to buy wedding items and order imported furniture. They're already in Tianjin and only now does she call."
>
> Discussion turned to Lin's visit to Zhongnanhai.
>
> Both Huang Yongsheng and I believed that the Chairman

hadn't met with Lin Biao because he was truly fatigued and needed to rest before his dinner guests arrived. We didn't think there was more to it than that.

But Li Zuopeng didn't agree. He said: "If the Chairman were really taking such a long nap, Wang Dongxing would have no reason to stay at Mao's quarters. Wang lives close by and it's easy for him to go back and forth. What would he be doing there for four or five hours?

"Premier Zhou didn't notify Chief Lin that Mao had returned to Beijing," he added. "He said he wasn't even going to meet him at the train station. Isn't that strange? For someone like the Chairman who enjoys ceremony, how is it that he slipped back into Beijing without a big to-do? It's not normal."

Ye Qun became even more distraught upon hearing his words. Huang Yongsheng and I began to feel that perhaps we had treated the matter too lightly. Qiu Huizuo warned that we should not become overly suspicious lest we make wrong moves, and suggested that Li Zuopeng calm down, saying he should not work himself into a state of anxiety.

Li Zuopeng responded with a rebuttal. He said that the Navy cable communications control and observation network had reported to him their discovery that in the last three days the Central Committee in Beijing had been using a new secret code to send out communications. The new code was not registered in any of the documents, which pointed to either espionage or internal secret activities.

He had consulted with Wang Hongkun of the signal corps and found that the secret code was not used for espionage activities, and that it indeed had been used for the first time by the Central Committee.

Li Zuopeng then asked me: "What the hell do you make of it?"

I was very nervous because the Air Force cable communications monitoring station had reported the same code phenomenon to me. The news was included in a "Special Daily Bulletin" submitted by the Chief-of-Staff of the Air Force, Liang Pu. But until that time I had failed to make the connection to the Chairman that Li Zuopeng had. Now I was beginning to feel there was

142

a real possibility that Mao had been making secret contact with Beijing while he was away.

This kind of situation was quite unusual. Mao was possibly plotting against some people in his own ruling circle. That "somebody" might well be us.

Qiu Huizuo still seemed puzzled. "The people he would be making contact with in Beijing would have to be important figures," he said. He thought for a moment, then asked hesitantly, "Could it be the Premier?"

Li Zuopeng nodded his head vigorously. "Right. That's exactly what I was thinking."

Huang Yongsheng then asked Ye Qun: "Do you think all this is possible? What are they making secret contacts about? Could it have anything to do with us?"

We all fell into a somber silence. Lin Liguo, Zhou Yuchi and Liu Peifeng had listened to our conversation without saying a word.

I finally asked Ye Qun impatiently, "What is Chief Lin doing? What does he think?"

Ye Qun replied: "He is resting and doesn't want to be interrupted. It's best not to bother him now."

She had barely finished her sentence when Lin Biao came into the room. His gray suit was wrinkled, his head was wrapped in a towel and on his feet he wore only a pair of thick woolen socks.

He didn't seem at all flustered and remained solemn. He looked at each of us with a faint smile. Ye Qun went over to try to help support him as he walked, but he refused the gesture by pushing her hands away. Instead he stood in the middle of the room with his hands behind his back in a state of contemplation, nodding his head continually. I can't say how many times he tried to speak, but each time his voice cracked and the sounds just didn't seem to come out.

He finally spoke coherently: "Liu Shaoqi and old Deng [Deng Xiaoping] got it in 1966. The old man was returning to Zhongnanhai from West Lake. Liu Shaoqi went to see him to report on his work. Mao wouldn't see him, said he was sleeping. And what was he really doing? In his home were seven or eight people scheming mischief against Liu Shaoqi. I was there. So was the Premier. There was also Jiang Qing, Kang Sheng, Zhang Chunqiao and Wang Dongxing. But the guy who got us all started was Mao, the original troublemaker himself.

"If he isn't sleeping right now, then he's working on a new act. I have a feeling that he's playing tricks behind closed doors. I bet there are people who arrived right before I did who are there with him now."

Ye Qun repeated for his benefit the news about the secret code that Li Zuopeng had reported. Lin Biao listened attentively, but didn't show any reaction.

He continued, "This dinner invitation tonight—is it a chance to shake hands again, or is he setting a trap for his guest? What do you people say? What should I do?"

Lin Biao sat down on the sofa.

Lin Liguo, who hadn't participated in our conversation up to now, said, "I think it's important we act first. The signs are obvious. The old man is much trickier than we thought. It seems likely that he's really got something up his sleeve. What will we do if he makes the first move?"

Huang Yongsheng then spoke. "We must indeed adjust our timetable. But if we are to continue with the 'Jade Tower Mountain Scheme,' we can't move it up by more than a few days." In his opinion, there didn't seem to be sufficient reason to abandon our preparation for the "Jade Tower Mountain Scheme" completely in favor of one of the emergency measures.

Huang believed that the most important question at the moment was whether Lin should go to Chairman Mao's that evening. Huang felt that Lin should not go unless we launched the coup immediately.

Ye Qun asked for my opinion. I didn't have any definite viewpoint. I didn't feel there was any conclusive evidence for suspecting Mao, although there were disconcerting signs.

I recognized, of course, that the planned date for the coup, September 25, was all of two weeks away. Huang Yongsheng had set that date based on Premier Zhou's report that Mao would be coming back about then. Not expecting his early and sudden return, we were unprepared for immediate action. I did think it was dangerous for Lin Biao to see the Chairman that night; if something were to happen, there would be no fall-back position. But it also seemed inconceivable that Lin Biao could put off the visit for very long, even if he didn't go that night. Perhaps the only solution would be for him to come down with a sudden illness. I responded to Ye Qun's question. "Chief Lin can excuse himself with claims of illness."

Ye Qun cut in: "He could always say that his legs caught a chill and are numbed. He had this problem in 1957, and I was worried to death. Or he could make up something else."

Lin Biao didn't like the idea of feigning sickness.

Qiu Huizuo still insisted, "I think what we really have to establish is whether or not he is going. If he doesn't, I believe that Liguo is right in saying that we should strike first!"

"We mustn't let the Chairman act first," Lin Liguo said. "There is hope for success only if we can be the aggressor. If the 'Jade Tower Mountain Scheme' is out, we'll just have to do something else more direct."

Huang Yongsheng remarked that if Mao had already made preparations to fight, it would be difficult for us to defend ourselves. At least the "Jade Tower Mountain Scheme" would confuse him, and therefore might succeed.

Lin Biao didn't say any more. He merely sat on the sofa with his eyes closed and listened.

Ye Qun asked him what he was thinking. He shook his head and said he and Lin Liguo had never fought a war together. But all the rest of us had fought to arrive at our present positions. He said we should know better than to fight a battle without preparation. He repeated his maxim that one should never engage in a war without absolute certainty of victory.

He said that dinner at "Jade Tower Mountain" would provide a good opportunity for getting a sense of what was going on and learning what the Chairman had up his sleeve. He could then decide whether it was wise to go ahead with the "Jade Tower Mountain Scheme" at an earlier date than planned, and if not, whether it would make sense later. He could also discover what the Chairman would be doing in the next days and weeks.

He said that Ye Qun would also have to attend the dinner at Mao's, but that at least two of us four (Huang, Wu, Li and Qiu) should take up duty at the "Number 0" installation at Western Hills to prepare for any emergencies.

It was decided that Huang and I would go to the Western Hills. Li Zuopeng, Qiu Huizuo and Lin Liguo would stay in touch with us. Each person would have his own duties. Lin Liguo would keep track of Lin Biao and Ye Qun; Li Zuopeng would be ready to establish a command post in the city; Qiu would coordinate the activities of Huang and Li. We would be ready to fight under the commander-in-chief, Huang Yongsheng.

At about three P.M. that day I received a phone call from my wife, Chen Suiqi. I went into the other room to receive it. She told me Premier Zhou had called, looking for me. She didn't know why. He had left word with the Air Force to find me and have me call him back.

It would have been awkward for me to call from Lin Biao's home because I wouldn't have been able to say where I was and he might find out from the operator. Yet I was anxious to know what he wanted to talk about. I decided to go to the Air Force Headquarters to return his call.

When I returned to the conference room, I learned that Lin Biao had just received a phone call from Jiang Qing. She had extended a warm invitation to Lin Biao for dinner at Mao's. She had also spoken for a while with Ye Qun about Lin Liheng's impending marriage. From the way Jiang Qing sounded over the phone, there was no sign that anything was wrong.

Ye Qun said she felt relieved. She requested her secretary, Li Wenpu, to get somebody to prepare some gifts. She also arranged for Lin Biao to have a massage.

I told them I had to go to the Air Force Headquarters to call Premier Zhou. I promised Ye Qun I would call her as soon as I found out what he wanted.

I was the first to leave. Everyone else stayed behind.

I called Premier Zhou as soon as I arrived at the headquarters.

I could not reach him. My guess is that he was at Chairman Mao's. Yang Dezhong (his secretary) told me he was not in the office and then asked me to stand by for a few minutes to wait for his call. When he called back, he asked me if I had any plans for that evening. He said he wanted to discuss some things with me, such as the production of planes by the Third Machine-Building Ministry as well as our donation of planes to the air forces of certain Third World countries. We arranged to talk later to arrange a mutually convenient time to meet late in the evening.

I called Ye Qun to tell her about what the Premier had said. After she spoke with Lin Biao, they decided I could meet the Premier without affecting my duties at the "Number 0" installation. She said that certainly by eleven P.M. we would know if anything was wrong. If someone were needed to stand by at the "Number 0" installation past that time, Qiu Huizuo could fill in. She also told me that Huang Yongsheng and Qiu Huizuo had already left and that I should notify them of my plans.

I arrived at the "Number 0" installation at about five P.M. Huang Yongsheng was already there. We examined the surface and underground command posts. We had the people in charge of the command posts begin their drills.

At 5:45 Liu Quanjue of the command post reported that the surface and underground practice exercises had already begun.

At this time Huang Yongsheng and I completed our procedural duties as command authorities. We would use two of the secret codes employed during battle to order all the troops of the entire armed forces to enter a state of emergency and to engage in war preparations. (All the troops except the 8341 Guards and the Seventh Technical Corps, designated to operate the hydrogen bomb, fell under our command.)

The nature of our activities, if discovered by Mao, would certainly lead him to believe that we were undertaking a coup. I was very nervous. I reminded Huang Yongsheng that secrecy was of deadly importance.

He told me not to worry. He said that he could draw up a legal document calling for a drill at the installation; as long as the five of us signed our names to the document, our use of the command post was legitimate and would not rouse Mao's suspicions. (The five he was referring to were himself, Ye Qun, Li Zuopeng, Qiu Huizuo and me.)

At 6:27 P.M. Ye Qun called. She and Lin Biao were coming immediately to the Western Hills. She told me not to ask any questions. She would explain later.

Huang Yongsheng and I were terrified. We hadn't the faintest idea what was going on. I tried to call Li Zuopeng and Qiu Huizuo to see if they knew anything. Li Zuopeng for some reason was not at the Navy compound. Qiu Huizuo's wife, Hu Min, told me he had already left for the Western Hills.

Huang Yongsheng said it was very possible something had gone wrong. Maybe Lin Biao had changed his mind and decided to act now.

I went outside and waited nervously in a car for Lin Biao. Huang Yongsheng stayed in the senior officers' room to wait for news.

Shortly thereafter I saw a Red Flag automobile speed toward me. It was Li Zuopeng. I asked him what was going on. He said that Lin Biao might have decided not to go to the "Jade Tower Mountain."

I asked him: "Is it that he's decided not to go ahead with the plan or that he's just not going to dinner?"

He replied, "Maybe both."

Li entered the command office and checked up on preparations.

Close behind him was Qiu Huizuo, who didn't seem to know anything either. Li Zuopeng had told him to come.

While the three of us waited for Lin Biao, Li Zuopeng said, "The situation we're faced with makes things very difficult. We might have to get a head start. It's too bad we're so rushed for time."

A fleet of three cars arrived carrying Lin Biao, Ye Qun, Lin Liguo, Yu Yunshen, Li Wenpu, Zhou Yuchi and Liu Peifeng.

Lin Biao got out and looked around him. His face was expressionless and he didn't acknowledge our presence. He headed immediately for the operations office and we nervously followed him.

Huang Yongsheng and Liu Quanjue switched on the electronic shield in the command office for extra protection from bugging.

Lin Biao asked Huang Yongsheng to recite for him the procedure for the "Jade Tower Mountain Scheme." Li Zuopeng was told to help him supplement his narration.

When they had gotten about halfway through, Lin Biao interrupted Huang Yongsheng and asked, "If I wanted to attack the Soviet Union now, could I? If the order were given now, how many minutes would be required for my order to be carried out?"

Huang Yongsheng didn't know how to answer. He looked at me. I was also unprepared. He looked at Li Zuopeng. Li Zuopeng said: " 'Intelligence Report #1577' [the false information prepared by Huang to justify the attack on the Soviet Union, which would be said to have arrived at the news-analysis center of the General Staff by telephone from the border regions] declares that the Soviet Union is posing serious threats to China's defense. We telephone you [Huang]. You recommend fighting, the conversation is recorded and your name is signed by proxy. Within twenty or thirty minutes, or even less, we will be able to submit the signed document to the Chief."

Li Zuopeng then said to Huang Yongsheng: "After the order to respond is given, I don't think it will take longer than one or two hours to begin a regimental-level attack. Within eight hours we could begin the division attack. However, this kind of procedure could easily be unmasked later on. If that happens, all you have to do is to pin the blame on certain people and have them sacrificed."

Lin Biao then asked to see "Intelligence Report #1577."

While we were waiting, both Huang Yongsheng and I asked Lin Biao whether the situation had changed.

Lin Biao denied that it had. He said that after much thought he had decided it was best to act immediately. Going to "Jade Tower Mountain" might be too dangerous. In the ten minutes it took to get there from here he could lose everything.

Lin Biao was wearing his military uniform and cap, and for some reason wore on his left hand a white half-glove exposing his fingers. He also had a small briefcase containing the necessities used by commanders-in-chief in case of emergency. Ye Qun carried a black briefcase for him. Both their secretaries were also carrying briefcases. Lin Biao's three medical advisors had also come to the Western Hills and were waiting for orders at Lin Biao's home.

"Intelligence Report #1577" was finally brought to us by Liu Quanjue. Huang Yongsheng had written at the top: "Transmit immediately to Faxian, Zuopeng and Huizuo for their review; to Administrative Office Head Ye; to Vice-Chairman Lin for his directives."

In the column reserved for the Chief-of-Staff's remarks, Huang wrote: "Immediately organize a counter-attack at the regiment level. Prepare with artillery at the army and division level.[2] Dispatch at least five regiments to the most advantageous location. Within two hours after the regiment counterattack, mobilize the divisions. Send in at least four divisions. The Shenyang Air Force will assist in the operations. The operations plan will be examined by Li Zuopeng and Yan Zhongchuan [deputy chief-of-staff of the PLA]."

"Intelligence Report #1577" was made to look entirely authentic, exactly simulating an emergency situation. It included many details, names, places, figures and other data, and had been created in such a way as to make verification difficult. It suggested convincingly that Lin Biao had sufficiently verified the information on which he based his orders, and at the same time made it awkward for Chairman Mao, Premier Zhou and the Shenyang Military Region's commanders to check the facts or make front-line investigations.

Lin Biao insisted that we immediately attack the Soviet border. But we hadn't yet drawn up the arrangements for the General Staff and Shenyang Military Region, and it didn't seem there would be time to do so now. It would be very risky to proceed. Li Zuopeng's attitude to this was cavalier. He didn't seem to think it mattered if it were necessary to kill off many people in starting the incident. I wasn't really able to give it all much careful thought at the time, but it still seemed crazy to me to undertake the coup immediately.

Huang Yongsheng handed me the "1577 Document." I didn't read it over in detail; nevertheless I added my remarks at the top of the page: "I agree with the Chief's proposals. For the sake of the honor of the Army and of the nation, I suggest we fight using our Shenyang Air Force attack-plane troops and the Second Artillery missile base."[3]

Then both Li Zuopeng and Qiu Huizuo signed the document.

Ye Qun wrote something to the effect of "Vice-Chairman Lin, please review."

Lin Biao took the document and rapped it with his knuckles. "What should we put down for the date?"

Li Zuopeng suggested we write down today's or tomorrow's date. Huang Yongsheng was about to take the document back to fill in the date when Lin Biao said, "Let's not worry about that for now."

He thought for a while, then dashed off a few lines at the top in cursive writing. "I agree with the comments of the Chief-of-Staff Yongsheng, Faxian, Zuopeng and Huizuo. If the Soviet revisionists take advantage of us, under the Chairman's guidance we will fight as best we can. We will not subject ourselves to humiliation.

"I hereby order the Chief-of-Staff to transmit to the Operations command the order to mobilize the Shenyang Military Region and prepare for Operations Plan Number 1 against the Soviet Union.

"Commanders and soldiers at every level must obey the command absolutely. All violators will be severely punished. No sacrifice is too great for us if we are to repel the invaders.

"The Beijing, Xinjiang and Lanzhou military regions are required to make war preparations of the first priority.

"To ensure the safety of the Great Leader and Chairman Mao Zedong, we must fight the bloody battle until the end, until we have achieved victory."

After each of us read Lin Biao's comments, Huang Yongsheng

said that he was now ready to have the command post transmit the operations order by secret code. The orders had been prepared in advance by Huang Yongsheng, Li Zuopeng and myself and were based on the original draft for the "Jade Tower Mountain Scheme" which Lin Biao had approved. The original had been drafted by Li Zuopeng.

Lin Liguo began to press Lin Biao to make a decision. "It's almost six o'clock. There's not much time."

Huang Yongsheng used a walkie-talkie to call in Liu Quanjue of the command post. Liu Quanjue arrived with the head of the communications office, the staff officer on duty in the Security Office and the head of the broadcasting station. They waited in another room, separated from us by two pairs of safety doors.

Suddenly Lin Biao shouted, "Be quiet!"

He looked at his watch, then grabbed the orders document again to look it over. "I'm sweating," he said, "I'm sweating."

Ye Qun and Yu Yunshen immediately rushed over to wipe the perspiration from his face and help him to a seat. He waved his hand in the air and shouted somewhat hysterically: "Heavens! What are these people doing here? Would you mind if I had a little peace and quiet for a change?"

Lin Liguo and his men retreated to the second lounge. Li Zuopeng, Qiu Huizuo and I went to the senior officers' lounge and were later joined by Ye Qun and Huang Yongsheng.

The five of us together didn't have much to say to one another. I didn't know what to do. I doubt anyone else did either. The atmosphere was extremely tense.

Lin Biao stayed alone in the Operations Office for about half an hour. We waited like idiots in the other room, without saying a word.

Finally Lin Biao pushed open the door to our room. He had become very calm and amiable.

First he shook hands with each of us. With great self-assurance he said: "We must not become too suspicious. We shouldn't blow things out of proportion. We have spent every second of every minute for years building up our strength. We mustn't use up all our blood and sweat at once. Meticulous preparation mustn't turn into wasted effort. There isn't yet enough evidence that he is at 'Jade Tower Mountain' waiting to stab me in the back. I can't make any judgments yet. Let's wait awhile, until everything is arranged. We'll act on the 17th or 18th of the month."

We all agreed to Lin's proposal with a sigh of relief.

When we returned to the Operations Office, we saw the remains of burned papers in the spittoon. Lin Biao pointed to the ashes and said to Huang Yongsheng: "Clean that up. I burned the thing."

He had burned "Intelligence Report #1577" and had returned the operations-order cable to Huang Yongsheng. Then he said, "Now it's up to you people to come up with an immediate plan of action in case something happens to me tonight. You'll have to base it on our 'Jade Tower Mountain' tactical and strategic model and simply be ready to act sooner than originally planned."[4]

What confused Wu Faxian and others was Lin Biao's strange behavior during the last three or four hours. After a long and difficult period of deliberation Lin Biao had seemed prepared to attend Mao's dinner party. Then he had come to the "Number 0" installation ready to launch the "Jade Tower Mountain Scheme" immediately. Then he had come full circle back to his original decision.

Lin Biao's sudden change of mind was partly a reflection of his own vacillating spirit, but mainly the result of desperate appeals by his son, Lin Liguo, at the urging of the members of the Joint Fleet, especially Lin Liguo's chief-of-staff, Zhou Yuchi.

After the Joint Fleet combined with Lin Biao's coup forces, especially after Lin Liguo announced the end of the missile operations, Zhou Yuchi felt an even greater affinity with his comrades of the Joint Fleet. Conversely, he felt distanced from Wu and others in the Lin Biao camp. Differences in age, position, background and status contributed to the alienation and antagonism. But perhaps even more important, Zhou had become truly convinced that the Joint Fleet was correct in wishing to act aggressively against Mao. At first merely "assigned" to the project, Zhou finally had grown deeply partisan as the Lin-Mao split grew wider. In addition, he had been strongly influenced by Jiang Tengjiao's arguments in favor of violent tactics.

While discussion among the top brass took place at Maojiawan regarding the advisability of Lin's attending Mao's dinner, Zhou Yuchi, although present, did not express any opinions. Nor did anyone ask him to.

But as soon as Lin Biao made his decision to go to Mao's party, Zhou Yuchi, Yu Xinye and Liu Peifeng began trying to persuade Lin Liguo to take action.

Anxious and distraught under the pressure, Lin Liguo solicited the views of Jiang Tengjiao and Wang Fei. They both staunchly agreed with Zhou.

Lin Liguo finally approached his father again, this time with even greater vehemence. According to Yu Yunshen, "At first Lin Biao and Ye Qun were quite affected by his desperate pleas. They called in Zhou Yuchi and Liu Peifeng to consult with them. Lin Biao at that point agreed to go first to the 'Number 0' installation to discuss further whether he should see Chairman Mao. At the installation Lin Biao, Lin Liguo and Ye Qun argued violently. Ultimately Lin Liguo was unable to convince his father not to go."[5]

The final decision of Lin Biao left Lin Liguo and the Joint Fleet vastly disappointed and angry. Yu Xinye had the unpleasant duty of announcing to Fleet members in Beijing that their last chance to carry out the 571 Project had been forfeited. Zhou Yuchi finally accepted the situation only after Lin Liguo practically collapsed before him and said: "We've been fighting for over an hour. I'm going to have a nervous breakdown if I go on. He won't listen to anyone. I guess we have to trust his experience."

As a precaution, Lin Liguo gave his mother a watch equipped with a signaling device, which she was to wear while she and Lin Biao were attending the dinner at Mao's home. It automatically transmitted an alarm by radio in the event that the wearer's pulse stopped. The watch could also be used by Ye Qun to send a specific signal indicating danger, while another device automatically sent an all-clear signal every five minutes when nothing was wrong.

The messages were to be received by two special patrol cars positioned 500 to 1800 meters away from Mao's home and then transmitted to Lin Liguo's post. In order to avoid being detected by the radio observation station in Beijing, Lin Liguo arranged to transmit on Air Force navigation frequencies.

At about 8:10 P.M. on September 12, 1971, Lin Biao arrived at Mao's home. The armed guards awaiting guests in front of Mao's courtyard hailed Lin Biao—the marshal, China's Vice-Chairman, the Minister of Defense and Mao's appointed successor—with the appropriately ceremonious salute.

XVI

The villas of "Jade Tower Mountain" are couched in a privacy ensured by a tall gray wall that surrounds the hill, and by the dense woods, a seemingly solid surface of leaves from which only an occasional rooftop emerges. At one time Mao Zedong, Zhu De, Liu Shaoqi and Zhou Enlai all possessed villas here.

In 1964 Lin Biao too secured a "Jade Tower Mountain" villa, and in 1967 he inherited the most attractive of the villas from Liu Shaoqi after the latter's fall from grace. Only seven months later, however, Lin Biao relinquished the dwelling. He was haunted by the tragic fate of Liu, whose disastrous struggle with Mao had played a large part in thrusting the nation into the violence of the Cultural Revolution.

When Lin Biao moved out, scratching his name off the list of onetime owners, the former Liu Shaoqi villa became successively the temporary residence of such Cultural Revolution leaders as Jiang Qing, Kang Sheng, Zhang Chunqiao and Chen Boda. The new masters of the villa, however, never occupied all of it, only a part.

At one time Lin Biao had attempted in vain to switch villas with Chairman Mao. Mao Zedong's own villa occupied one half of the southeast corner of the hill and was encircled by towering trees, a carpet of green grass and a brick wall. Within the villa were several courtyards, flower and bamboo gardens, ancient stone tablets and fountains, and both ancient and modern living quarters, offices and banquet compounds.

Mao Zedong used these quarters only sporadically during the summer and fall months. In a small vegetable patch in the corner of one of the courtyards he sometimes scattered a few handfuls of seeds himself. Often the seeds were planted out of season—as a strangely symbolic gesture. At harvest time he liked presenting a bunch of green beans or peppers to his friends, gloating affectionately over his "magic tonics."

For dinner at Chairman Mao's on September 12, Lin Biao and Ye Qun had spared no trouble in procuring the best gifts. Wu Faxian flew in live lobster and salmon on a military plane, and a surveying team picked wild ginseng fresh in the field. Lin also brought with him a letter from the residents of Beidaihe in which they paid their respects and pledged their loyalty to the Chairman.

Lin Biao knew that protocol prevented his bringing any secretaries or assistants to the dinner itself, but his chief of security, Zhu Bingliang, arranged for an entourage of fifteen people, including security personnel, drivers and four bodyguards, to accompany Lin on the journey.

When the motorcade arrived at the front gate of Mao's villa, only Lin's limousine was allowed to enter the inner courtyard of the residence. Mao Zedong's secretaries and attendants received Lin Biao and Ye Qun at their car. The driver, Yang Zhengang, and the chief of security, Zhu Bingliang, presented the attendants with the gifts to Mao from Lin Biao, then drove to a parking area near the gate designated by Mao's guards.

Waiting to greet Lin Biao and Ye Qun at the end of the garden path were Jiang Qing, Zhou Enlai, Kang Sheng and Wang Dongxing. They chatted courteously and amicably, Lin Biao asking after the Chairman's health and saying how much better he himself felt after a rest at Beidaihe.

Mao Zedong waited for his guests in the flower garden outside his study. He beamed as he shook hands with Lin Biao and Ye

Qun. He commented jokingly that Lin Biao appeared to have eliminated ten years from his age. Ye Qun's suggestion of a rest at Beidaihe had obviously made a world of difference.

In the meantime Lin Liguo, at his station at the headquarters of the 34th Air Force Regiment in the Beijing Western Suburbs Airport, had just received Ye Qun's first signal of safety. He then commented to his companions, Zhou Yuchi and Liu Shiying: "I only hope this sudden dinner invitation is just a false alarm."[1]

Among those who witnessed the events that evening were the direct participants, the members of the 8341 Guards, Mao's body-guards. Wang Dongxing coined an elegant name for this select group of soldiers: "The Experts Unit."

To call these men soldiers does not do them justice. Although dressed in military uniforms, they were not ordinary troops but members of an intellectual elite who had the added advantage of choice military training and discipline. Courageous, suave, dynamic, they were a diverse group of individuals with broad interests. What bound them together was a blind submission and loyalty to Mao Zedong which made them ruthless, and paranoid about keeping secrets. They were expected to be, paradoxically, both ignorant and knowledgeable regarding their boss's affairs.

The structure of the 8341 Guards resembled that of a division in the People's Liberation Army, but with a personnel strength greater than a division's. The force consisted of eighteen troops, each troop being the size of a battalion and composed of 500 to 870 people. A troop was subdivided into four to five squadrons, which were further subdivided into platoons. Each platoon leader answered directly to Wang Dongxing. The smallest unit was the squad.

In addition to these troops, the corps included other battalions which carried out emergency tasks, or filled in for those in training or on temporary duty elsewhere; there was a large secret service that conducted espionage activities; there were vast numbers of "office workers"; and there was a sort of logistics department, nearly one half the size of the entire 8341 unit, in charge of equipment, weaponry, communications, transportation and warehouse facilities.

The following extract from Zhao Yanji's memoirs is based on conversations with Wang Dongxing.

Wang Dongxing sighed as he spoke of the events of that evening of September 12, Lin Biao's last meeting with Mao Zedong. He said that the Chairman and Lin Biao had met on innumerable occasions spanning dozens of years. The very last evening the two men were to spend together, despite its significance, was marked by conversation that was unusually banal.

Mao Zedong began by speaking of the South, from which he had just returned, and of the pleasures of traveling. The conversation then turned to an investigative report he had recently read on longevity. They discussed longevity in China, Japan and other countries.

From the reception room connected to Mao Zedong's study they proceeded toward the banquet hall to embark on what Zhou Enlai was later to call "the last supper."

Mao Zedong began the ceremonies by opening a bottle of imperial wine sealed in its original Ming Dynasty porcelain vessel 482 years earlier. He then lit some incense.

The dinner was elaborate—sea cucumbers and other land and sea delicacies, some caught or hunted down that very day and delivered by plane. Mao Zedong used his chopsticks to heap Lin Biao's plate with the precious tendons of tiger shot recently in Manchuria. Lin Biao reciprocated. The atmosphere of the banquet was very warm.

Wang Dongxing commented on the evening later on: "I thought the last meal given in Lin Biao's honor would be a very tense affair. It turned out that all the precautions taken were superfluous. Of course, our inner feelings were quite mixed beneath the veneer of perfect calm."

Around ten o'clock Mao Zedong invited everybody into another banquet room to eat fresh fruit from southern China. At some point Ye Qun mentioned that perhaps they should let the Chairman rest from his long and tiring journey. Lin Biao and the Premier agreed with her. At Mao Zedong's urging, they stayed another thirty minutes.

Premier Zhou, Kang Sheng and Jiang Qing said their good-byes first. Lin Biao and Ye Qun stayed to chat with Chairman Mao another twenty minutes. At 10:54 they too bade farewell. Wang Dongxing joined Mao Zedong in seeing them to their car, which was waiting for them at the entrance to the banquet room.

At eleven o'clock the sound of explosions could be heard throughout the villa. The Chairman's only comment to Premier Zhou and Wang Dongxing upon hearing the noise was: "As to who in this is guilty, it doesn't matter what anyone says. I don't really give a damn."

When the Premier returned after verifying the death of Lin Biao and Ye Qun, he said to the Chairman: "This is the first time since coming into the capital that we have had to act like this. We must find the proper explanation, and not let him get away with looking like a hero."

The Chairman responded: "I trust you can take care of the rest."[2]

Among the 8341 Guards present at Mao Zedong's villa on September 12 was a man called Tan Shu, a transportation expert. In the course of investigating the Lin Biao Affair, Zhao Yanji secured a copy of Tan Shu's memoirs. The following excerpt from those memoirs describes Tan Shu's own involvement and the preparations made for the operation.

Shortly after Mao Zedong returned to Beijing, Wang Dongxing called in several of us from the 8341 Guards for a meeting. He wanted us to set up a plan within an hour. Our objective was simple. Where the blacktop road descending from Chairman Mao's residence turned, we were to destroy a car and kill the passengers inside.

My specialty is vehicle safety, so I didn't need much time to come up with a method of destroying a car that I assumed to be armored and bulletproof.

I was one of a small technical group of eleven. Wang Rongyuan, an expert on explosives, was in charge; I was his deputy. There was also an operations group of sixty men. We were ready within the allotted time, after which Wang Dongxing assigned Wang Zigang to assemble us at the Security Office at the East Gate of Zhongnanhai to wait for further instructions before moving out to "Jade Tower Mountain."

An hour and a half later Wang Dongxing arrived, met with the eleven of us first and then with the operations group. Except for my suggestion that we plant land mines for insurance, he agreed to my plan. He then ordered us to proceed directly to the scene and lie in ambush. He said that before we arrived there, the regular guards stationed at the "Jade Tower Mountain" would have been replaced with our own units.

The plans for our ambush were as follows: A car would be parked horizontally across the blacktop road where it turns left at the curve. When the target car descended, we would be ready with two sections of rocket-launchers, one in front of the car and one behind. According to my estimation, a single 40 mm. rocket on target would kill everyone in the car. But just to make extra sure, we prepared four 40 mm. rockets and three 60 mm. anti-tank rockets. The launching sites were 15.7 meters from the target.

Most members of the operations group lay in ambush farther down the road, on both sides. Other operations-group members occupied two open cars; they were armed with light machine guns and submachine guns to cut off the road behind, should the target car attempt to turn back.

Bright streetlights would give a very clear view of the road. The rocket-launchers wouldn't need aiming devices as they were so close to the target.

We were to communicate by wire supplemented by a walkie-talkie. At my station was Wang Zigang with his signal gun.

While we were drilling, Wang Dongxing came by four times to check on our preparations. At about 7:10 P.M. he came to where I lay in ambush. He pointed to where the operations group was stationed a little farther down the road. "Can they get hurt? They're so close."

I replied, "The 60 mm. rocket is very powerful. Those men are less than five meters from the target. There could be deaths or injuries."

Wang Dongxing quickly responded: "We mustn't fear sacrificing ourselves. We are offering our devotion to Chairman Mao. It would be an honor to die. Everybody must remember this."

A few minutes before eleven o'clock, signals were sent out. We heard the car and saw its headlights shining. It was our target. We prepared to fire.

It was the largest model of the Red Flag, driving at a speed of about fifteen kilometers per hour. Under the bright street-lamps the entire body of the car glittered. Just after the car started making its turn, it skidded to a halt seven or eight meters short of the roadblock. At that moment the signal was sent out to launch the rockets. I heard the deafening sound of explosions and saw a rocket land squarely on the back of the car. The car was now in flames.

A second rocket was fired toward the middle of the car, but I couldn't distinguish its sound from the first. I could only see the flare of light and parts of the car fly into the air. Those responsible for extinguishing the fire leaped into action.

I moved hastily with Wang Zigang and Wang Rongyuan toward the skeleton of the car. The frame of the car was twisted, the doors had fallen off and all its windows were shattered. The fire-extinguishing chemicals had further devastated the already indistinct flesh and blood of the four corpses.

The two individuals in the front seat were completely mashed, while the woman in the back seat was a heap of rags and bones from the waist up. The man beside her had only one side of his face and body partially intact.

The remains of the blood-drenched corpses were moved to an air-conditioned room before Wang Dongxing and Premier Zhou came to look at them. Premier Zhou asked for the names of all of us present in the room. He said to us: "You have achieved meritorious service in the protection of Chairman Mao. You are all heroes."

Wang Dongxing pointed at the two corpses that a minute ago were sitting in the back seat of the car and asked: "Do you know who they are? That was Lin Biao, a traitor who forsook the Chairman. And that was his stinking wife, Ye Qun."

His words stunned us all. The person we had just killed was Chairman Mao's successor, Lin Biao.[3]

Pictures of those who died in the Lin Biao Affair (which included several members of the technical unit and the operations group) were kept on file at Zhao Yanji's investigative office. According to Zhao, in the photographs made after his face was wiped clean of blood Lin Biao was recognizable by the right eye (which had remained intact), by his eyebrows (only scorched) and by the area surrounding the partially opened eye, which was thick with wrinkles.

These photographs are in stark contrast to the pictures later exhibited to high-level cadres by the Central Committee General Office at the Jingxi Hotel. The exhibited photographs were purportedly taken by staff from the Chinese embassy in Mongolia early in the morning of September 13 at the site of a plane crash. Needless to say, the pictures of Lin Biao in the wreckage, like those of Ye Qun and Lin Liguo, were doctored.

XVII

On the evening of September 12, when Lin Biao finally agreed to attend dinner at Chairman Mao's home, Lin Liguo had made the following arrangements:

- Wang Fei, Yu Xinye, Li Weixin, Wang Yongkui and others were stationed at the Air Force Headquarters in the Y-shaped building to await Lin Liguo's orders. Jiang Tengjiao stayed home, at Lin's request, to maintain communication with the headquarters of the Air Force military regions in Shanghai, Hangzhou and Guangzhou; one of Lin Liguo's girlfriends, an actress in the Air Force, and Cheng Hongzhen would remain with Lin himself.

- Lin Liguo, Zhou Yuchi, Liu Peifeng, Liu Shiying and others placed themselves at the Western Suburbs Airport to observe activities at the "Jade Tower Mountain," keeping in constant touch with Huang Yongsheng's group.

- Lin Liguo's personal driver was Wang Zhuo, the deputy head of the automobile corps at the Air Force Headquarters, who was also responsible for the dispatch of vehicles.

- In case Lin Biao or Ye Qun encountered any trouble, Huang Yongsheng was to begin the military coup immediately by announcing that counterrevolutionary forces had kidnapped Chairman Mao, arrested Vice-Chairman Lin and begun an armed rebellion. As Chief-of-Staff of the armed forces, he would order the Western Hills command-post area to be completely closed off. He would then command the Beijing Military Region and Shenyang Military Region to dispatch armed forces under their control, in particular the 38th Army, to surround Beijing.

• All the military units in Beijing and all the military regions across the country would be notified of the coup. The Beijing Garrison unit would be ordered to surround Mao's 8341 Guards to make sure that the orders emanating from the command post were obeyed. Navy and Air Force troops would be deployed to surround "Jade Tower Mountain," the state guest house and Zhongnanhai. The Instruction Unit of the Air Force (the Joint Fleet contingent), having just arrived at the Western Suburbs Airport from Shanghai, would be sent in as an assault team to rescue Lin Biao and Ye Qun and kill Mao Zedong, Wang Dongxing and other important figures in Mao's circle.

• Within four hours, three divisions of the Airborne Corps of the Air Force would be sent to Beijing to strengthen the anti-Mao forces.

After the necessary arrangements had been made, Lin Liguo concentrated his attention on the signals coming from Ye Qun's wrist device. The system had tested out perfectly, and now he found it was not transmitting. He thought there was something wrong with it. He did not yet realize that the transmitter had been destroyed by rocket shells at the same instant his mother was killed.

While puzzling over the absence of signals, Lin Liguo received a report from the patrol cars stationed at the "Jade Tower Mountain" that two inexplicable explosions had been heard. There had been no sounds of gunfire or any other unusual events. The news was enough to convince Lin Liguo and his Joint Fleet colleagues that Lin Biao had been the target of an ambush.

Lin Liguo called Huang Yongsheng to report the news. Huang questioned the reliability of the signaling device. When Lin pleaded with him to give the order that would set the "Jade Tower Mountain Scheme" in motion, Huang replied that launching the *coup d'état* based on an inaccurate assumption would jeopardize the safety of Lin Biao and Ye Qun.

Zhou Yuchi, who was with Lin Liguo, overheard the conversation. Zhou was infuriated by Huang's paralytic behavior, and utterly convinced that everything was lost.

Without consulting anyone, Zhou suddenly got up to call Pan Jingyin, telling him to prepare a Trident jet for a long-distance flight. He also called his helicopter instructor, Chen Shiyin, at the Air Force Academy with the request that he be ready at any moment to carry out an emergency task.

In his later confessions Joint Fleet member Liu Shiying described the succession of events that day:

> Lin Liguo walked out of the room and told the head of the Shanghai Group of the Air Force Instruction Unit to wait for orders. Zhou Yuchi went into another room. I followed him and found that he was on the phone with Pan Jingyin.
>
> Zhou Yuchi then said to me, "Hurry up and tell Li Weixin to clean up my things in the office and pack them all in a suitcase. It looks like tonight's the night to burn all the bridges behind us. If you can't win, you have to escape before they come get you!"
>
> Zhou Yuchi told me to remain calm. I should reveal to no one that we were escaping. He said that if Lin Liguo wasn't willing to leave when the time came, we would have to drag him onto the plane. "We can't leave him here to face death," Zhou said.
>
> Lin Liguo called his home at Maojiawan. Yu Yunshen answered the phone. Yu answered none of the succession of questions that Lin Liguo asked him. Instead Yu responded with questions of his own: Was he still at the Western Suburbs Airport? How was Lin Biao doing? What was Huang Yongsheng up to?
>
> Yu Yunshen seemed to be acting very strangely. Lin Liguo guessed that he couldn't talk over the phone. Zhou Yuchi and others nearby were also surprised by his behavior.
>
> Lin Liguo finally asked him if something was wrong at his end. The line was suddenly disconnected.
>
> Lin Liguo dialed the number again. No one answered. He called several more times. Still no answer.

Zhou Yuchi suddenly cried out: "Dammit! Maojiawan must be occupied. Yu Yunshen probably has a gun at his head."

After Zhou Yuchi's outburst, everyone became frightened. Then Huang Yongsheng called. He said he had used the excuse of an emergency to call Lin Biao at Mao's home. Zhou Enlai answered the phone and said that Lin was in the midst of a talk with the Chairman. Zhou said that they might ask Huang Yongsheng to join them later and that he should prepare to come over for a chat.

Huang said that perhaps things weren't as serious as Lin Liguo had imagined.

Lin Liguo told him that something was wrong at Maojiawan. Lin Liguo demanded that Huang order a mutiny immediately. Huang Yongsheng said he would consult with Wu Faxian, Li Zuopeng and Qiu Huizuo by phone. After he had hung up, Lin Liguo kept cursing and said, "I really regret not putting my gun up against their old heads and forcing them to listen to me."

Someone told me that those were once Yu Xinye's words.

After about ten minutes Huang Yongsheng called back and said that he had to go to "Jade Tower Mountain." He would make contact with Wu Faxian at a designated time, and if he failed to do so, the others could assume that something was wrong. Wu Faxian, Li Zuopeng and Qiu Huizuo would then take over command of the coup.

Lin Liguo did not agree with Huang Yongsheng's proposal. But he had no way of influencing his decision. He kept saying to me, "What can you do? The old chieftains are totally lame."

Then he said, "You all come with me to the Western Suburbs command post to get Huang Yongsheng back here to talk reason. If we can't get him to change his mind, we'll put a gun to Wu Faxian's head and make him act."

Zhou Yuchi led the chorus of approval. Just at this time one of the patrol cars reported that when returning to the Western Suburbs Airport it had been passed by a military vehicle. The patrol car said it might be carrying armed troops ready to occupy the Western Suburbs Airport.

The other patrol car also reported at the same time that the road to the Western Suburbs Airport was blocked off by a military vehicle. Apparently all the roads to the airport were guarded.

Zhou Yuchi said, "They're moving in. They've got us surrounded."[1]

In another set of confessional materials Liu Shiying described in detail the activities later that day:

Lin Liguo, the person among us who had all along been acting as the decisive supreme commander, suddenly found himself at a loss.

Zhou Yuchi wanted the Instruction Unit of the Fourth Air Force Army to enter a position of defense in preparation for battle.

He requested Pan Jingyin to board a plane with an air crew, then call the airport with orders from the chief of the Air Force, Wu Faxian, to start the engine of the Trident plane immediately in preparation for flight.

Lin Liguo asked him what he was doing.

He replied that they were surrounded, and that the Western Hills command post was also surrounded. There was still enough time to escape. If they waited any longer, it would all be over.

Lin Liguo asked him where they could escape to.

Zhou Yuchi said to the Soviet Union.

Lin Liguo looked at each of us and asked: "What do you think?"

We all felt that the old chieftains were useless. None of the military regions would support us. And we had no power to control them. It seemed that the only path was to escape abroad.

Zhou Yuchi wanted Liu Peifeng and me to accompany Lin Liguo aboard the plane first. He would contact Wang Fei and others at the Air Force to complete last-minute work, then hurry to join us.

Liu Peifeng and I took Lin Liguo in a car driven by Wang Zhuo to the aircraft parking area of the airport.

The Trident was waiting there ready for flight. I forget its exact number.

Aboard the aircraft Pan Jingyin advised us that the entire crew was on hand. The plane had been fully fueled and, he joked, we could practically live up in the sky without ever having to come down. He didn't know how close to the truth that was.

I remember there being seven crew members. One of the communications officers was a middle-aged female and the rest were male: two pilots (including Pan Jingyin), a navigator, a chief mechanic and two mechanic's assistants.

From the plane we spoke by phone to Zhou Yuchi. Pan Jingyin told him that they hadn't yet given the air-control tower the plane's route and number. Zhou Yuchi said that he had already spoken to Deputy Chief-of-Staff Wang Fei and everything was taken care of. He asked that Pan Jingyin simply listen to Deputy Chief Lin's orders.

When Lin Liguo and Zhou Yuchi had spoken by phone, Zhou Yuchi said that he would be bringing about 100 men to the airport to board the plane in the next few minutes. He told Lin that I [Liu Shiying] should go help lead the troops.

When I got off the plane, Wang Zhuo asked me to help him carry several machine guns from his car onto the aircraft.

We used a ladder to get on and off the plane and at one point I fell and hurt my leg pretty badly. Lin Liguo asked me if I was okay, and both he and Pan Jingyin came over to see how I was.

It was about then that Pan Jingyin asked Lin Liguo in a low voice where we were going.

Lin Liguo said, "Can you handle the crew?"

Pan Jingyin replied, "With the Deputy Chief here, there should be no problem."

Lin Liguo said, "Whoever doesn't obey orders tonight gets this." As he said the words, he tapped Pan Jingyin's holster.

Wang Zhuo and I left by car to locate Zhou Yuchi. As we passed the control tower we heard many cars revving up their engines. Before we reached the command center of the Joint Fleet, we saw a whole column of vehicles, with armed soldiers jumping out of them.

Wang Zhuo said, "Dammit! We can't get through."

Then we saw three jeeps leaving the command center and heading toward the airport. I thought Zhou Yuchi was in one of the jeeps and told Wang Zhuo to overtake them. As we approached, we saw that they were military cars. The people in the cars got out and pointed guns at us, shouting for us to halt.

We turned around and headed back to the airfield. Wang Zhuo kept shouting, "Damn!"

I also saw searchlights from the control tower sweeping the runway. A group of soldiers was running toward the Trident. But the plane had already picked up speed for takeoff.

Zhou tried to catch up to the plane, while I shouted at him to turn around. He finally did. We detoured into a residential section and left the airport through a side gate, then headed back to the Air Force Academy to seek refuge.[2]

After Lin Liguo had boarded the plane, Zhou Yuchi told Wang Fei to gather everyone together and come up with a single consistent story. They agreed on a common response to investigators, and to feign ignorance about the affairs of Lin Liguo and the Joint Fleet.

Zhou had Wang Fei and Li Weixin contact all the members of the Joint Fleet at their command posts, instructing them to burn all documents, destroy all other evidence of their presence and preserve their strength.

He said, "We have suffered a setback, but we are not yet defeated. Victory will ultimately be with the Joint Fleet."

As Liu Shiying was heading to meet Zhou Yuchi, Zhou received word that the army troops had entered the airport and were approaching the aircraft parking area. The Instruction Unit could see the troops from their position.

After Zhou Yuchi realized he had lost any chance of boarding the plane, he radioed to Lin Liguo and urged him to take off immediately.

The Joint Fleet communications officer, Xu Limin, wrote in his confessions:

> Zhou Yuchi told Lin Liguo he shouldn't wait even one second. To take off was safety. He wanted Lin Liguo to use his submachine gun to disarm the crew, including Pan Jingyin.

Lin Liguo asked him what he was going to do. Zhou said he would escape by helicopter. They would meet at their agreed destination. Lastly, he shouted two slogans: "Long live Lin Biao! Long live Lin Liguo!"

Without first notifying the Instruction Unit, he took me, the driver Lin Jianping, the secretary Xu Xiuxu and two guards from the Air Force Academy's secret meeting place, Lu Yang and Qi Yaofang, to an electric car and drove us from the maintenance shop at the airport through the fields onto a small road, and by a roundabout route to the secret meeting place at the Air Force Academy.

Chen Shiyin was waiting there.

Zhou Yuchi ordered everybody to collect written materials and divide them into two groups: one group to be packed in suitcases, one to be burned.

I took care of some of the documents by soaking them in alcohol and burning them in a washbasin in the bathroom. Before long Liu Shiying and Wang Zhuo came in.[3]

Joint Fleet member Li Weixin described Zhou Yuchi's activities in his confessions:

I arrived at the secret meeting place at the Air Force Academy at about one in the morning on September 13. I went by car carrying two suitcases full of papers selected by Zhou Yuchi. The papers were mostly important files compiled by the Joint Fleet. They included top-secret documents, manuals, maps, magnetic tapes and microfilms which Lin Liguo had obtained from Lin Biao. Some were originals and some copies of the originals. These were highly classified materials involving military and national security. In addition, there was $30,000 in American currency, Soviet intelligence materials, air route maps, drugs, narcotics and a signal pistol.

At the request of Zhou Yuchi, before leaving the Air Force compound I went to see his family. Using a secret code, I informed them that he was going on a "test flight."

Zhou Yuchi examined the things I had taken. He asked about Wang Fei, Jiang Tengjiao and others and told the people with him to coordinate their stories with those of Wang Fei.

He said, "Shanghai [meaning the Shanghai Group] has really suffered." He wanted me to call the Shanghai Group and have its members establish their own defensive measures based on specific need.

He never ceased to curse Huang Yongsheng, calling him a true blockhead and a criminal. If he had the chance, he would kill him to relieve his hatred. He said that history had fallen into the hands of a group of useless, rotten individuals. If the Joint Fleet had had its own way, the situation would be entirely different.

Zhou Yuchi made contact with the secret hideouts of the Joint Fleet at the Technical Institute, 5 Fandi Road and the Air Force compound. He arranged to disperse all those stationed there except a few who would remain behind. At the end of the telephone conversation he used a secret code word to indicate the discontinuation of all future communication.

As we were about to leave, Yu Xinye, Liu Shiying and Wang Zhuo arrived. Zhou Yuchi was violently angry and went into a fit of cursing. We were all practically in tears and followed Zhou Yuchi as he banged his handgun rhythmically against the table and walls and recited the Joint Fleet's pledge of loyalty.

By the time we left the Air Force Academy, it was probably about two o'clock. Zhou Yuchi, Yu Xinye, Liu Shiying, Wang Zhuo, Chen Shiyin and I then headed by car for the Shahe Airport.

On our way there our car broke down and we had to spend some time fixing it, so I don't know exactly when we arrived. It was probably about four or five o'clock.

We arrived at the 101st Regiment of the 34th Division. Chen Shiyin, following the orders of Zhou Yuchi, had helicopter pilot Chen Xiuwen called out of his house in the city. Zhou Yuchi and I told Chen Xiuwen that we had an emergency duty to carry out.

Chen Xiuwen asked if he could tell his family. Liu Shiying replied that it would all be over by tomorrow and that he should not tell his family.

Once in the car, Chen Xiuwen asked about the flight plan. Zhou Yuchi said that we were going to the Sino-Soviet border to pick someone up. He said that a member of our high-level intelligence organ and a representative from an anti-Brezhnev Soviet organization were waiting for us immediately on the other side of the border.

Because Chen Xiuwen had been called upon to perform similar duties before, he didn't think it unusual. He merely asked about the route. Zhou Yuchi said that he would give his orders along the way. He wouldn't go into the details right now.

Zhou Yuchi had the driver send Chen Xiuwen, Chen Shiyin and Liu Shiying to the airfield first. He, Yu Xinye and I went again to look for a portable generator truck. When we arrived at the quarters of the ground service unit at the Shahe Airport, Chen Shiyin went to wake the head of the group.

Zhou Yuchi asked him, "Are you or are you not loyal to Vice-Chairman Lin?"

Without immediately replying, the unit head went over to his desk to get something. Thinking he might be looking for a weapon, Liu Shiying and I pointed our guns at him.

He fished out his *Quotations from Chairman Mao* and, standing erect, waved it in the air, shouting, "To Vice-Chairman Lin's health! Good health to him always!"

We rode in the portable generator truck, with the unit head at the wheel, to the airfield. I handed the guard documents I had prepared at the Air Force Headquarters authorizing our use of helicopter #3685.

The guards said we needed the approval of the head of the 101st Regiment or the stationmaster.

Zhou Yuchi became furious and yelled at the two guards. They didn't speak after that.

Later I saw one of the guards walk into the gatehouse about 150 meters away. He was probably going to make a phone call.

We swiftly prepared the aircraft and soon it was ready to go.

The guard came out of the office and started running toward us. Liu Shiying and Wang Zhuo jumped off the helicopter and drove away in the car.

We immediately took off. Zhou Yuchi ordered the pilot to fly in a northwest direction and to turn off the lights.

After we had been flying for about twenty minutes, we saw a small high-speed craft pass diagonally to our right. Yu Xinye and I guessed that it was a fighter plane.

I said to Zhou Yuchi, "There may be a plane following us." Zhou Yuchi replied, "Shut up."

Yu Xinye, without using the intercom, reminded me, "They can hear you."

Zhou Yuchi asked Chen Xiuwen, "Did you hear anything?" Chen Xiuwen said, "I didn't hear a thing."

Zhou Yuchi then said, "Don't be scared. He [meaning me] said it, didn't he? There's a plane that wants to intercept us. You must fly a little lower, closer to that mountain ridge. We're in a net of fire now. We'll be safe if we can just get across the border."

"Aren't we carrying out duties? Why are we to be intercepted? I don't understand." Chen Xiuwen was truly puzzled.

Zhou Yuchi finally told him the truth about the escape. He asked Chen for his reaction. Chen replied, "I have lived for Vice-Chairman Lin. I would also die for Vice-Chairman Lin."

Zhou Yuchi praised him gratefully.

After that exchange I didn't put on the earphones. I was completely in the dark about what was happening in the front of the cabin.

We had probably been flying for about an hour when the aircraft became unsteady. Only then did I put on my earphones again. I heard Zhou Yuchi yelling at Chen Xiuwen that he was tampering with the navigation monitoring system to deceive him.

I was very nervous and told Yu Xinye what had happened.[4]

Chen Shiyin in his confessions gave his version of his story:

When I discovered that the aircraft was not going in the right direction, I didn't dare say anything right away for fear of there being a fight. I knew that if I made it to the Soviet Union, there would be no telling when I might see my family again, or when I might be able to step on the soil of my motherland once more. I was deeply distraught.

Zhou Yuchi had had some experience piloting helicopters. He had studied with me in the Skylark. He learned that we were not heading in the right direction when he saw a large block of lights below. We ought to have been flying over rather desolate areas. When he looked at the monitoring board, he thought the compass was broken. At this point he sat behind Chen Xiuwen and me with a gun in his hand.

He interrogated Chen Xiuwen, pointing at the group of lights below. "Isn't that Beijing? You're just going around in circles, aren't you?"

Chen Xiuwen said that perhaps the monitor was not working properly. He fidgeted with the knobs of the electric compass and magnetic compass and made a show of fixing an electric switch behind him (though the electric switch was not located there).

Just as Zhou Yuchi was yelling at me to take command of the helicopter, Chen Xiuwen suddenly grabbed Zhou Yuchi's submachine gun with one hand and threw it aside, and with the other hand seized the gun at Zhou's waist. He stuck his head against Zhou's chin and knocked him over backward. Zhou struggled to regain balance. The two of them wrestled for a few moments.

Because Chen Xiuwen was still at the controls, the helicopter rocked back and forth violently. I tried to steady the craft, but didn't dare do anything else.

Zhou Yuchi screamed at me to help him subdue Chen Xiuwen. I pleaded with Chen: "If there's something wrong, we should talk about it. But don't fight."

Chen Xiuwen shouted, "Who do you think you're fooling? You thought you could fool me. You wanted me to follow you blindly and end up a traitor with the rest of you."

His saliva spattered me. Now I was getting angry.

Zhou Yuchi started screaming at me again. "Chen Shiyin, you damn fool, are you looking for death? Why are you standing there like an idiot? Take the gun and smash his head in."

I didn't have a handgun. I grabbed one of Chen Xiuwen's hands from behind. Zhou Yuchi freed one of his hands and pushed Chen Xiuwen away from him, then kicked him against

The downed Skylark helicopter in which a number of the conspirators attempted to escape. Li Weixin is shown in the inset. (From *Criminal Materials of Lin Biao's Anti-Party Clique*)

the cabin wall. Finally he used his submachine gun to shoot him. Chen Xiuwen died on the spot.

In the seconds before he died, Chen Xiuwen managed to turn off the fuel and electric supply and push the fire-alarm button. The engine of the helicopter died and the aircraft floated powerless in the air before gradually descending.

I did my best to execute a safe landing.

Behind me I heard two shots go off successively which penetrated the cabin walls. One of the shots hit Zhou Yuchi in the arm and tore his clothing and flesh. He started cursing. As we were getting off the helicopter, he asked who had fired those shots.

Then we saw Li Weixin run limping into the fields. Zhou Yuchi called to him, but he didn't turn around. Zhou asked Yu Xinye what Li Weixin was doing. Yu Xinye shook his head and said he didn't know. But he added that Li Weixin had said that because we were forced to land, it was all over for us.

Shortly thereafter Li Weixin disappeared into the fields.

Zhou Yuchi then asked me if it was possible to start up the helicopter again. He said we could use the storage batteries carried in the aircraft.

I re-entered the cabin. I saw that the engine fire-control system had already been used up and that the engine had completely stopped. I knew there was no possibility of getting the helicopter off the ground. Then I saw Chen Xiuwen's bloody body and felt very guilty.

Chen Xiuwen had been my longtime superior, colleague and aircraft technical instructor. He had always treated me well.

Now it seemed we wouldn't even get to the Soviet Union. If I didn't kill myself, I probably would either be shot by Zhou Yuchi or end up in jail as a criminal.

I didn't particularly want to commit suicide; even less did I care to be killed by someone else. As a prisoner I might be able to atone for my crimes through hard work. But with Zhou Yuchi by my side I probably would have to prove my loyalty to Lin Biao with death.

As I was examining the helicopter, I reached a decision. I said the engine could be started. I asked Zhou Yuchi and Yu Xinye to help me get Chen Xiuwen's body off the aircraft. While they were helping with the body, I stood behind them with a gun behind my back. Just as Yu Xinye was straightening up, I put a bullet right through the middle of his forehead. He fell onto Zhou Yuchi.

Zhou's immediate reaction was to block Yu's fall with his arm. Before he realized what had happened, I shot him four times in the back of his head and killed him.

After I left the aircraft, I wanted to kill Li Weixin too, but I couldn't find him.

This morning during my confessions I lied by saying I had killed three people, Zhou Yuchi, Chen Xiuwen and Yu Xinye. Li Weixin, also a traitor, had escaped.

Later, because I learned Li Weixin had been arrested and knew he would be interrogated too, I decided to tell the whole truth. I in fact killed only two people.[5]

The two survivors from the helicopter were caught and arrested in a distant suburb of Beijing by local militia and soldiers.

The remains of the Zhi-5 helicopter[6] were collected by the Department of Public Security as part of the evidence of the crimes of Lin Biao, Lin Liguo and the Joint Fleet. The head of Public Security, Li Zhen, his wife and his closest assistants spent that whole night sorting through the items found in the helicopter.

Among the materials recovered were not only extremely confidential documents involving national security but also information about the clandestine intrigues of such individuals as Mao Zedong, Zhou Enlai, Jiang Qing, Zhang Chunqiao, Kang Sheng, Wang Dongxing, Xie Fuzhi and others, including Li Zhen himself.

XVIII

Zhou Enlai's handling of the remaining members of Lin Biao's clique at the eleventh hour once again revealed his experience and cunning.

When Huang Yongsheng arrived at "Jade Tower Mountain," Zhou Enlai met with him for a "frank" discussion. Zhou told Huang that Lin Biao had already confessed to his clandestine divisive activities and had agreed to suspend them. Lin would listen to orders and allow himself to be interrogated.

Zhou Enlai asked Huang Yongsheng to respond. Huang knew that he had little remaining room for maneuver. If Lin Biao had surrendered, then he had to follow suit.

Zhou Enlai subsequently had Huang Yongsheng escorted back to the Western Hills compound and placed under house arrest.

Before being taken away, Huang was ordered by Zhou to make calls to Wu Faxian, Li Zuopeng and Qiu Huizuo revealing his confession. Zhou Enlai took the opportunity to speak to each of them on the phone. His message was simple and straightforward and he expected the responses that he received. Advised that both Lin Biao and Huang had surrendered, they had no alternative but to admit their own guilt and offer full cooperation.

What surprised everybody, including Mao Zedong, was that none of the conspirators attempted suicide. Instead, in the limited time available before being arrested they tried to destroy as much incriminating evidence as possible.

Wu Faxian, for one, raced back to his home at the Air Force compound and ordered his secretary to gather all documents and letters from his office and bring them to his study at home. Wu, his secretary and his wife, Chen Suiqi, then proceeded to burn every piece of material related to his clandestine activities with Lin Biao, Lin Liguo, Ye Qun, Huang Yongsheng, Li Zuopeng and Qiu Huizuo.

Wu Faxian describes those remaining hours in his written confessions:

> While I was burning documents and materials, I kept calling Li Zuopeng and Qiu Huizuo. Li Zuopeng told me he had already transmitted via secret telegraph and telephone a message to everyone stationed at the Shenyang, Xinjiang and Beijing military regions to destroy all materials related to our planned instigation of a Sino-Soviet battle.
>
> He added that this was really the end. There would be no climbing up again from this fall. He sounded glum, to say the least.
>
> Qiu Huizuo said that he was about to take some sleeping pills, getting ready for a long sleep.
>
> I asked him if he meant to commit suicide. He said he didn't, but that he meant to be too groggy to talk. His wife, Hu Min, had told him to make believe he didn't know what had happened tonight.
>
> Qiu Huizuo also said that he had had no idea Lin Biao would give in so easily. He said he couldn't make his head stop spinning. He said all of us should expect to be demoted or go to jail.
>
> We tried to protect ourselves by making our explanation consistent. We promised each other we wouldn't reveal more than we had to.
>
> At about midnight the Air Force command center notified me that a plane had taken off from Beijing without reporting its flight plan or responding to calls from the air-traffic control station. I ordered them to continue attempting contact and in the meantime to investigate the type of aircraft involved and the airport from which it had departed.
>
> Very quickly the command center replied that the aircraft was

a Trident with the number 256, with Pan Jingyin at the controls, and that it had taken off in a hurry from the Western Suburbs Airport.

I, of course, was fairly certain that Lin Liguo was on the plane. I guessed that the entire plane, in fact, was occupied by people connected with the attempted coup.

I asked the command center to have my Chief-of-Staff, Liang Pu, join me at the center and to instruct the commander of the Air Force of the Beijing Military Region, Li Jitai, to go to his headquarters immediately. The center was unable to locate Liang Pu in the middle of the night. Later his family was able to locate him somewhere near Tiananmen.

As soon as I arrived at the command center, I called Premier Zhou about the event. Premier Zhou wanted me to issue emergency orders to all the Air Force military regions and command centers forbidding any takeoffs or landings at any airport nationwide except under special orders.

Premier Zhou asked me if I could force the plane down. I replied that I couldn't guarantee anything, but that I had already sent another plane to intercept it.

Acting on my orders, Li Jitai sent four Jian-7[1] planes from the Yangcun Airport, which overtook the Trident jet in Inner Mongolia.* The Trident did not obey the orders of the fighters to land. It continued flying north, then started veering west.

I ordered the Beijing Air Force anti-aircraft artillery and surface-to-air missile troops to prepare for action, then reported to the Premier that the Trident might be heading across the Chinese border.

The Premier asked me what I thought should be done. I advocated shooting the plane down.

The Premier agreed and asked me to carry out the task.

Because the plane was flying along the border, I was afraid our attacking planes might accidentally penetrate Mongolian air space, so I ordered Li Jitai to use ground-to-air missiles to shoot down the plane.

Li Jitai ordered three battalions from the missile camps

*Inner Mongolia is part of China.—Translator.

located at the 10457 and 11959 Air Defense System sectors to take action.

After the Trident jet entered the Mongolian People's Republic, it disappeared from the radar screen. I immediately contacted the Premier.

The Premier asked if the plane had already been shot down. I told him we had already fired twice with three missiles each time. I believed the target was definitely hit.

The Premier then said: "You have made a great contribution tonight. I will report it to Chairman Mao."

I left Liang Pu at the command center and returned home. Chen Suiqi and I discussed what we should do if we were separated. We burned some more materials. Chen Suiqi wanted to call our son, Wu Xinchao, who happened to be at the Shenyang airplane factory representing the Air Force. I was afraid of alarming him and stopped her from calling him.

Jiang Tengjiao, then Wang Fei called, with Chen Suiqi answering both times. They asked about me. She said I was very well, and that I had just done the Chairman a great service. She reminded them that under any circumstances they should protect Commander Wu.

Jiang Tengjiao said on the phone: "Without Commander Wu there would be no Jiang Tengjiao." Wang Fei also expressed his loyalty to me.

At about four A.M. Liang Pu reported to me that at the Shahe Heliport (in Beijing) a helicopter had taken off in violation of the new order. The direction of flight was northwest from Beijing. He guessed it was heading for Inner Mongolia or the Mongolian People's Republic. The aircraft refused to respond to radio queries from the air-traffic control station.

I reported this incident to Premier Zhou. The Premier had already returned to Zhongnanhai from "Jade Tower Mountain." He wanted me to think of a way of bringing the helicopter down. But, he added, he wanted the passengers alive this time.

I consulted with Chen Suiqi, who felt that the helicopter passengers were all Joint Fleet members. Perhaps it was this aircraft that Lin Liguo and Zhou Yuchi were aboard.

I was afraid that if the passengers survived a forced landing, their testimonies would harm me. Chen Suiqi asked me what the alternatives were. I said, "I'll shoot it down!"

I called Liang Pu at the Air Force command center and told him to be sure to shoot down the helicopter. I said, "If they're allowed to live, both you and I will be in serious trouble. We are their superiors, aren't we?"

Liang Pu was very tense. He didn't understand exactly what I meant and wanted to know more details. I said he would understand in time.

Premier Zhou called me at least a dozen times. He kept emphasizing that he wanted them alive.

But I still ordered Liang Pu to have Li Jitai use Beijing's artillery and missile troops to shoot the helicopter down. I also ordered the artillery and missile divisions under the Air Force to participate in the attack.

Two fighter planes, a Jian-6 Jia and a Jian-5, took off from the Yangcun Airport a total of fourteen times to search for the helicopter.[2] But because the helicopter had followed an irregular route, the search was in vain.

The anti-aircraft artillery station at Beikanzi spotted the helicopter, but was not able to get a clear shot at it. It was flying at a low altitude in a mountainous area.

Liang Pu and I kept pushing Li Jitai. Li Jitai said, "I've done the best I can. If the aircraft doesn't land, we can definitely shoot it down."

In the meantime Premier Zhou called to say he was sending people over to help me with my work. Soon Yang Dezhong, Li Desheng and others arrived at the Air Force command center.

Once they arrived, Liang Pu and I changed our orders, instructing that the helicopter be forced down.

Before long the helicopter disappeared from the radar screen.

Yang Dezhong wanted me to go with him to the Great Hall of the People to meet with Premier Zhou. Li Desheng and Liang Pu stayed at the command center.[3]

The wreckage of Trident jet #256 photographed in the vicinity of Öndörhaan in Outer Mongolia. (From *Criminal Materials of Lin Biao's Anti-Party Clique*)

Trident jet #256 crashed on the soil of the Mongolian People's Republic, in a desolate area, to the east of Ulan Bator near Öndörhaan, several hundred kilometers north of the Chinese border. It is not known exactly what caused the airplane to crash, but speculation within Chinese military circles suggested that the first salvo of missiles fired at it damaged it, and that the pilot, Pan Jingyin, a very skilled man, had immediately reduced altitude to escape the radar. This would explain why the aircraft disappeared from the radar screen at that point. Presumably the Trident continued to fly north until it finally crashed.

After the crash the Chinese embassy in Ulan Bator began an investigation at the site. The secret report sent by the embassy to the Foreign Ministry in Beijing by telegraph was labeled "Top Secret Document Number 81029" and submitted to Premier Zhou Enlai. The document stated that the staff members of the Chinese embassy in Mongolia concluded that the passengers in the crashed plane were between the ages of about twenty and fifty.

Zhou Enlai ordered that the document be sealed in the Security Bureau of the Central Committee. The time he spent reading the document in the Foreign Ministry was unusually short—only forty-five minutes.

The Chinese embassy worked hard at making arrangements for the bodies recovered from the wreckage to be shipped back to China. Only later did the embassy receive an order—which actually emanated directly from Mao Zedong—that the bodies were to be buried near the site of the crash.

According to several reliable sources, both the Soviet Union and the Mongolian People's Republic had sent technicians to perform autopsies on the buried bodies, and to try to discern their ages and identities. At least some of the members of the Soviet team did not believe that Lin Biao was among those who died in the crash.[4]

XIX

The concluding chapter of this book once again excerpts from the memoirs of Zhao Yanji, the man from whom we heard in the first chapter.

Despite the voluminous materials I had collected about the Lin Biao Affair, I was unable to piece them together to form a comprehensive and coherent whole. I was able, however, to make some educated guesses about what happened and to come up with explanations that both seemed plausible and did not contradict my information. It was for this reason that I harbored the desire to find an appropriate opportunity to speak personally with Wang Dongxing, to clarify some hazy points and perhaps find out more than I already knew.

That opportunity finally came one day in 1973 when Wang invited me to his house in Zhongnanhai. I thought he might have called the meeting to discuss a case I had been working on at the time about a cadre in the 8341 Guards named Xu Shiguang. Xu had been given a sentence of life imprisonment for killing his wife. He was now appealing the sentence. His case landed on my desk because he was one of the individuals involved in the assassination of Lin Biao.

Wang Dongxing was concerned about the Xu case because he was afraid others who participated in the events of September 12 would also attract attention by requesting special treatment or clemency. I was told by Wang to eliminate such possibilities. The "special treatment" Xu and others most often faced was a sudden and inexplicable death.

I arrived at Wang's palatial home near the lake at Zhongnanhai to find a different reason for the visit. Wang had just had a hemorrhoid surgically removed and was sitting awkwardly in a special chair in his reception room. With him was Mao Yuanxin.

Mao Yuanxin was a nephew of the Chairman and was obviously being cultivated by him as a key figure in China's future. The question of a successor had been troubling Mao ever since he had Lin Biao killed, and although he never formally announced Lin's replacement by Mao Yuanxin, it was clear to many people that he had it in mind. Both Wang Dongxing and I at least found ourselves treating Mao Yuanxin like a crown prince.

This was of course before Jiang Qing had used both "hard" and "soft" tactics to win him over. Although a powerful figure in his own right, as a top leader in the Shenyang Military Region and as one of Mao Zedong's top aides, Mao Yuanxin was still eager to curry favor with the rapidly rising Gang of Four. He became deeply involved in the factional fighting led by Jiang Qing and Zhang Chunqiao and in the end retreated from the position of Mao's potential successor in favor of serving as a nuclear member of the Cultural Revolution group.

Mao Yuanxin had evidently come to see Wang Dongxing at the suggestion of the Chairman. The Chairman had said Mao Yuanxin ought to have a profound understanding of the "practice of violence by the proletariat," and suggested he find out from Wang Dongxing how the Lin Biao problem had been resolved.

I had the impression that I had been called in to take on the task of describing Mao's gallant victory over Lin Biao because Wang was extremely busy and had little time to go into the details. As it turned out, Wang did most of the talking while Mao and I listened. At times I introduced questions of my own, which propelled him into fuller and deeper explanations than he had previously been willing to give. Points that had once eluded me were now clarified. My investigative work on the Lin Biao Affair had of course gained me a clearer and more objective understanding of the event than many had who were actually present. Therefore, probably no one but Mao Zedong, Zhou Enlai, Wang Dongxing and Yang Dezhong could have provided me with the answers that I sought.

Wang Dongxing had an excellent memory, and when I pointed out details that he had previously neglected or did not accurately recall, he was able to provide full explanations that were, to the best of my knowledge, devoid of exaggeration or fabrication.

When Wang spoke of the Lin Biao Affair, it always was as if he himself had had no direct involvement. This was curious, and something I had noticed on many occasions in the past. Wang seemed to view himself as an omniscient observer—both anonymous and objective. He rarely made mention of his own role or thoughts in the matter. It was as if he didn't care to go down in the annals of Chinese history. Ironically, ever since Mao had come into power, virtually no high-level political struggle or policy decision saw Wang sitting on the sidelines. He was in the thick of it all, and yet he rarely spoke of what he knew.

His inconspicuous behavior was almost certainly due to his utter loyalty to Mao. Faced with any situation, he was always calculating countless ways to turn it to advantage for Mao Zedong. It seemed almost second nature to him. It was probably the result of both voluntary and involuntary training; having moved up in the world from a child beggar to one of Mao's orderlies, finally to become his most trusted guard and military politician, Wang was a product of Mao's thought and style.

Wang's character was in fact similar to Mao's in some ways. They both had an uncanny power of locution, an ability to state —and sometimes distort—facts so as to present Mao in a positive light. Descriptions of Mao's actions were frequently rationalized and linked in their speech with theoretical phrases such as "historical necessity," "the significance of the era" and "the cause of revolution."

When our discussion turned to the dramatic events of September 12, however, Wang spoke dryly and precisely, without any embellishment.

He said that Mao had been in Hangzhou when he received the information secured by Lin Yamei while she was spying on her lover, Lin Liguo, and heard reports of Lin Liheng's confessions regarding her brother and mother. These reports confirmed other information Mao had received about Joint Fleet activities, Lin Biao's attempt at secret negotiations with the Soviet Union and Lin's planned *coup d'état*. Mao was convinced of the need to act immediately.

He gave Wang Dongxing three directives. First, Wang should request Premier Zhou by telegram to continue pursuing any pertinent information and to act on it as he saw fit. Mao also wanted to know from the Premier if and when he could safely return to Beijing. Second, Wang was to devise an appropriate method for doing away with Lin Biao. And, third, Wang should prepare for an immediate departure from the South. Mao requested that the special security measures normally adopted at each train station along his journeys by train should not be put into effect on this trip. While the measures were customarily confidential, there were always certain individuals whose peripheral duties caused them to be alerted and learn of Mao's schedule. Mao chose in this case to forfeit the extra protection in exchange for the utmost secrecy.

Wang said the method was successful. Apart from the guards stationed along Changan Boulevard for the short distance between the Beijing train station and Mao's home at Zhongnanhai, the arrival was accomplished without any special security coverage.

Wang then proceeded to describe the conversation that took place on the train. Mao had slept all the way from Nanjing to Henan province. After entering Henan province he called Wang and Ji Zechun, a high-level officer in the 8341 Guards, to join him in his car. He wished to discuss with them his strategy against Lin Biao.

Mao asked Wang what he thought should be done. Wang suggested that they first arrest Lin Biao, then quietly but quickly kill him. Wang said he had already begun drawing up detailed preparations.

Mao Zedong shook his head, but didn't respond verbally. He merely leaned his head back and chain-smoked.

Ji Zechun then made the comment that the problem was compounded by the fact that Lin Biao was the Chairman's appointed successor.

The comment caused Mao to launch into a lengthy exposition of his own views: "My successor—if I can raise him up, why can't I push him down? If I can push him down, what's stopping me from killing him? If people want to damn me, let them. One hell of a difference it makes!"

Mao continued: "Zhong Kui was an ugly man, but he could kill the devil.[1] There is a lesson to be learned from him. You can't have a widow look for a new spouse while she's afraid her deceased husband will rise up from the grave. The world is full of situations which must be dealt with by thick-skinned people like me.

"When explaining the problem of Lin Biao, don't be afraid of others criticizing my methods. Don't worry about the talk behind our backs. We have to get rid of him, so we use whatever tactics are necessary."

Mao asked Wang Dongxing: "What is the best way to subdue a powerful general?" Wang Dongxing didn't answer. Mao replied for him: "The best way is to make his head fall to the ground in the time it takes to blink an eye."

Mao continued by recounting the tale of Liu Bang, the founder of the Western Han Dynasty. Liu Bang, with the help of Empress Lü, dealt with Han Xin and other strong generals. Mao was fond of citing this particular historical allusion.

According to Wang, the train was traveling at about 110 or 120 kilometers an hour. Enroute from Tianjin to Beijing, Mao told him what his plans were.

They were anything but elaborate. Mao simply wanted Lin killed on the spot. He also insisted that he be an actor in the scene.

Wang said he asked Mao how many people he needed. Mao

asked him to guess. Wang gave a number—1600 people, maybe. Two battalions to surround the area, and one to move in with the assault.

The Chairman smiled, held up a finger and asked: "Is my number bigger or smaller than yours?" Wang said, "Smaller." Mao asked him, "Smaller by how much?" Wang said by a thousand.

The Chairman then said he only needed a hundred people. "And that includes me and you. I really need fewer than a hundred people."

Wang said he and Mao shared the unspoken understanding of where the hundred people would be drawn from.

Wang departed from the events of September 12 to describe for us the creation and subsequent function of the notorious 8341 Guards. He said that following liberation Mao had commented to him, "I don't need the blood disciples that Yong Zheng[2] had. I just want some soldiers who will stick with me through thick and thin."

Wang remarked, "It doesn't matter if he's some illiterate from the countryside. As long as he can speak with a gun, he's qualified to be a soldier in the 8341 Guards."

As to the counter-coup, Wang said that the only point on which he disagreed with the Chairman was his site for the activities. Mao Zedong had insisted on carrying out the closing battles of his conflict with Lin at the very place where Lin had chosen to launch his coup. He felt it was only appropriate.

Wang was afraid that Lin would have had sufficient opportunity to set some traps of his own. Furthermore the invitation to "Jade Tower Mountain" alone might rouse his suspicion. Wang tried, but failed, to convince Mao to choose another location.

In my opinion, Mao Zedong's almost perverse insistence on accomplishing his counter-coup at "Jade Tower Mountain" was a reflection of his feudalistic, superstitious nature. At the threshold of a very important decision or action Mao would often rely on divination with *suan-gua* or *zhan bu* in the *Yi Jing* [*I Ching*]. I once personally drew bamboo lots for him from his divination cylinder during the War of Liberation. His colleagues

Chen Yi and Xu Xiangqian also had divination cylinders, but they did not seem to take them as seriously as did Mao. They used them more for gambling purposes.

Further demonstrations of Mao's superstitions were evident in his sleeping habits. No matter where he slept, his bed had to be positioned in an east-west direction. He often said that his name included the word *dong,* "east"; therefore, when he slept, his head had to be at the eastern end while his feet pointed west.

His relationships with women were also highly influenced by superstition. He felt that younger women had the power to extend his longevity. However, he attached even greater importance to their birthdays. If a girl had an inauspicious birthday, no matter how beautiful she was, he would refuse any relationship with her whatsoever.

Wang Dongxing agreed with me that Mao was a highly superstitious man. But he said nothing more.

I continued contemplating how a man who was such a masterful writer on the theory of materialism, a man who advocated "Seek truth from facts," was able to live his life steeped in feudalism and idealism. It certainly made him a very colorful, strange and unpredictable personality.[3]

EPILOGUE

The aftermath of the Lin Biao Affair included the public disgrace of Lin Biao, which in most respects resembled the fate of any number of other political enemies of Mao Zedong following their fall. A fervent anti-Lin campaign was launched and his supporters were swept into prison.

Lin Biao's death had larger political consequences, because in connection with the anti-Lin campaign Madame Mao (Jiang Qing) and her Gang of Four were able to gain support for their attacks on opponents and increase their own influence. The three-way power struggle that had prevailed during the beginning of the Cultural Revolution in 1966—with Jiang Qing, Lin Biao and Zhou Enlai in mutual opposition—now became a two-sided battle. Backed by Mao, Jiang Qing could afford to act aggressively. Zhou Enlai was on the defensive. With Mao's health failing, Jiang Qing felt fully prepared to rule China after his death.

In early 1976 Zhou Enlai died of cancer. On April 5 that year 100,000 people spontaneously poured into Tiananmen Square to express a double message: Premier Zhou was good, the Gang of Four was bad. When Mao squelched the demonstration, his popularity suffered.

In the autumn of 1976 Mao himself died. Acting Premier Hua Guofeng, with the help of Wang Dongxing, very quickly placed the Gang of Four under arrest. Hua then attempted to solidify his strong hold over China.

Instead Deng Xiaoping, having twice fallen from grace, emerged as the new leader, and Hua Guofeng and Wang Dongxing suffered accordingly. In 1980 the Deng-led ruling party set out to reject the whole idea of the Cultural Revolution by establishing a special court to try the cliques of Jiang Qing and Lin Biao. For Lin Biao's men the results of the trial were as follows:

Huang Yongsheng, eighteen years imprisonment
Wu Faxian, seventeen years imprisonment
Li Zuopeng, seventeen years imprisonment
Qiu Huizuo, sixteen years imprisonment
Jiang Tengjiao, eighteen years imprisonment

In each case the period spent in custody prior to sentencing was to be deducted.

Members of the Joint Fleet, all of whom had been imprisoned since the end of the Lin Biao Affair, also received sentences, of unspecified lengths. According to Chinese law, once the prisoners complete their sentences they are permitted to lead normal lives. The author believes that these men will continue to be held under strict supervision; their knowledge of certain party and military secrets remains dangerously extensive.

In 1982, Huang, Wu, Li and Qiu were released from Qincheng Prison and allowed to live under more comfortable conditions outside of prison, albeit separated from one another and their families and kept under close surveillance. New prison facilities for the four have been under construction since 1981. The decision to move them stemmed partly from the worsening health of Huang and Li, and partly from a government wish to draw a distinction between those who complied with Central Committee orders to confess their crimes and those (like Jiang Qing and Zhang Chunqiao) who refused to do so.

A number of innocent persons drawn into the Lin Biao Affair have also been gravely affected. Lin's daughter, Lin Liheng, for instance, was forced to adopt a pseudonym and now works and lives under conditions specified by the organizational department of the Central Committee security and safety organs. While her life is still somewhat privileged, her spirits are low.

The women who once served as Lin Liguo's "angels" were also imprisoned, but after several years of investigation they were sent back into society with new names. They are sworn to secrecy not to reveal what they know, and most now lead ordinary, inconspicuous lives as wives and mothers.

The wives of Huang Yongsheng, Wu Faxian, Li Zuopeng, Qiu Huizuo and Jiang Tengjiao live in seclusion apart from their husbands, most of whom are suffering from poor health. Their children for the most part attempt to carry on normally, under no particular restrictions except shame.

Mao's chief conspirator, Wang Dongxing, although credited with helping to bring about the downfall of the Gang of Four, was implicated in too many crimes of the Cultural Revolution era to keep his reputation intact. Since being forced out of the political arena by Deng Xiaoping, he has been allowed to live in Beijing under conditions that restrict his movement. Nevertheless he is cooperating with the Central Committee in writing his memoirs; he more than anyone else is in a position to contribute to the investigation of Mao and his daily work.

On reflection, one realizes that all the major factional leaders during the Cultural Revolution have now been eliminated in one way or another. Mao Zedong, Lin Biao, Zhou Enlai and Kang Sheng are dead. The cliques of Lin Biao and Jiang Qing are tucked away, either in jail or in complete isolation. They live in close proximity, but are forbidden to speak to one another.

The leader of China's Communist revolution for over forty years managed to live out a legend. Not once, before or after death, has he suffered defeat at the hands of a political opponent. Not even Lin Biao, who had all the strength of the military behind him, could triumph. Yet although Mao was able to undermine the conspiracy of his appointed successor, he was not able to control the succession altogether. China's road today is not the one he mapped out. It is perhaps fortunate that this is so.

BIBLIOGRAPHY

The following documents contain the principal official account of the Lin Biao Affair. They have been widely circulated and at least in part published in China:

Criminal Evidence for a Counter-revolutionary Coup by Lin Biao's Anti-Party Clique (Party Central Committee document, June 26, 1972)

Criminal Materials of Lin Biao's Anti-Party Clique, Parts 1, 2, 3 (Party Central Committee document, September 3, 1972)

The following documents received limited circulation within official circles:

A Letter from Comrade Gong Peng to the Military Science Academy of the People's Liberation Army (Classified document, 1963)

"The Soviet Response to Chinese Broadcasts," from *"The Joint Chiefs-of-Staff Daily Report on Key Issues"* (Classified document, 1971–72)

The following documents and materials, all labeled "Class 1," have never been circulated inside or outside of China:

"Compilation of Confessions of Li Zuopeng Concerning the Plot at [Jade Tower Mountain]" (Class 1 document, September 17, 1972)

"Compilation of Ye Qun's Notes," Volume 17 (Class 1 materials, November 1973)

"Comrade Wang Dongxing's Explanation of the Arrest of the Nine Chief Criminals Involved in the Case of Lin Biao" (Class 1 document, February 1980)

"Confessional Materials of Huang Yongsheng on Secret Preparations for a Plot Discussed by Lin Biao and Wu Faxian on July 10, 1971" (Class 1 document, February 1972)

"Confessional Materials of Wu Faxian on Secret Conversations with Lin Biao on July 10, 1971" (Class 1 document, April 18, 1972)

"Confessional Materials of Xi Zhuxian, Zhou Deyun and Zu Fuguang on Their Illegal Activities in the 'Search Group'" (Class 1 materials, 1972)

"Confessions of My Criminal Activities in Participating in the Plot to Harm Our Great Leader, Chairman Mao," by Jiang Tengjiao (Class 1 materials, January 1972)

"Confessions of Wu Faxian: Admitting His Crimes to the People" (Class 1 materials, November 1974)

"Confessions of Xu Limin" (Class 1 document, 1972)

"Criminal Materials of Lin Biao's Diehard Supporter Huang Yongsheng" (Supplementary materials: Huang Yongsheng's confessions of his activities from September 12 to September 13; Huang Yongsheng's confessions regarding the plot at [Jade Tower Mountain]; Huang Yongsheng's confessions regarding Wu Faxian and Li Zuopeng; Huang Yongsheng's memoirs of conversations with Lin Biao and Ye Qun at Maojiawan on August 24, 1971) (Class 1 document, March 1972)

"The Decision to Award and Promote Those Who Contributed in the Struggle to Smash Lin Biao's Anti-Party Clique: A Talk by Comrade Wang Dongxing on the Significance of Confidentiality of the Facts Behind the Lin Biao Affair" (Class 1 document, September 20, 1971)

"Directives of Comrade Wang Dongxing to Those Who Participated in the Struggle to Smash Lin Biao's Anti-Party Clique Concerning the Rechecking of Confidentiality" (Class 1 document, April 1972)

"Document on the Twenty-four Directives of Comrade Wang Dongxing Since 1971 Concerning the Handling of Possessions of Lin Biao and Lin Biao's Family" (Supplementary materials: Two letters from Comrade Lin Liheng requesting the return to her of all property of Lin Biao's family: Comrade Lin Liheng's explanation of her role in the Lin Biao Affair) (Class 1 document, April 1980)

"How Lin Biao Made His Last-Minute Decisions," by Wu Faxian (Class 1 materials, April 8, 1972)

"I Was Lin Biao's Secretary," by Yu Yunshen (Class 1 document, 1972)

"Important Talks by Comrade Zhou Enlai to Deng Xiaoping and Qi Zujia on the Lin Biao Incident" (Class 1 document, January 7, 1975)

"Investigative Report of Sub-group No. 2 on the Investigation of the Cause of the Crash of Trident #256 Concerning the Target of the Missiles

Launched from the Xiao Shanzi* Missile Base at 00:14 on September 13, 1971" (Class 1 document, February 1972)

"Investigative Report of the Ding Siqi Incident; Records of Testimony and Oral Confessions of Those Involved in the Ding Siqi Incident; File on the Air Force Personnel Secretly Killed by Lin Biao's Anti-Party Clique" (Class 1 document, 1972)

"Investigative Report on the Escape of the Helicopter," Part 4, "Oral Confessions" (Class 1 materials, 1973)

"Letter from Comrade Wang Dongxing to Comrades Hua Guofeng and Deng Xiaoping" (Supplementary materials: Materials on Comrade Wang Dongxing's introduction to the 9/13 Incident and fifteen suggestions concerning the trial of Lin Biao's anti-Party clique (Class 1 materials, February 15, 1980)

"Letters Comrade Lin Liheng Wrote to the Central Committee" (Class 1 document, September 28, 1972)

"Memoirs of Chen Suiqi" (Class 1 document, May 1972)

"Memoirs of Comrade Yang Dezhong on Certain Actions Taken by Premier Zhou Before and After the 9/13 Incident" (Class 1 document, December 1976)

"Memoirs of Zhao Yanji" (Class 1 document, 1974)

"My Criminal Activities in Revealing Lin Liguo's Secret Activities to Lin Biao and Ye Qun," by Wu Faxian (Class 1 document, August 4, 1972)

"My Criminal Activities in the 9/13 Incident," by Liu Shiying (Class 1 document, October 18, 1971)

"My Exposure of the Criminal Activities of Lin Biao's Diehard Supporter Zhou Yuchi," by Wang Fei and "Confessions of My Criminal Activities," by Li Weixin, Part 17 from "Criminal Activities of the Counter-Revolutionary Zhou Yuchi" (Class 1 materials, 1973)

"Oral Confessions of Joint Fleet Members," Part 7 of "Crimes of Lin Biao's Counter-revolutionary Clique in Its Plot to Kill Chairman Mao" (Class 1 document, 1973)

"Oral Confessions of Li Weixin," from the supplementary materials of the "Secret Work Report of the Double Case Office of the General Political Bureau on the Interrogatory Materials of Lin Biao's Eleven Diehard Supporters in the Air Force" (Class 1 document, February 18, 1980)

*Xiao Shanzi is located near the border of Hebei province and Inner Mongolia.—Translator.

"Oral Confessions of Wang Fei," from the supplementary materials of the "Secret Work Report of the Double Case Office of the General Political Bureau on the Interrogatory Materials of Lin Biao's Eleven Diehard Supporters in the Air Force" (Class 1 document, February 18, 1980)

"Original Documents of 'Plot at [Jade Tower Mountain],' Plans of Lin Biao's Anti-Party Clique for a Military *Coup d'État*" (Class 1 document, October 20, 1971)

"Party Central Committee Document Concerning the Verification of and Methods for Confidentiality in the Confessions of Members of Lin Biao's Anti-Party Clique" (Class 1 document, January 1972)

"Pictorial Materials of the Scene of Death of the Criminal Counter-revolutionary Leader Lin Biao" (Class 1 document, August 1974)

"Recommendations of Comrade Wang Dongxing to Vice-Premier Deng Xiaoping" (Class 1 document, August 1980) (Note: Wang Dongxing believed that cautious handling of the Lin Biao Affair was crucial to the preservation of the reputations of both Chairman Mao and the party)

"Report of the Administrative Office of the Party Central Committee on Several Analyses of the Cause of Li Zhen's Death," Part 101 (Class 1 document, 1973)

"Report of the Engineering Department of the Air Force Concerning the Investigation of the Crash of the Number 256 Trident" (Class 1 document, May 15, 1972)

"Report of the Fifth Investigative Research Office of the State Council on the Handling of the Corpses of Lin Biao and Ye Qun" (Class 1 document, September 28, 1971)

"Report of the Fifth Investigative Research Office of the State Council to Premier Zhou on the Sixth Piece of Circumstantial Evidence for the Case of Wu Zonghan: Li Zhen's Handling of the Case on Illicit Relations Between the General Staff and Foreign Countries" (Class 1 document, June 7, 1972)

"Report of the General Political Department of the People's Liberation Army on the Confessions of Lin Biao's Diehard Supporter Cheng Hongzhen, from June 8, 1972, to September 1, 1972" (Class 1 document, 1972)

"Report of the Security Bureau of the Party Central Committee to Chairman Mao and Comrade Wang Dongxing Concerning the Problem of Filing of Records of Conversations Between Chairman Mao and Lin Biao during the 9/13 Incident" (Supplementary materials: Transcriptions of the recordings) (Class 1 document, December 1971)

"Report of the Security Section of the Party Central Committee's Special Case on Lin Biao's Anti-Party Clique, Submitted to Comrade Wang Dongxing"; Section 5, containing "The Summary and Original Text of the Seven-Part Confessional Materials of Lin Biao's Diehard Supporter Wu Faxian, Written October 7–December 11, 1971" (Class 1 document, December 20, 1972)

"Report on Comrade Lin Yamei's Work" (Class 1 document, February 1973)

"Report on the Deaths of Lin Biao, Ye Qun and Lin Liguo" (Class 1 document, December 1979)

"Report on the Request for Instructions from the Central Committee by the Security Bureau of the Party Central Committee Concerning the Problem of Sealing the Records on the Four Talks Given by Chairman Mao on the Lin Biao Affair," File No. 7 (Supplementary materials: Complete transcription of Mao's four talks) (Class 1 document, December 1979)

"Secret Conversations Between Lin Biao and Huang Yongsheng on July 4, 1971" (Class 1 materials, 1972)

"Secret Work Report of the Double Case Office* of the General Political Bureau on the Interrogatory Materials of Lin Biao's Eleven Diehard Supporters in the Air Force" (Supplementary materials: Former Beijing Air Force Commander Li Jitai's explanation of orders from Wu Faxian and Liang Pu to intercept two aircraft; Record of communications of the Beijing Air Force Command Post from 23:00 September 12, 1971, to 5:55 September 13, 1971; Confessional materials of Former Chief-of-Staff of the Air Force Liang Pu regarding the Air Force Command Post's handling of the escape of aircraft on September 13, 1971; Confessional materials of key members of the Joint Fleet: Wang Fei, Li Weixin, Jiang Guozhang and ten others) (Class 1 document, February 18, 1980)

"Selection of Wu Faxian's Confessions, 1972–1973" (Class 1 document, April 23, 1975)

"Testimonial Materials of Qi Zhijing," Part 3 (Class 1 materials, 1972)

"Top-Secret Foreign Ministry Document No. 81024" (Class 1 document, September 19, 1971) (Note: Report of the Chinese embassy in the Mongolian People's Republic on the examination and handling of corpses found at the site of the crash of plane #256)

"Work Diary of Ye Qun" (Class 1 materials, 1972)

"Yu Sang's Notes on Two Pieces of Information Regarding the Li Zhen Case" (Class 1 document, 1973)

*The "Double Case Office" handled the cases of Lin Biao and the Gang of Four. The name was coined in 1976.

NOTES

CHAPTER I

As described in the text, the source for this chapter is the unpublished memoir of Zhao Yanji. The author is not able to reveal how the document came into his hands.

1. "8341" refers to the Party Central Committee Security Troops headed by Wang Dongxing. When Wang lost his political power in 1980, the military designation 8341 was eliminated and the troops were reorganized under new leadership.
2. The Baqi Sanatorium in Dalian (Dairen), once a foreign facility, now serves high-level military officers. It is under the control of the Shenyang Military Region.
3. The 34th Division of the Air Force is the transport division, equipped with various types of aircraft including helicopters. One of its responsibilities is to provide air transport for high-level Chinese officials. The unit is stationed at the Beijing Western Suburbs Airport.
4. The Red Army did not have ranks before 1949, nor did the People's Liberation Army until 1954–55. In that year the PLA established a system whereby the Military Commission of the Party Central Committee and the Ministry of Defense jointly conferred ranks on officers of the various military units. This system was abolished in 1965 by Mao Zedong and Minister of Defense Lin Biao.
5. Besides Wang Liangen, the other two directors of the Special Case were Li Zhen and Yu Sang.
6. "Three Doors" refers to one of the major office buildings occupied by the Military Commission, an ancient, elaborate and heavily guarded structure located on Jingshan Front Street in Beijing.

CHAPTER II

It is difficult to describe Lin Liguo's "racy" private life with assurance that every detail is correct. Rumors of all kinds, including many that are clearly implausible, have been current in China during the past ten years, especially among young Chinese military personnel. The personal accounts excerpted here have been drawn from Class I documents containing oral confessions of various Joint Fleet members. These accounts have been supplemented with information from other Class I documents and personal interviews conducted by the author, on such matters as Lin Liguo's increasing interest in politics, his relationship with Lu Min and the role of his mother, Ye Qun.

1. "Confessional Materials of Xi Zhuxian, Zhou Deyun and Zu Fuguang."
2. "Testimonial Materials of Qi Shijing."

CHAPTER III

The contents of this chapter are extracted mainly from the Class I file titled "Report of the Security Section of the Party Central Committee's Special Case on Lin Biao's Anti-Party Clique, Submitted to Comrade Wang Dongxing," Section 5, "Containing the Summary and Original Text of the Seven-part Confessional Materials of Lin Biao's Diehard Follower Wu Faxian, Written on October 7–December 11, 1971," and referred to below as "Confessions of Wu Faxian." Other Class I files were used in providing background information.

1. "Memoirs of Chen Suiqi."
2. "Confessions of Wu Faxian."
3. Henceforth referred to as the "Lushan Plenum."
4. "Investigative Report of the Ding Siqi Incident." From the confidential documents of the Party Central Committee on the handling of the Ding Siqi Incident.
5. "Confessions of Wu Faxian."

CHAPTER IV

This chapter is based largely on Wu Faxian's confessions and Yu Yunshen's memoirs, neither of which have been published, and which contain detailed transcriptions of conversations. Virtually none of the details of the story told here—for example, the conversation between Wu and Lin, and Wu's deliberation and response—have been touched upon in official documents.

1. The Administrative Group of the Military Commission was the highest

organ of the Chinese military during the Cultural Revolution. It was composed of Huang Yongsheng, Wu Faxian, Ye Qun, Li Zuopeng, Qiu Huizuo, Li Xuefeng and others.

2. "Mixing different grains of sand" was a phrase coined by Mao Zedong. It means to infiltrate the enemy camp with your own men, to gather intelligence, interfere with and disrupt the enemies' activities, ultimately causing their dissolution.

3. "Memoirs of Chen Suiqi."

4. "I Was Lin Biao's Secretary," by Yu Yunshen.

5. "Confessions of Wu Faxian"; "Confessional Materials of Wu Faxian on Secret Conversations with Lin Biao"; "Compilation of Ye Qun's Notes"; "I Was Lin Biao's Secretary," by Yu Yunshen; "Confessional Materials of Huang Yongsheng on Secret Preparations for a Plot"; and other sources.

6. Babaoshan, meaning "Eight-Jeweled Mountain," refers to China's most elite crematorium, which is located in the western suburbs of Beijing.

7. "Three-in-one policy" is a phrase coined by Mao.

8. Yu Yunshen's confessional material quotes Lin Biao as saying: "He [Mao] is going away and leaving me here in Beijing to watch what my next move will be. But I refuse to be trapped. I'm going to go away on vacation too and give him the impression that Lin Biao isn't up to anything in Beijing, that 'all is quiet on the Western Front.' "

CHAPTER V

Apart from the historical and biographical material presented here, which is generally known, this chapter makes use of various Class 1 documents. The author has also drawn upon personal conversations with individuals familiar with the relationships between the members of the Lin family and Lin Biao's "anti-party clique."

1. "Work Diary of Ye Qun"; "I Was Lin Biao's Secretary," by Yu Yunshen.

2. "Confessions of Wu Faxian"; "Selection of Wu Faxian's Confessions."

3. "I Was Lin Biao's Secretary," by Yu Yunshen.

4. "Compilation of Confessions of Li Zuopeng."

CHAPTER VI

What the author here calls the "Jade Tower Mountain Scheme," Lin Biao's attempt to apply his military strength in a *coup d'état* against Mao Zedong, and the ultimate cause of his own death, is never mentioned in the official circulated documents. Plainly, public knowledge of the full participation of China's most powerful military leaders in the plot would have made too obvious the weakness of Mao himself, who as chairman of the Military Commission of the Party Central Committee was the nominal head of the Chinese armed forces. Furthermore Mao's counterattack against Lin was directly associated with the "Jade Tower Mountain," and those events too Mao wished to keep secret. Mao therefore chose to characterize the Lin Biao Affair as one involving mainly the activities of Lin Biao's son, Lin Liguo, and his Joint Fleet.

The original confessional materials of members of Lin Biao's clique, solicited by Wang Dongxing after the Lin Biao Affair, provide the full details of Lin's failed plot. As the author is unfortunately not in a position to quote directly from these materials, the conversation between Lin Biao and Huang Yongsheng cannot be considered verbatim, but the meaning and tone is representative of the original sources, and circumstantial details may be regarded as accurate. The precise dates of some documents are not available.

1. "I Was Lin Biao's Secretary," by Yu Yunshen; "Compilation of Confessions of Li Zuopeng."
2. "Original Documents of 'Plot at [Jade Tower Mountain].' "
3. "Criminal Materials of Lin Biao's Diehard Supporter Huang Yongsheng."
4. "Secret Conversations Between Lin Biao and Huang Yongsheng."

CHAPTER VII

The name of Wu Zonghan (a pseudonym) does not appear in any of the documents describing the Lin Biao case that were circulated to high-level Chinese cadres. Yet an appreciation of this man's role is crucial to any understanding of the way Zhou Enlai was able to discover—and forestall—Lin Biao's attempt at secret negotiations with the Soviet Union.

The principal sources for the story told in this chapter are certain Class 1 documents whose titles, for reasons of special sensitivity, cannot be revealed. The titles of various supporting documents are cited below.

1. "Report of the Fifth Investigative Research Office . . . on . . . the Case of Wu Zonghan."
2. "Report of the Administrative Office . . . on . . . the Cause of Li Zhen's Death"; "Memoirs of Comrade Yang Dezhong on Premier's Zhou's Actions."
3. "Yu Sang's Notes on . . . the Li Zhen Case."

CHAPTER VIII

The fact that Lin Biao submitted false personal medical reports to Mao, and was found out, was omitted from the documents circulated to high-level cadres. This discovery, along with Zhou Enlai's revelation of Lin's attempted covert negotiations with the Soviet Union, was the proximate cause of Zhou, and then Mao, taking action against Lin.

The sources for this chapter, in addition to the documents indicated in the notes below, are certain original documents whose titles cannot be given for security reasons.

1. *A Letter from Comrade Gong Peng* (1963), an official document in the archives of the Military Commission, not distributed but seen by a handful of top military leaders. Gong Peng was a secretary to Zhou Enlai. In the latter part of the Cultural Revolution she was married to the then foreign minister, Qiao Guanhua. She later died of illness.

2. "Memoirs of Comrade Yang Dezhong on Premier Zhou's Actions"; "Important Talks by Comrade Zhou Enlai . . . on the Lin Biao Incident"; and other Class 1 materials that discuss Premier Zhou's actions.

   In a manuscript written by the late Zhou Rongxin, a onetime secretary of Zhou Enlai's and Minister of Education (now kept as a top-secret file in the Security Bureau of the Central Committee), the author describes in great detail his private conversations with the Premier regarding actions taken in the Lin Biao case.

3. "Memoirs of Comrade Yang Dezhong on Premier Zhou's Actions."

4. "Report of the Fifth Investigative Research Office . . . on . . . the Case of Wu Zonghan."

CHAPTER IX

In the officially circulated documents Lin Yamei is mentioned only as one of Lin Liguo's numerous mistresses. Her full role in the story of Lin Liguo and his father is told here for the first time. As the information on which it is based is particularly sensitive—only a handful of people know exactly how Wang Dongxing was able to use his knowledge of Lin Liguo's sexual life to expose him—the author cannot divulge his chief sources.

1. The Whampoa Military Academy in Guangzhou (Canton) was a famous institution established by the Guomindang (Kuomintang) in 1924, not long before the start of the Northern Expedition. Some students later went on to become Communist Party leaders.

2. "Report of the General Political Department . . . on the Confessions of . . . Cheng Hongzhen."

3. Ibid.; "Report on Comrade Lin Yamei's Work."

CHAPTER X

Descriptions of the activities of the Joint Fleet are very full in the officially circulated documents. The plan to attack Mao's train as drawn up in the so-called "571 Project Outline" is presented in detail. The reason for this emphasis seems to have been twofold: to implicate Lin Biao in the subversive plot while at the same time diverting attention from Lin's own activities—and Mao's.

General descriptions of the meetings of the Joint Fleet in its preparation of the "571 Project Outline" as well as the summary of the outline itself are taken from the documents released to the cadres. The information contained in them is consistent with information in unadulterated Class 1 documents. The latter documents are, however, able to add some specifics about certain meetings and discussions.

1. "Oral Confessions of Wang Fei." The first department was the Secretariat of War Operations; the second department was the General Administration Office; and the third department was the Party Office.
2. "Oral Confessions of Joint Fleet Members."
3. *Criminal Materials of Lin Biao's Anti-Party Clique.* This includes a full transcription of the "571 Project Outline."
4. Zhu Tiesheng, Li Weixin, Cheng Hongzhen and Wang Yongkui were all arrested and imprisoned after the Lin Biao incident.
5. "Confessions of My Criminal Activities in Participating in the Plot to Harm Our Great Leader, Chairman Mao" by Jiang Tengjiao.
6. In actuality, both the Shanghai and Hangzhou missile bases fell under the jurisdiction of the Air Force Headquarters in the Nanjing Military Region.

CHAPTER XI

Although the Joint Fleet's plans to attack Mao's train were repeatedly referred to in the secret materials released by the government for circulation among high-ranking cadres, details of the plans have never been divulged. This chapter, by making use of the hitherto unpublished confessions of a participant, elaborates the story very considerably. The author was not able to learn the name of the man whose testimony is quoted here; since he was not one of the key members of the Joint Fleet, his identity cannot easily be deduced.

1. "Oral Confessions of Joint Fleet Members."
2. "Secret Work Report of the Double Case Office of the General Political Bureau . . . (Supplementary Materials: . . . Confessional Materials of Key Members of the Joint Fleet.)"

CHAPTER XII

The fact that the Joint Fleet's attack on Mao's train failed is widely known, but the cause for the failure has never been explained, nor has it hitherto been known that it was Lin Biao who obstructed his son's plans, with Wu Faxian's help.

The official documents cite many instances in which Lin Liguo and Lin Biao made contact, but they are used to support the argument that Lin Liguo was working under the direction of his father rather than in opposition to him.

The sources for this chapter are supplemented principally by the circulated reports on the activities of Joint Fleet members, Class 1 documents (Wu Faxian's "Confessions" and Yu Yunshen's memoirs).

1. "Oral Confessions of Joint Fleet Members."
2. "I Was Lin Biao's Secretary," by Yu Yunshen.
3. "My Criminal Activities in Revealing Lin Liguo's Secret Activities to Lin Biao and Ye Qun," by Wu Faxian.
4. "I Was Lin Biao's Secretary," by Yu Yunshen.

CHAPTER XIII

The official documents released to cadres made no mention of what is here called the "Jade Tower Mountain Scheme" devised by Lin Biao. The author's description of this plan, derived from various sources that cannot be further identified for security reasons, is not intended to be exhaustive, as it is felt that a more detailed account could still jeopardize national defense.

CHAPTER XIV

The official account credits Lin Liheng, Lin Biao's daughter, with informing Zhou Enlai of her father's activities. What she actually told him is never spelled out. Class 1 documents reveal, as this chapter describes, that Zhou Enlai coerced Lin Liheng into telling what she knew about the activities of the various members of her family. This fact was apparently suppressed because of what it said about Zhou's espionage and intelligence operations.

The principal sources for this chapter are Class 1 documents detailing Zhou Enlai's activities, as recounted by Zhou himself in later conversations with various associates. Yang Dezhong was Zhou's longtime secretary. The conversations with Deng Xiaoping apparently took place not long before Zhou's death in 1976; Deng was under house arrest at the time. Qi Zujia is not a name familiar to the author.

1. "Memoirs of Comrade Yang Dezhong on Premier Zhou's Actions"; "Im-

portant Talks by Comrade Zhou Enlai on . . . the Lin Biao Incident." The documents include Zhou Enlai's own evaluation of what can be learned from the Lin Liheng case, which he divides into the following:

a. The effect of Lin Biao's defeat on Lin Liheng
b. The work that Zhou Enlai and others did regarding Lin Liheng
c. All about Yang Dingkun
d. The importance of "transparent relationships" in inner-party struggle
e. A successful realization of the style of using secret work in inner-party struggle

CHAPTER XV

A large part of this chapter is quoted from Wu Faxian's confessions, a Class 1 document. In contrast to the official story contained in the circulated documents, it places Lin Biao in Beijing rather than Beidaihe during the last day of his life, and makes clear the extent of his plans to oppose Mao. Also it points up the degree of conflict that existed between the Joint Fleet and those in Lin Biao's personal camp.

1. "I Was Lin Biao's Secretary," by Yu Yunshen.
2. "Army artillery" refers to the weapons customarily used by artillery troops: heavy artillery and rockets.
3. "The Second Artillery missile base" refers to the headquarters of the Second Artillery troops, a unit whose weapons are rockets and missiles.
4. "How Lin Biao Made His Last-minute Decisions," by Wu Faxian.
5. "I Was Lin Biao's Secretary," by Yu Yunshen.

CHAPTER XVI

This chapter, which describes the events in Beijing on the last day of Lin Biao's life, is largely quoted directly from the hitherto unpublished memoir of the investigator Zhao Yanji. It is in evident conflict with the doctored official version of Lin Biao's death, which placed him aboard the Trident jet that took off from Beidaihe and crashed in Mongolia.

The author cannot discover whether the name of the transportation expert Tan Shu, whose memoirs as quoted by Zhao Yanji are excerpted here, is his actual name or a pseudonym. Many names used in Class 1 documents are pseudonyms, and the author is not familiar with this one.

1. "My Criminal Activities in the 9/13 Incident," by Liu Shiying.
2. "Memoirs of Zhao Yanji."
3. Ibid.

CHAPTER XVII

Official sources discuss at length the flights of Trident jet #256 and helicopter #3685. In the case of the jet, they wrongly describe its point of departure and the passengers aboard and omit the reason for the crash. In the case of the helicopter, much of what was officially revealed is the truth: it did leave from the Shahe Airport near Beijing; it did carry Zhou Yuchi, Yu Xinye, Li Weixin and pilots Chen Xiuwen (who was killed by Zhou Yuchi) and Chen Shiyin; it did contain vast quantities of secret documents, weapons and money; and it was forced to land.

This chapter makes use of the personal testimonies of actual participants, taken from Class 1 documents, to clarify many of the gaps and inconsistencies of the official story.

1. "My Criminal Activities in the 9/13 Incident," by Liu Shiying.
2. Ibid.
3. "Confessions of Xu Limin."
4. "Oral Confessions of Li Weixin."
5. "Investigative Report on the Escape of the Helicopter," Part 4, "Oral Confessions."
6. The Zhi-5 helicopter is Chinese-made and modeled after the Soviet Mi-4.

CHAPTER XVIII

The account of Trident #256 given in official circulated documents is widely different from the account given here, in regard both to the persons on board and to the cause of its crash in Mongolia. The official story had Lin Biao and his wife both killed in the crash, and said nothing about the fact that the plane had been the target of Chinese missile batteries operating under orders from Wu Faxian, who was in turn instructed by Zhou Enlai.

The official version of the helicopter incident accords better with the account presented here, though it does not mention Wu Faxian's efforts to bring the helicopter down.

A principal source for this chapter is again Wu Faxian's memoir, an unpublished Class 1 document. It also makes use of the unreleased Report 81029 detailing the investigation of the crash in Mongolia conducted by Chinese embassy officials.

1. The Jian-7 is Chinese-made and modeled upon the Soviet MiG-21.
2. The Jian-6 Jia is a Chinese-made fighter designed for night operations and modeled upon the Soviet MiG-19. The Jian-5 is also Chinese-made, modeled upon the Soviet MiG-17.

3. "Confessions of Wu Faxian."
4. "The Soviet Response to Chinese Broadcasts."

CHAPTER XIX

The source for this chapter is again Zhao Yanji's unpublished memoir. Much of the material in it is supported by various Class 1 documents. Official accounts of the Lin Biao Affair circulated to cadres of course said nothing of any of this; release of any part of the story, from the use of the 8341 Guards to the intimate involvement of Mao himself, would have caused deep political repercussions.

1. Zhong Kui was a legendary figure who could eliminate evil spirits. The Chinese people like to hang his picture on their door to scare ghosts away.
2. Yong Zheng, second emperor of the Qing Dynasty, developed one of the most extensive intelligence networks in Chinese history. In his later years the activities of his agents, the so-called "blood disciples," aroused widespread resentment and disapproval.
3. "Memoirs of Zhao Yanji."

GLOSSARY OF NAMES

BAI CHONGSHAN　白崇善
Commander of the Fifth Air Force Army

BI JI　毕　纪
Chief-of-Staff of the Missile Regiment of the Air Force Missile Division in Shanghai

CAO LIHUAI　曹里怀
Senior Deputy Commander of the Chinese Air Force

CAO YI-OU　曹轶欧
Wife of Kang Sheng; member of the Central Committee of the Communist Party

CHEN BODA　陈伯达
Member of the Standing Committee of the Politburo; a leading Maoist ideologue and polemicist; onetime editor of *Red Flag* magazine; in 1966, named head of the Cultural Revolution Group; attacked during the Second Plenum of the Ninth Party Congress. Arrested and sentenced to eighteen years in prison.

CHEN DAYU　陈达昱
Officer in the Soviet Military Intelligence Section of the General Staff

CHEN LIYUN　陈励耘
Political Commissar of the Chinese Fifth Air Force Army; important leader in Zhejiang province; imprisoned following the Lin Biao Affair

CHEN LUNHE　陈伦和
English translator at the Intelligence Department of the Air Force; Member of the "Joint Fleet"

CHEN SHIYIN 陈士印
Squadron leader of the 101st Regiment of the 34th Division of the Air Force

CHEN SHOU 陈 授
Real father of Yang Dingkun; Kuomintang landlord, police chief and county magistrate during the Nationalist period

CHEN SUIQI 陈绥圻
Wife of Wu Faxian; Deputy Director of the General Office of the Party Committee of the Air Force; currently under house arrest

CHEN XILIAN 陈锡联
Member of the Politburo; member of the Military Commission; Vice-Premier of the State Council; Commander of the Shenyang Military Region and, later, of the Beijing Military Region; important military leader during the Cultural Revolution; supporter of Hua Guofeng after the arrest of the Gang of Four

CHEN XIUWEN 陈修文
Wing leader of the 101st Regiment of the 34th Division of the Air Force; favored pilot of the Air Force; participated in many flights during Sino-Soviet border disputes; an expert at long-distance flights and night flights

CHEN YI 陈 毅
Member of the Politburo; one of China's ten marshals; Minister of Foreign Affairs; major target of Red Guards at the beginning of the Cultural Revolution; died in 1972 of physical and mental abuse

CHENG HONGZHEN 程洪珍
Member of the "Joint Fleet"; Secretary of the General Office of the Party Committee of the Air Force; arrested during the Lin Biao Affair

CHI YUTANG 池玉堂
Cadre in the 8341 Guards

CHIANG CHING-KUO 蒋经国
Son of Chiang Kai-shek; current leader of the Nationalist Party and President of the Republic of China

CHIANG KAI-SHEK 蒋介石
President of the Republic of China on the Chinese mainland until 1949; after the People's Republic of China was founded, ruled Taiwan until his death in 1975

DENG XIAOPING 邓小平
Secretary General of the Secretariat of the Chinese Communist Party; Vice-Chairman of the Politburo; Vice-Premier of the State Council; Chief-of-Staff of the Armed Forces; twice arrested; rehabilitated in 1977 and arguably the most powerful man in China

DI XIN 狄辛
One of Lin Liheng's boyfriends

DING SIQI 丁思奇
Low-ranking officer in the Air Force in the Nanjing Military Region who attempted to expose the activities of the "Joint Fleet" to Wu Faxian and was killed as a result

FENG YINJIE 冯银洁
Cadre in the communications station in the Air Force

GAO GANG 高岗
Member of the Politburo; Chairman of the State Planning Commission; Deputy Commander and Deputy Political Commissar of the Northeast Military Region in late 1940's; purged and dismissed from party in 1955

GU TONGZHOU 顾同舟
Chief-of-Staff of the Air Force in the Guangzhou Military Region

GUO YUFENG 郭玉峰
Minister of the Organization Department of the Central Committee

HAN HONGKUI 韩洪奎
Secretary of Wang Weiguo

HE LONG 贺龙
One of China's ten marshals; Director of the National Physical Education Committee; arrested by Mao and died in prison during the Cultural Revolution

HOU TINGFANG 侯廷芳
Leader of a missile regiment of the Air Force Missile Division in Shanghai

HU MIN 胡敏
Wife of Qiu Huizuo

HU PING 胡萍
Commander of the 34th Division of the Air Force; Deputy Chief-of-Staff of the Air Force

HU XIAODONG 胡小冬
One of Lin Liheng's boyfriends

HUA GUOFENG 华国锋
Party Secretary of Hunan province before the Cultural Revolution; member of Politburo and Acting Premier during Cultural Revolution; responsible for the arrest of the Gang of Four while Chairman of the Party and Premier; lost both posts in 1980–81

HUANG YONGSHENG 黄永胜
Member of the Standing Committee of the Politburo; Chief-of-Staff of the People's Liberation Army; important member of Lin Biao's "diehard" clique; arrested during the Lin Biao Affair and sentenced to eighteen years in prison

JI ZECHUN 吉泽春
Squadron leader in the 8341 Guards

JIANG GUOZHANG 蒋国璋
Director of the Military Affairs Bureau of the Fourth Air Force Army; important member of the "Joint Fleet"

JIANG QING 江 青
Member of the Politburo; fourth and last wife of Mao Zedong; head of the Gang of Four; arrested in 1976 and sentenced to death; currently on probation

JIANG TENGJIAO 江腾蛟
Political Commissar of the Fourth Air Force Army; Political Commissar of the Air Force in the Nanjing Military Region; important member of the "Joint Fleet"; arrested during the Lin Biao Affair and sentenced to eighteen years in prison

KANG SHENG 康 生
Vice-Chairman of the Standing Committee of the Politburo; leader of investigative and espionage work

KE QINGSHI 柯庆施
Member of the Standing Committee of the Politburo; First Secretary of the East China Bureau of the Chinese Communist Party; Mayor of Shanghai; "ultra-leftist" cadre and Mao's confidant

LI DESHENG 李德生
Member of the Politburo; current commander of the Shenyang Military Region

LI JITAI 李际泰
Commander of the Air Force in the Beijing Military Region

LI KENONG 李克农
High official in charge of intelligence and investigation in the Chinese Communist Party

LI WEIXIN 李伟信
Deputy Director of the Secretariat of the Fourth Air Force Army in Shanghai; arrested during the Lin Biao Affair

LI WENPU 李文普
Secretary to Ye Qun

LI XUEFENG 李雪峰
Member of the Politburo; First Party Secretary of the Beijing Military Region; lost all his posts during the Second Plenary Session of the Ninth Party Congress

LI ZHEN 李震
Chief of the Military Commission of the Public Security Ministry; Acting Minister of the Public Security Ministry; died under suspicious circumstances

LI ZUOPENG 李作鹏
Member of the Standing Committee of the Politburo; First Political Commissar of the Navy; Deputy Chief-of-Staff of the People's Liberation Army; important member of Lin Biao's "diehard" clique; arrested during the Lin Biao Affair and sentenced to seventeen years in prison

LIANG JUN 梁 军
Political Commissar of the Second Technical Institute of the Air Force

LIANG PU 梁 璞
Chief-of-Staff of the Air Force; in charge of illegal flights out of the country during the Lin Biao Affair; dismissed during the Lin Biao Affair and later arrested

LIN BIAO 林 彪
The third of China's ten marshals; Minister of Defense; Vice-Chairman of the Communist Party; Mao's appointed successor; died on September 12, 1971

LIN JIANPING 林建平
Driver at the Air Force Academy

LIN LIGUO 林立果
Son of Lin Biao and Ye Qun; Deputy Chief of the Operations Department of the Air Force and head of the "Joint Fleet"; died during the Lin Biao Affair

LIN LIHENG (nicknamed LIN DOUDOU) 林立衡
Daughter of Lin Biao; Associate Editor of the Air Force Press

LIN YAMEI 林雅妹
Soldier in the Air Force; chosen to become Lin Liguo's lover; in 1972, transferred out of the Air Force and had her name changed

LIU JINPING 刘锦平
Chinese People's Civil Aviation Bureau Chief

LIU PEIFENG 刘沛丰
Deputy Director of the General Office of the Party Committee of the Air Force; important member of the "Joint Fleet"; died during the Lin Biao Affair

LIU QUANJUE 刘荃觉
Cadre at the command post at the "Number 0" installation

LIU SHAOQI 刘少奇
Chairman of the People's Republic of China; Vice-Chairman of the Standing Committee of the Politburo; purged at the beginning of the Cultural Revolution; died in 1967

LIU SHIYING 刘世英
Deputy Director of the General Office of the Party Committee of the Air Force; important "Joint Fleet" member

LIU YALOU 刘亚楼
Chief-of-Staff of the Fourth Field Army; first commander of the Chinese Air Force; died in 1965

LU MIN 鲁 珉
Chief of the Operations Department of the Air Force; arrested in September 1971

LU YANG 鲁 杨
Air Force Academy guard

LUO RUIQING 罗瑞卿
Minister of the Public Security Ministry; Chief of the General Staff; arrested and imprisoned during the Cultural Revolution; after the Cultural Revolution, named General Secretary of the Military Commission

MAO YUANXIN 毛远新
Nephew of Mao Zedong; technical worker in the Missile Troops of the Air Force; during the Cultural Revolution, became Political Commissar of the Shenyang Military Region and Political Commissar of the Air Force in the Shenyang Military Region; arrested and punished by Hua Guofeng

MAO ZEDONG 毛泽东
Chairman of the Chinese Communist Party; Chairman of the Military Commission; died in 1976

PAN JINGYIN 潘景寅
Deputy Political Commissar of the 34th Division of the Air Force; experienced pilot favored by Chinese leaders

PENG DEHUAI 彭德怀
Member of the Politburo; Minister of Defense; ranked second among China's ten marshals; clashed with Mao at the Lushan Plenum in 1959; arrested and put on public trial in 1966

QI YAOFANG 齐杳方
Air Force Academy guard

QI ZHIJING 祁智静
Candidate to be Lin Liguo's fiancée

Qiu Huizuo 邱会作
Member of the Standing Committee of the Politburo; Chief of the Logistics Department; important member of Lin Biao's "diehard" clique; arrested and imprisoned during the Lin Biao Affair and sentenced to sixteen years in prison

Rao Shushi 饶漱石
Leader in the Northeast Bureau of the Chinese Communist Party; attacked by Mao, along with Gao Gang, in the 1950's

Shi Niantang 时念堂
Director of the General Aviation Dispatchers' Office of the Air Force

Su Quande 苏荃德
Cadre in the 8341 Guards

Tan Shu 潭 述
Transportation expert in the secret service of the 8341 Guards

Wang Bingzhang 王秉璋
Deputy Commander of the Air Force; Minister of the Seventh Machine-Building Ministry

Wang Dongxing 汪东兴
Vice-Chairman of the Politburo; Director of the General Office of the Party Central Committee; Mao Zedong's most trusted aide in charge of security work; leader of the 8341 Guards; lost his posts in 1979

Wang Fei 王 飞
Deputy Chief-of-Staff of the Air Force; important member of the "Joint Fleet"; arrested and imprisoned during the Lin Biao Affair

Wang Hongkun 王宏坤
Deputy Political Commissar of the Navy; placed under house arrest in 1980 for his involvement in the Lin Biao Affair

Wang Hongwen 王洪文
Member of the Standing Committee of the Politburo; Vice-Chairman of the Party; member of the Gang of Four; most influential leader of mass organizations during the Cultural Revolution; arrested in 1976 and sentenced to life imprisonment

Wang Liangen 王良恩
Deputy Director of the General Office of the Party Central Committee; assistant to Wang Dongxing

Wang Ming 王 明
General Secretary of the Party Central Committee in the 1930's; replaced by Mao as number-one leader in 1935; lost power in Yanan in early 1940's; left for the Soviet Union

WANG PU 王 璞
Commander of the Air Force in the Guangzhou Military Region

WANG RONGYUAN 汪荣元
Secret-service officer in the 8341 Guards

WANG SHAOYUAN 王绍渊
Commander of the Air Force in the Lanzhou Military Region

WANG WEIGUO 王维国
Political Commissar of the Fourth Air Force Army in the Nanjing Military Region; leader of the Military Control Commission in Shanghai; important member of the "Joint Fleet"; arrested and imprisoned during the Lin Biao Affair

WANG YONGKUI 王永奎
Director of the Administrative Bureau of the Air Force; arrested and imprisoned during the Lin Biao Affair

WANG YUANYUAN 王圆圆
One of Lin Liheng's boyfriends

WANG ZHUO 王 琢
Deputy leader of the transportation corps in the Air Force; Lin Liguo's personal driver

WANG ZIGANG 汪子刚
Secret-service officer in the 8341 Guards

WU DAYUN 吴达云
Member of the confidential personnel in the office of the Party Committee of the Air Force

WU DEFENG 吴德峰
Member of China's intelligence network who had worked with Kang Sheng

WU FAXIAN 吴法宪
Member of the Standing Committee of the Politburo; Commander-in-Chief of the Air Force; Deputy Chief-of-Staff of the People's Liberation Army; important member of Lin Biao's "diehard" clique; arrested during the Lin Biao Affair and sentenced to sixteen years in prison

WU XINCHAO 吴新潮
Son of Wu Faxian; Air Force representative in Shenyang airplane factory

WU ZONGHAN (Pseudonym) 吴宗汉
Military engineering expert; spy for the Soviet Union; intelligence agent for the General Staff of the People's Liberation Army

XI ZHUXIAN 席著堃

Deputy Political Commissar of the 8th Artillery Division of the Fourth Air Force Army; important member of the "Joint Fleet" in Shanghai

XIAO JINGUANG 肖劲光

Commander in the Navy; Vice-Minister of Defense

XIAO KE 肖 克

Principal of the Military Political Academy

XIAO QUANFU 肖全夫

Division Commander of the ninth column of Lin Biao's Fourth Field Army; Deputy Commander of the Shenyang Military Region; Commander of the Urumqi Military Region

XIE FUZHI 谢富治

Member of the Standing Committee of the Politburo; Minister of Public Security Ministry; Commander of Public Security Troops; Vice-Premier of the State Council; a Cultural Revolution leader and supporter of the Gang of Four

XU LIMIN 徐立敏

Communications officer in the Air Force

XU SHIGUANG 许士光

Cadre in the 8341 Guards

XU SHIYOU 许世友

Commander of the Nanjing Military Region

XU XIANGQIAN 徐向前

Member of the Politburo; one of China's ten marshals

XU XIUXU 许秀绪

Secretary of the General Office of the Party Committee of the Air Force

YAN ZHONGCHUAN 阎仲川

Commander of the 43rd Army of the Fourth Field Army; Deputy Chief-of-Staff of the People's Liberation Army

YANG CHENGWU 杨成武

Replaced Luo Ruiqing as Chief of the General Staff at the beginning of the Cultural Revolution; later purged; currently commander of the Fuzhou Military Region

YANG DEZHONG 杨德中

High-ranking secretary to Zhou Enlai in charge of security

YANG DINGKUN 杨定坤

Officer in the military hospital and Lin Biao's medical consultant; Lin Liheng's fiancé

YANG JIDA 杨继达
Stepfather of Yang Dingkun; military officer at the division level

YANG ZHENGANG 杨振刚
Lin Biao's personal driver

YAO WENYUAN 姚文元
Member of the Politburo; Secretary of the Party Committee of Shanghai; influential literary figure and theorist during the Cultural Revolution; member of the Gang of Four; arrested in 1976 and sentenced to twenty years in prison

YE JIANYING 叶钊英
The tenth of China's ten marshals; Vice-Chairman of the Politburo; Minister of Defense; Chairman of the National People's Congress; Vice-Chairman of the Party

YE QUN 叶 群
Member of the Politburo; wife of Lin Biao; Director of Lin Biao's General Office; member of the Administrative Group of the Military Commission

YU BOKE 遇波克
One of Lin Liheng's boyfriends

YU SANG 于 桑
Vice-Minister of the Public Security Ministry

YU XINYE 于新野
Director of the First Section of the General Office of the Party Committee of the Air Force; important member of the "Joint Fleet"

YU YUNSHEN 于运深
Lin Biao's chief secretary

ZENG GUOHUA 曾国华
Deputy Commander of the Air Force

ZHANG CHUNQIAO 张春桥
Member of the Standing Committee of the Politburo; Vice-Premier of the State Council; First Secretary of the Party Committee of Shanghai; Director of the General Political Department; member of the Gang of Four; influential leader during the Cultural Revolution; arrested in 1976 and sentenced to death

ZHANG TINGFA 张廷发
Member of the Politburo; Chief of Operations Section in Liu Bocheng's and Deng Xiaoping's Second Field Army; Vice-Commander of the Air Force; purged during Cultural Revolution; Commander of the Air Force

ZHANG YONGGENG 张雍耿
Political Commissar of the Air Force of the Shenyang Military Region

ZHAO SHANGTIAN 赵尚田
Director of the Political Office of the Missile Regiment of the Air Force Missile Division in Shanghai

ZHAO YANJI (Pseudonym) 赵研极
High-level cadre in the Classified Office on the Special Case on Lin Biao; head of the General Office of the Special Investigative Division on the Lin Biao Affair

ZHOU DEYUN 周德润
Cadre in the Fourth Air Force Army; member of the "Joint Fleet" in Shanghai in charge of training the Instruction Unit

ZHOU ENLAI 周恩来
Vice-Chairman of the Party; Premier of the State Council; died in 1976

ZHOU XIHAN 同希汉
Deputy Commander of the Navy

ZHOU YUCHI 周宇驰
Deputy Director of the General Office of the Party Committee of the Air Force; important member of the "Joint Fleet"; died during the Lin Biao Affair

ZHU BINGLIANG 朱炳亮
Chief of Lin Biao's security force

ZHU DE 朱 德
First of China's ten marshals; Vice-Chairman of the Party Central Committee; Vice-Chairman of the Military Commission; Vice-Chairman of the State; Chairman of the National People's Congress

ZHU TIESHENG 朱钦笙
Director of the Second Department of the Party Committee of the Air Force; member of the "Joint Fleet"; arrested and imprisoned during the Lin Biao Affair

ZU FUGUANG 祖付光
Officer in the Air Force of the Nanjing Military Region; member of the "Joint Fleet"

INDEX

229

Shanghai Military Region, 164
Shanhaiguan Airport, 6, 8, 47, 116, 138
Shanxi Province, 43
Shaoxing, 107
Shenyang Military Region, 14, 15, 43,
  57, 63, 64, 66, 72, 74, 126, 128, 150,
  151, 165, 180, 187, 203
Shi Niantang, 128
Shumchun, 27, 134
Skylark helicopter #3685, 172-6 and
  illus., 177-8, 182-3, 211
Soviet Union, 4, 6, 22, 32, 38, 54, 63-4,
  69-71, 73-4, 77, 168, 174, 185; Lin
  Biao's plans to involve in coup, 62-8,
  80-3, 123-4, 125, 129, 135, 138, 139,
  149-51, 180, 189, 206-7
Stalin, Joseph, 22, 23
State Council, 56, 73, 76, 79, 81, 83,
  125
Su Quande, 16-17
Suzhou, 27

Tan Shu, 160-3, 210
Tiananmen Square (Beijing), 3-4, *illus.*
  5, 17, 67, 124, 193
Tianjin (Tientsin), 22, 54, 135, 141
Tianjin Garrison Command, 43
trials (of "counter-revolutionaries"),
  11-12, 97 and *n.*, 194
Trident jet #256, 6, 8, 21, 138, 180-2,
  illus. 184, 185, 210-11

United States, 23, 32, 38, 64, 74, 80-1,
  100, 134-5

Vietnam, 67, 100
Vladivostok, 139

Wang Bingzhang, 128
Wang Dongxing, 10, 13, 87-9, 193-4,
  195, 203, 207; as aide to Mao, 44, 45,
  55, 87, 96, 98, 99, 106, 137, 140-1, 142,
  144, 157, 165, 178, 188, 192; and
  cover-up of Lin Biao Affair, 9, 10,

17-20, 24, 186-92, 206; and murder of
  Lin Biao, 158, 159-62, 189-91
Wang Fei, 182; and plots against Mao,
  91, 98, 100, 106-8, 110-12, 114-16, 138,
  154, 164, 168-9, 170, 171-2
Wang Hongkun, 142
Wang Hongwen, 80
Wang Liangen, 19, 24, 203
Wang Ming, 61
Wang Pu, 127
Wang Rongyuan, 160-3
Wang Shaoyuan, 128
Wang Weiguo, 28; and plots against
  Mao, 95, 99, 100, 101, 102, 105, 110-11,
  128
Wang Yongkui, 98, 164, 208
Wang Yuanyuan, 131
Wang Zhuo, 164, 168, 169-73 *passim*
Wang Zigang, 161-3
Western Hills compound, 43, 46, 64,
  124-5, 126, 146, 148, 150, 164, 168, 179
Western Suburbs Airport, 16, 91, 123,
  138, 158, 164-5, 167-8, 181, 203
Whampoa Military Academy, 78, 87,
  207
World War II, *see* Anti-Japanese Wars
Wu Dayun, 128
Wu Defeng, 15
Wu Faxian, *illus. 48,* 59-60, 87, 157,
  179-83, 195, 205; as Air Force
  Commander-in-Chief, 4, 32, 35-41,
  43, 46-7, 63, 113, 137, 168, 211; in Lin
  Biao clique, 4, 21, 41, 44-52, *illus. 57,*
  60, 136; and Lin Liguo, 26-7, 30, 32,
  35-40, 41-2, 44, 119-20, 209; and plot
  against Mao, 58, 61-2, 119, 125, 128-9,
  138-53, 167, 180; trial and
  imprisonment of, 12, 20, 194, 204, 210
Wu Xinchao, 182
Wu Zonghan, 69-74, 81, 82-3, 206
Wuhan, 99, 102

Xi Zhuxian, 27, 106, 111-12
Xiao Jinguang, 58

230